Two pies.
One fork.

by Cathy Guisewite

Selected Cartoons from
Wake me up when I'm a size 5
Volume II

FAWCETT CREST • NEW YORK

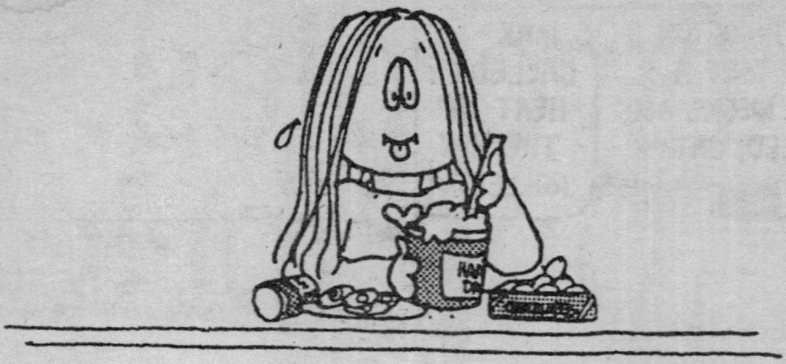

A Fawcett Crest Book
Published by Ballantine Books

This book comprises a portion of WAKE ME WHEN I'M A SIZE 5 and is reprinted by arrangement with Andrews, McMeel and Parker, Inc.

Library of Congress Catalog Card Number: 86–61452

ISBN 0-449-21249-1

Manufactured in the United States of America

First Ballantine Books Edition: August 1987
Second Printing: July 1988

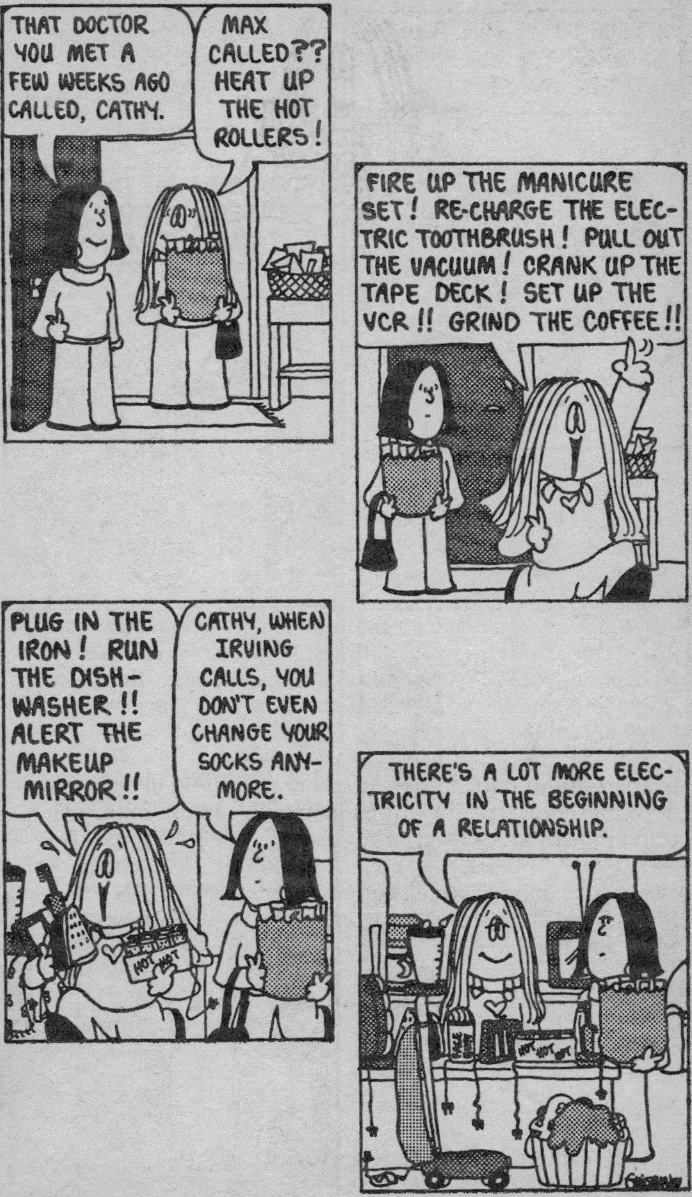
THAT DOCTOR YOU MET A FEW WEEKS AGO CALLED, CATHY.
MAX CALLED?? HEAT UP THE HOT ROLLERS!
FIRE UP THE MANICURE SET! RE-CHARGE THE ELECTRIC TOOTHBRUSH! PULL OUT THE VACUUM! CRANK UP THE TAPE DECK! SET UP THE VCR!! GRIND THE COFFEE!!
PLUG IN THE IRON! RUN THE DISHWASHER!! ALERT THE MAKEUP MIRROR!!
CATHY, WHEN IRVING CALLS, YOU DON'T EVEN CHANGE YOUR SOCKS ANYMORE.
THERE'S A LOT MORE ELECTRICITY IN THE BEGINNING OF A RELATIONSHIP.

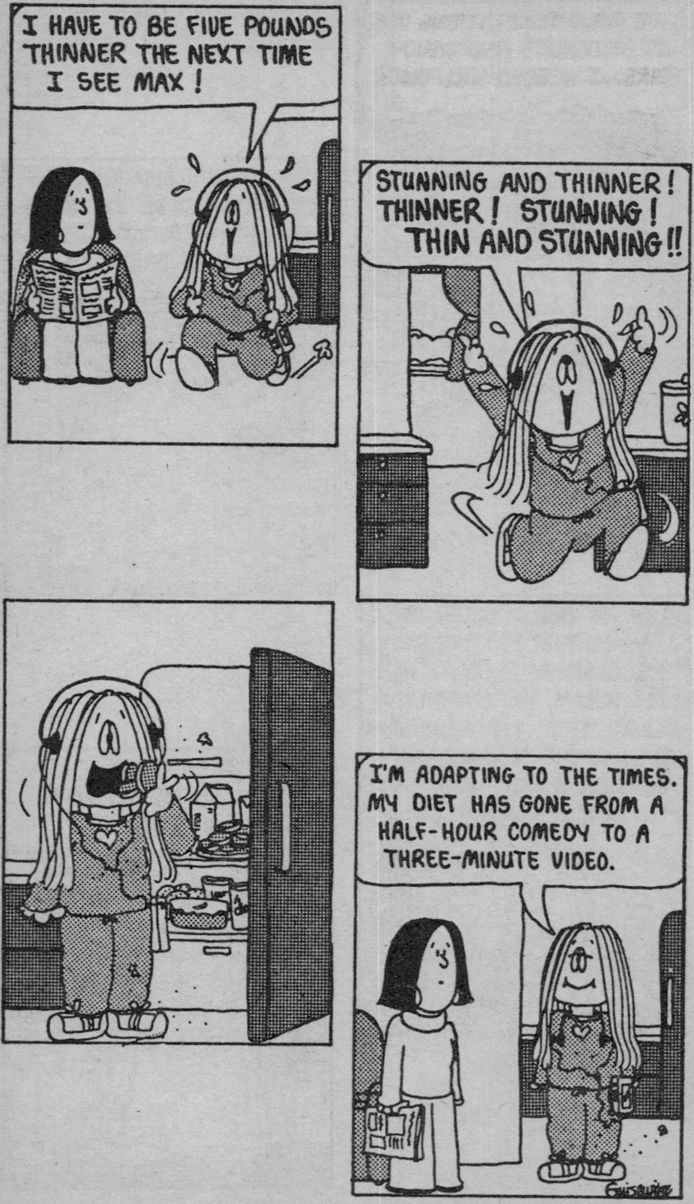
I HAVE TO BE FIVE POUNDS THINNER THE NEXT TIME I SEE MAX !
STUNNING AND THINNER ! THINNER ! STUNNING ! THIN AND STUNNING !!
I'M ADAPTING TO THE TIMES. MY DIET HAS GONE FROM A HALF-HOUR COMEDY TO A THREE-MINUTE VIDEO.

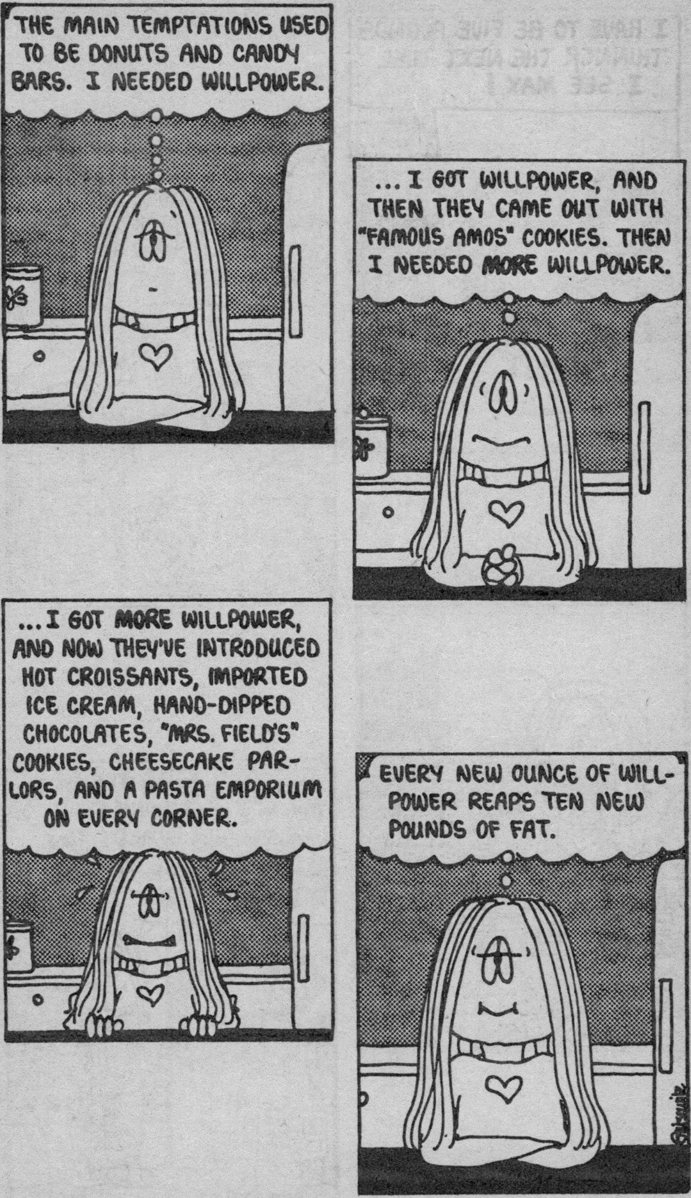
THE MAIN TEMPTATIONS USED TO BE DONUTS AND CANDY BARS. I NEEDED WILLPOWER.
... I GOT WILLPOWER, AND THEN THEY CAME OUT WITH "FAMOUS AMOS" COOKIES. THEN I NEEDED MORE WILLPOWER.
... I GOT MORE WILLPOWER, AND NOW THEY'VE INTRODUCED HOT CROISSANTS, IMPORTED ICE CREAM, HAND-DIPPED CHOCOLATES, "MRS. FIELD'S" COOKIES, CHEESECAKE PARLORS, AND A PASTA EMPORIUM ON EVERY CORNER.
EVERY NEW OUNCE OF WILLPOWER REAPS TEN NEW POUNDS OF FAT.

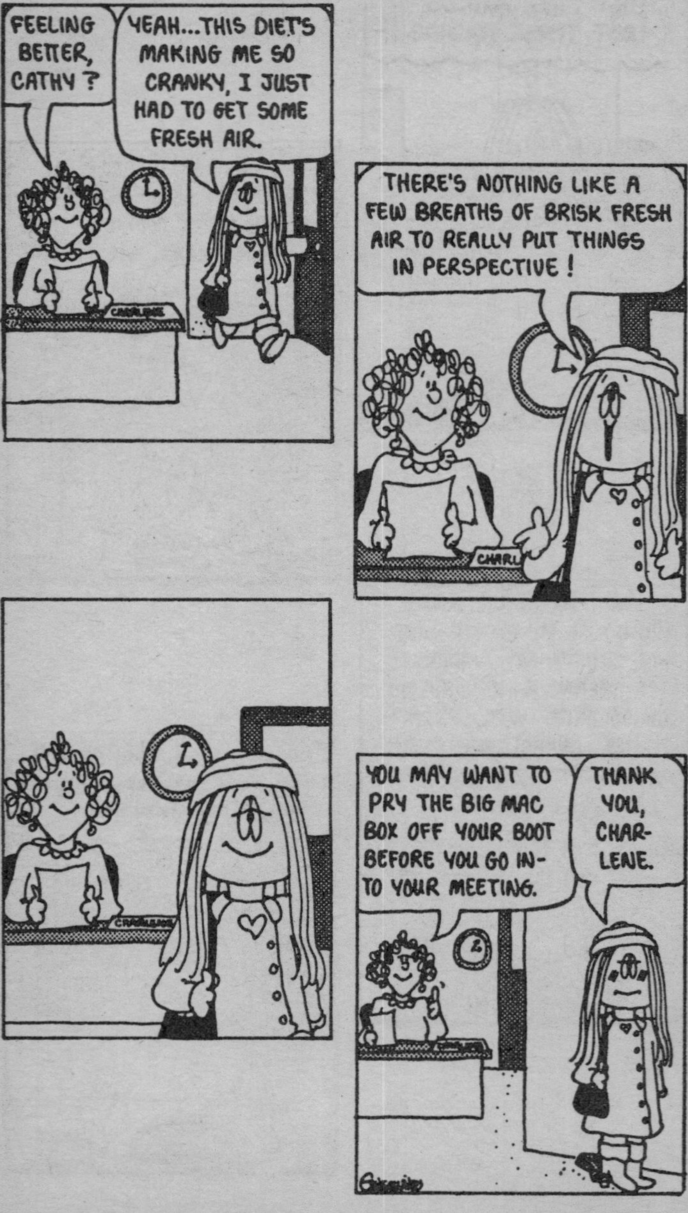
FEELING BETTER, CATHY ?
YEAH...THIS DIET'S MAKING ME SO CRANKY, I JUST HAD TO GET SOME FRESH AIR.
THERE'S NOTHING LIKE A FEW BREATHS OF BRISK FRESH AIR TO REALLY PUT THINGS IN PERSPECTIVE !
YOU MAY WANT TO PRY THE BIG MAC BOX OFF YOUR BOOT BEFORE YOU GO IN-TO YOUR MEETING.
THANK YOU, CHAR-LENE.

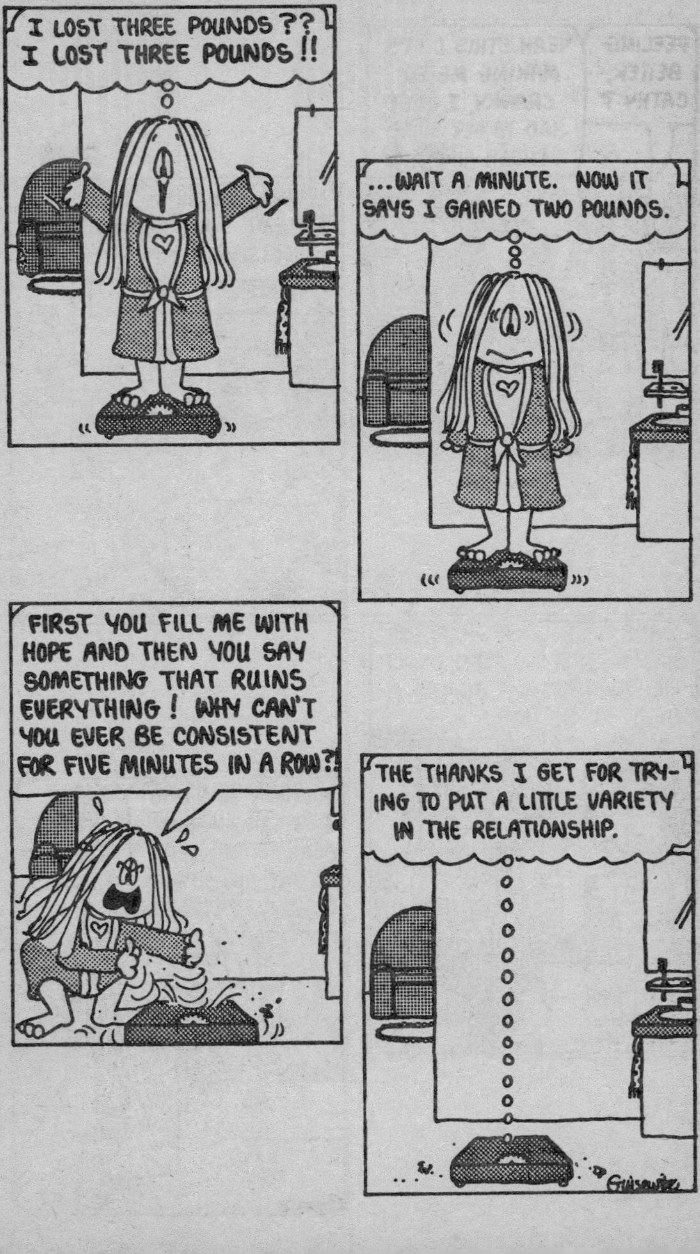
I LOST THREE POUNDS?? I LOST THREE POUNDS!!
...WAIT A MINUTE. NOW IT SAYS I GAINED TWO POUNDS.
FIRST YOU FILL ME WITH HOPE AND THEN YOU SAY SOMETHING THAT RUINS EVERYTHING! WHY CAN'T YOU EVER BE CONSISTENT FOR FIVE MINUTES IN A ROW?!
THE THANKS I GET FOR TRYING TO PUT A LITTLE VARIETY IN THE RELATIONSHIP.
Guisewite

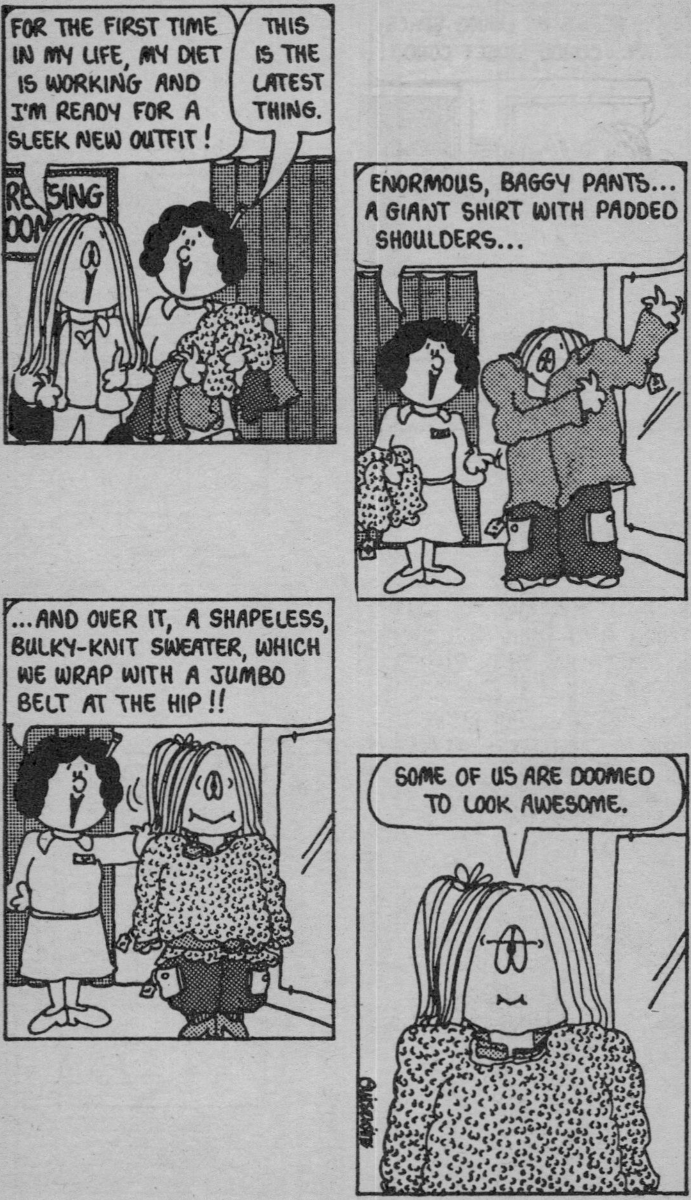
FOR THE FIRST TIME IN MY LIFE, MY DIET IS WORKING AND I'M READY FOR A SLEEK NEW OUTFIT!
THIS IS THE LATEST THING.
ENORMOUS, BAGGY PANTS... A GIANT SHIRT WITH PADDED SHOULDERS...
...AND OVER IT, A SHAPELESS, BULKY-KNIT SWEATER, WHICH WE WRAP WITH A JUMBO BELT AT THE HIP!!
SOME OF US ARE DOOMED TO LOOK AWESOME.

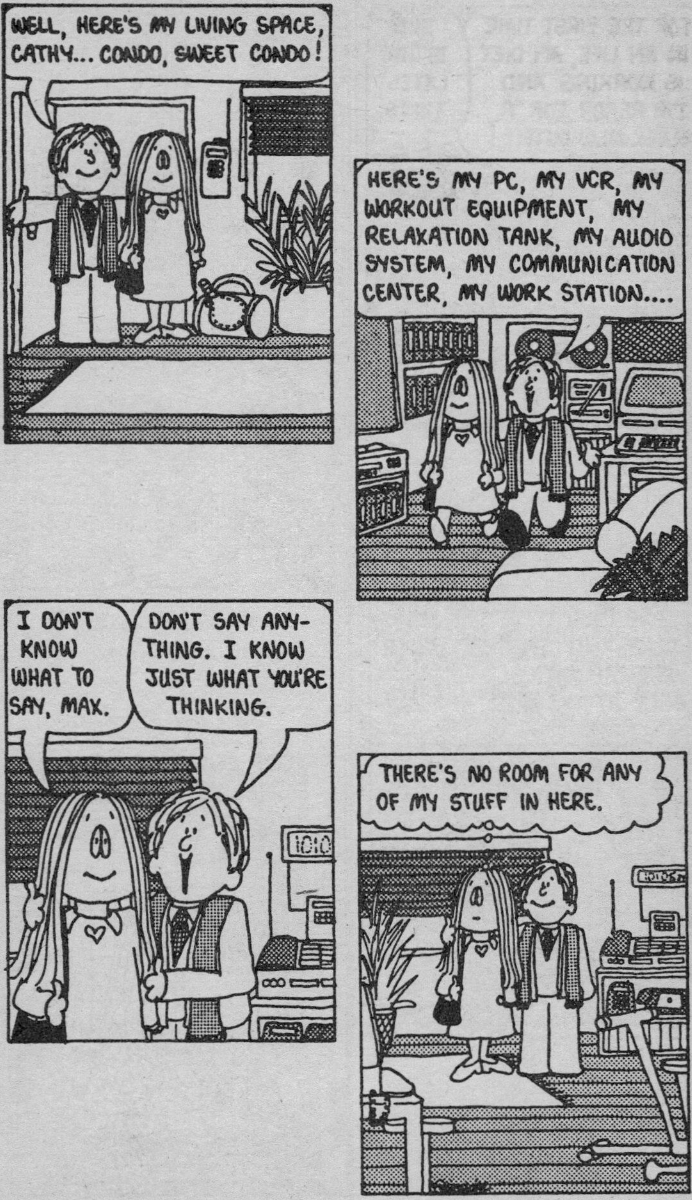
WELL, HERE'S MY LIVING SPACE, CATHY... CONDO, SWEET CONDO!
HERE'S MY PC, MY VCR, MY WORKOUT EQUIPMENT, MY RELAXATION TANK, MY AUDIO SYSTEM, MY COMMUNICATION CENTER, MY WORK STATION....
I DON'T KNOW WHAT TO SAY, MAX.
DON'T SAY ANYTHING. I KNOW JUST WHAT YOU'RE THINKING.
THERE'S NO ROOM FOR ANY OF MY STUFF IN HERE.

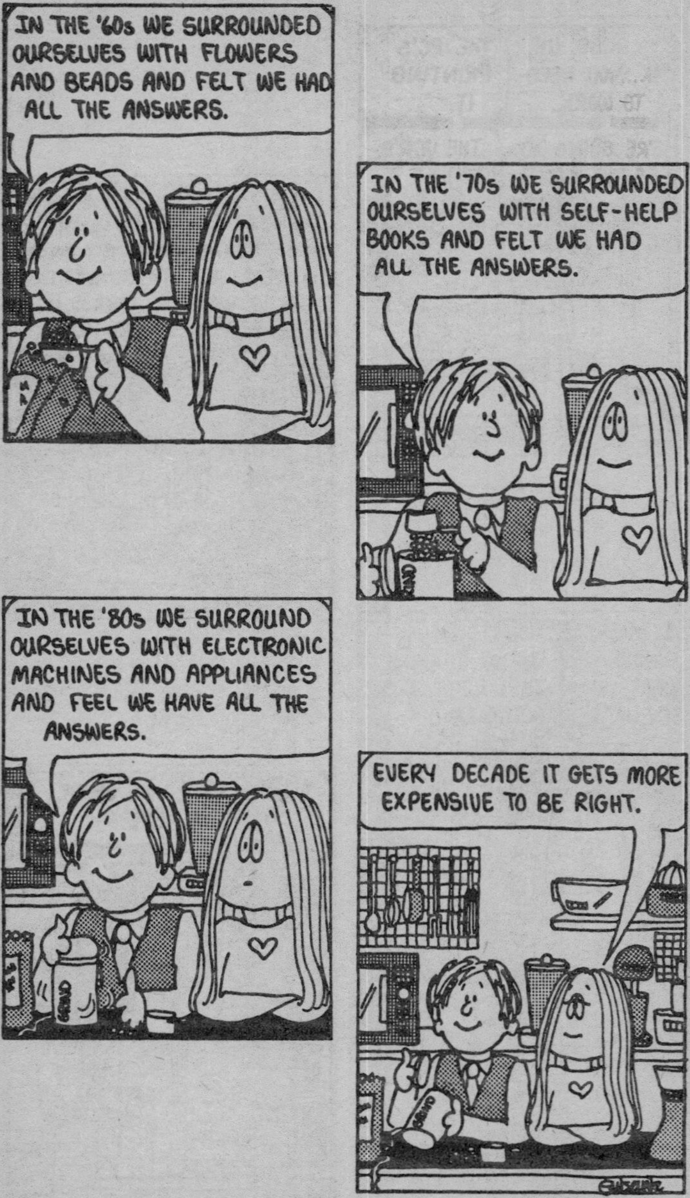
IN THE '60s WE SURROUNDED OURSELVES WITH FLOWERS AND BEADS AND FELT WE HAD ALL THE ANSWERS.
IN THE '70s WE SURROUNDED OURSELVES WITH SELF-HELP BOOKS AND FELT WE HAD ALL THE ANSWERS.
IN THE '80s WE SURROUND OURSELVES WITH ELECTRONIC MACHINES AND APPLIANCES AND FEEL WE HAVE ALL THE ANSWERS.
EVERY DECADE IT GETS MORE EXPENSIVE TO BE RIGHT.

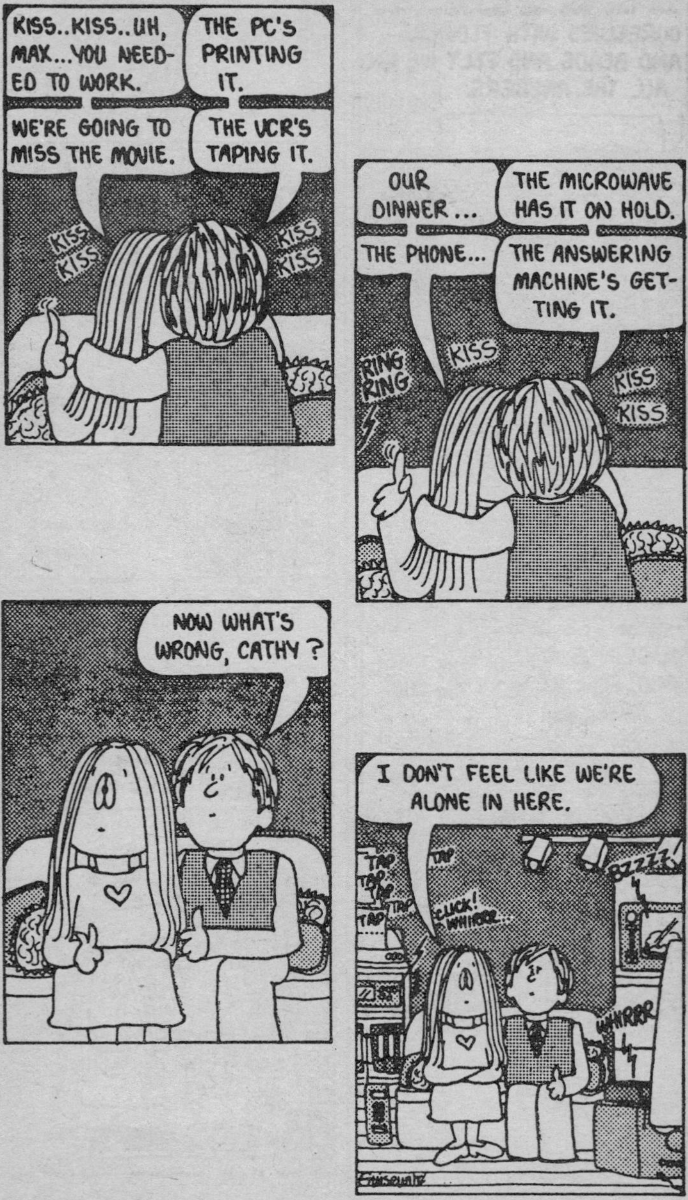
KISS..KISS..UH, MAX...YOU NEEDED TO WORK.
THE PC'S PRINTING IT.
WE'RE GOING TO MISS THE MOVIE.
THE VCR'S TAPING IT.
KISS KISS
KISS KISS
OUR DINNER...
THE MICROWAVE HAS IT ON HOLD.
THE PHONE...
THE ANSWERING MACHINE'S GETTING IT.
RING RING
KISS
KISS KISS
NOW WHAT'S WRONG, CATHY?
I DON'T FEEL LIKE WE'RE ALONE IN HERE.
TAP
CLICK! WHIRR...
BZZZZ
WHIRRR

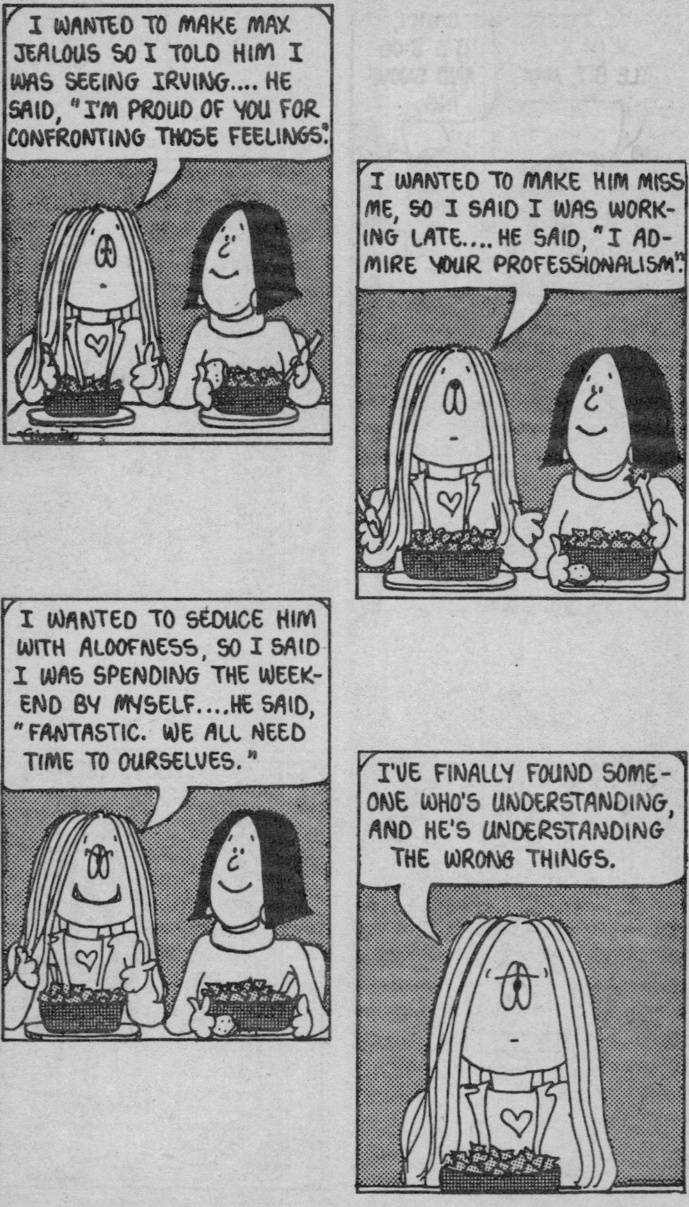
I WANTED TO MAKE MAX JEALOUS SO I TOLD HIM I WAS SEEING IRVING.... HE SAID, "I'M PROUD OF YOU FOR CONFRONTING THOSE FEELINGS."
I WANTED TO MAKE HIM MISS ME, SO I SAID I WAS WORKING LATE.... HE SAID, "I ADMIRE YOUR PROFESSIONALISM."
I WANTED TO SEDUCE HIM WITH ALOOFNESS, SO I SAID I WAS SPENDING THE WEEKEND BY MYSELF....HE SAID, "FANTASTIC. WE ALL NEED TIME TO OURSELVES."
I'VE FINALLY FOUND SOMEONE WHO'S UNDERSTANDING, AND HE'S UNDERSTANDING THE WRONG THINGS.

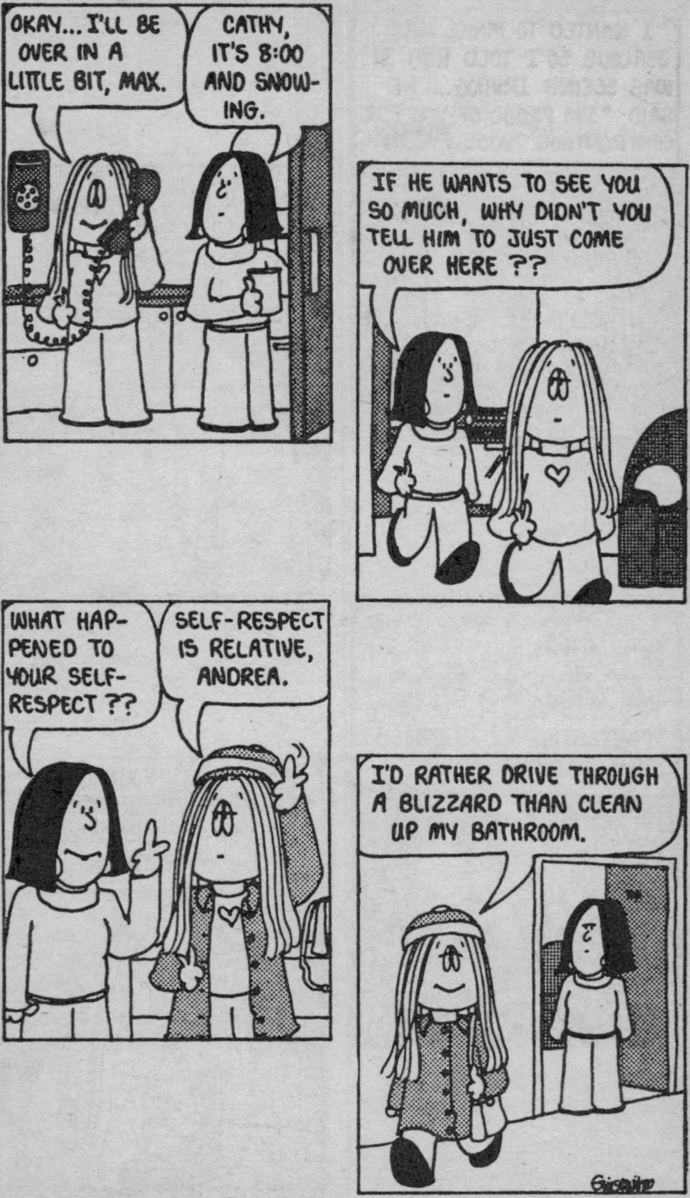
OKAY... I'LL BE OVER IN A LITTLE BIT, MAX.
CATHY, IT'S 8:00 AND SNOWING.
IF HE WANTS TO SEE YOU SO MUCH, WHY DIDN'T YOU TELL HIM TO JUST COME OVER HERE ??
WHAT HAPPENED TO YOUR SELF-RESPECT ??
SELF-RESPECT IS RELATIVE, ANDREA.
I'D RATHER DRIVE THROUGH A BLIZZARD THAN CLEAN UP MY BATHROOM.

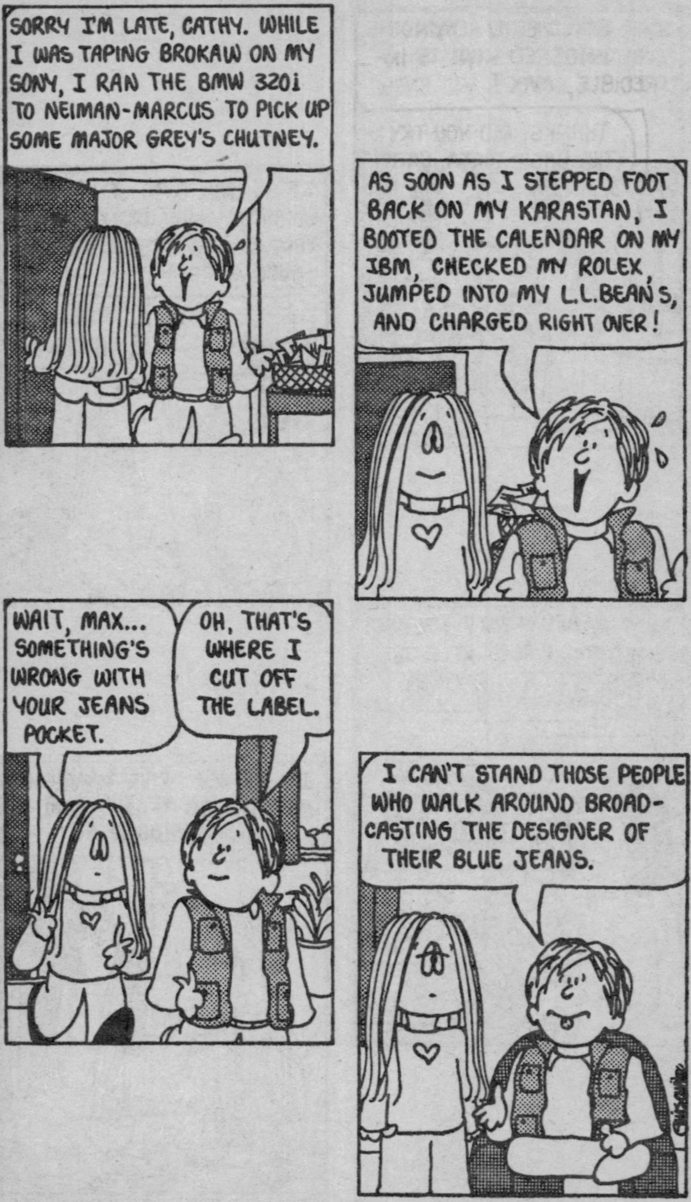
SORRY I'M LATE, CATHY. WHILE I WAS TAPING BROKAW ON MY SONY, I RAN THE BMW 320i TO NEIMAN-MARCUS TO PICK UP SOME MAJOR GREY'S CHUTNEY.
AS SOON AS I STEPPED FOOT BACK ON MY KARASTAN, I BOOTED THE CALENDAR ON MY IBM, CHECKED MY ROLEX, JUMPED INTO MY L.L.BEAN'S, AND CHARGED RIGHT OVER!
WAIT, MAX... SOMETHING'S WRONG WITH YOUR JEANS POCKET.
OH, THAT'S WHERE I CUT OFF THE LABEL.
I CAN'T STAND THOSE PEOPLE WHO WALK AROUND BROAD-CASTING THE DESIGNER OF THEIR BLUE JEANS.

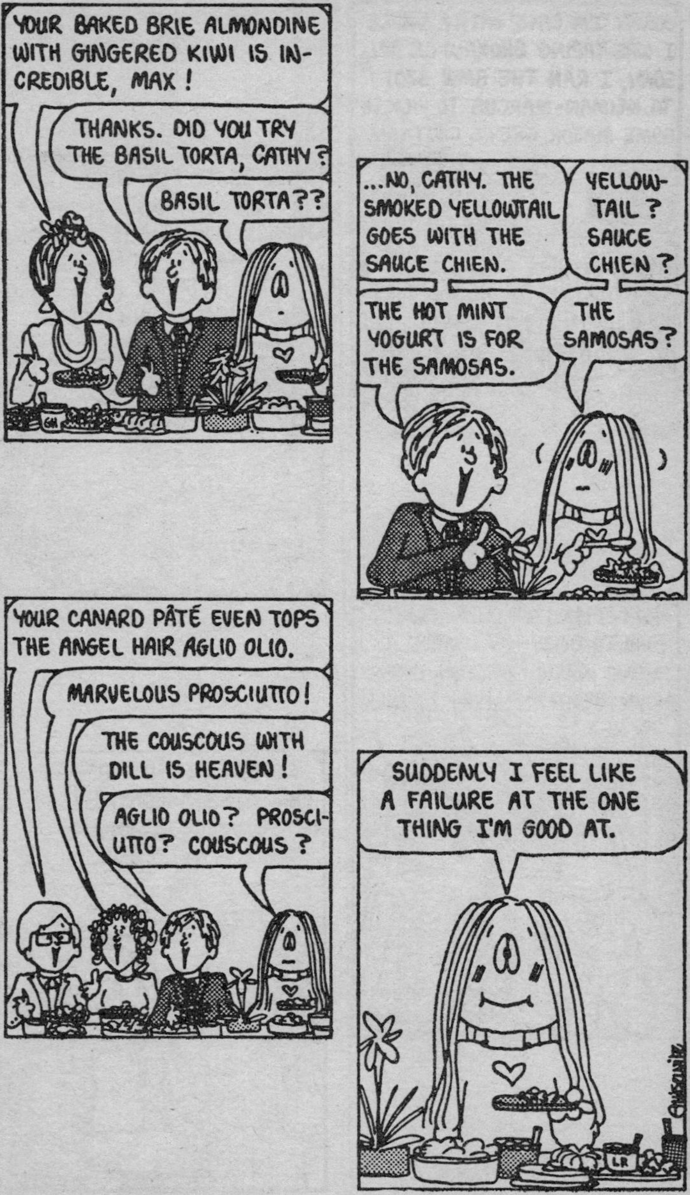
YOUR BAKED BRIE ALMONDINE WITH GINGERED KIWI IS INCREDIBLE, MAX!
THANKS. DID YOU TRY THE BASIL TORTA, CATHY?
BASIL TORTA??
...NO, CATHY. THE SMOKED YELLOWTAIL GOES WITH THE SAUCE CHIEN.
YELLOWTAIL? SAUCE CHIEN?
THE HOT MINT YOGURT IS FOR THE SAMOSAS.
THE SAMOSAS?
YOUR CANARD PÂTÉ EVEN TOPS THE ANGEL HAIR AGLIO OLIO.
MARVELOUS PROSCIUTTO!
THE COUSCOUS WITH DILL IS HEAVEN!
AGLIO OLIO? PROSCIUTTO? COUSCOUS?
SUDDENLY I FEEL LIKE A FAILURE AT THE ONE THING I'M GOOD AT.

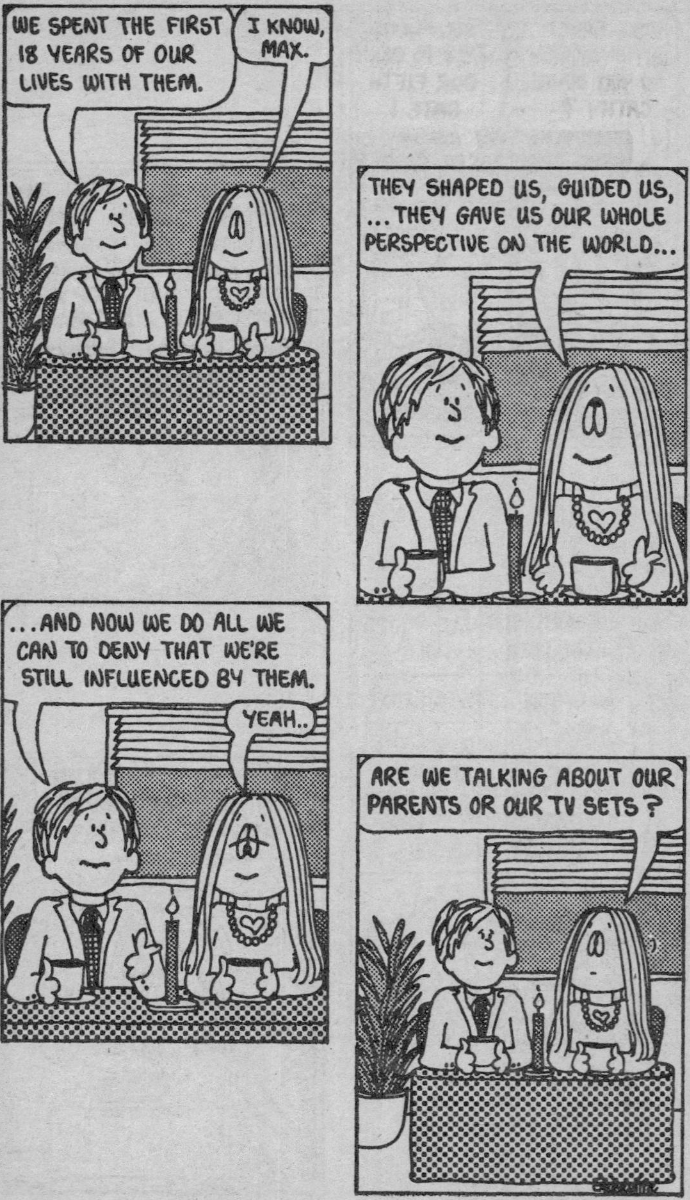
WE SPENT THE FIRST 18 YEARS OF OUR LIVES WITH THEM.
I KNOW, MAX.
THEY SHAPED US, GUIDED US, ...THEY GAVE US OUR WHOLE PERSPECTIVE ON THE WORLD...
...AND NOW WE DO ALL WE CAN TO DENY THAT WE'RE STILL INFLUENCED BY THEM.
YEAH..
ARE WE TALKING ABOUT OUR PARENTS OR OUR TV SETS?

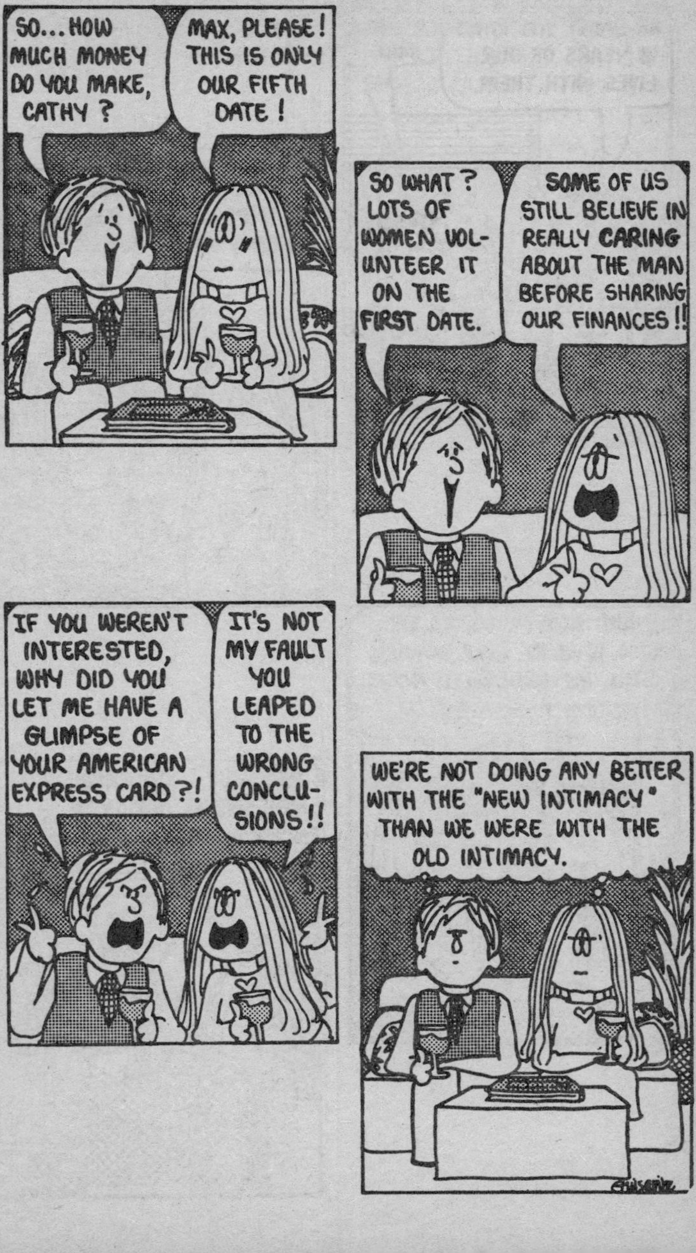
SO... HOW MUCH MONEY DO YOU MAKE, CATHY ?
MAX, PLEASE! THIS IS ONLY OUR FIFTH DATE !
SO WHAT ? LOTS OF WOMEN VOL-UNTEER IT ON THE FIRST DATE.
SOME OF US STILL BELIEVE IN REALLY CARING ABOUT THE MAN BEFORE SHARING OUR FINANCES !!
IF YOU WEREN'T INTERESTED, WHY DID YOU LET ME HAVE A GLIMPSE OF YOUR AMERICAN EXPRESS CARD ?!
IT'S NOT MY FAULT YOU LEAPED TO THE WRONG CONCLU-SIONS !!
WE'RE NOT DOING ANY BETTER WITH THE "NEW INTIMACY" THAN WE WERE WITH THE OLD INTIMACY.

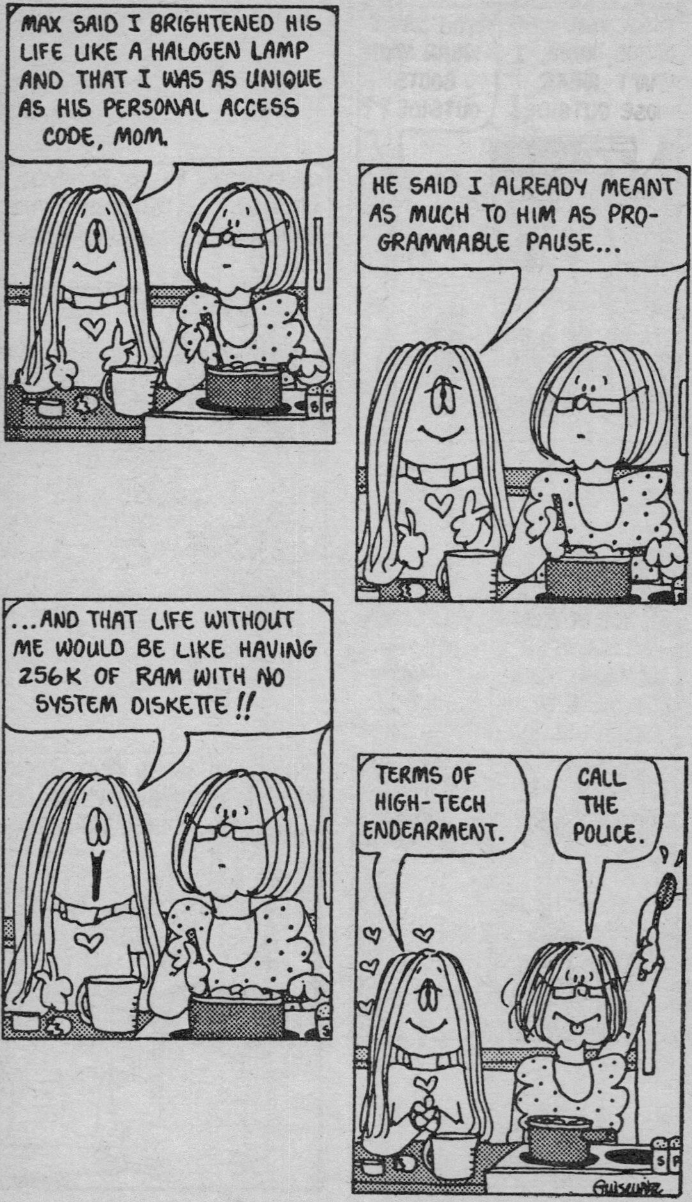
MAX SAID I BRIGHTENED HIS LIFE LIKE A HALOGEN LAMP AND THAT I WAS AS UNIQUE AS HIS PERSONAL ACCESS CODE, MOM.
HE SAID I ALREADY MEANT AS MUCH TO HIM AS PRO-GRAMMABLE PAUSE...
...AND THAT LIFE WITHOUT ME WOULD BE LIKE HAVING 256K OF RAM WITH NO SYSTEM DISKETTE !!
TERMS OF HIGH-TECH ENDEARMENT.
CALL THE POLICE.

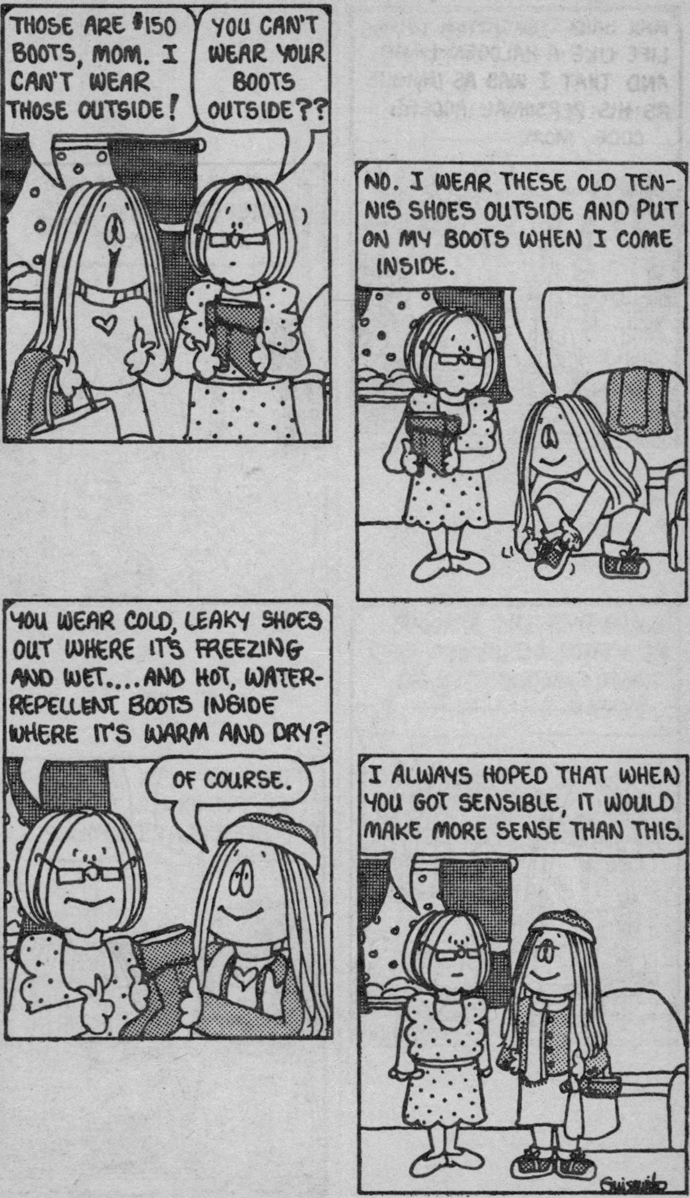
THOSE ARE $150 BOOTS, MOM. I CAN'T WEAR THOSE OUTSIDE!
YOU CAN'T WEAR YOUR BOOTS OUTSIDE??
NO. I WEAR THESE OLD TENNIS SHOES OUTSIDE AND PUT ON MY BOOTS WHEN I COME INSIDE.
YOU WEAR COLD, LEAKY SHOES OUT WHERE IT'S FREEZING AND WET....AND HOT, WATER-REPELLENT BOOTS INSIDE WHERE IT'S WARM AND DRY?
OF COURSE.
I ALWAYS HOPED THAT WHEN YOU GOT SENSIBLE, IT WOULD MAKE MORE SENSE THAN THIS.
Guisewite

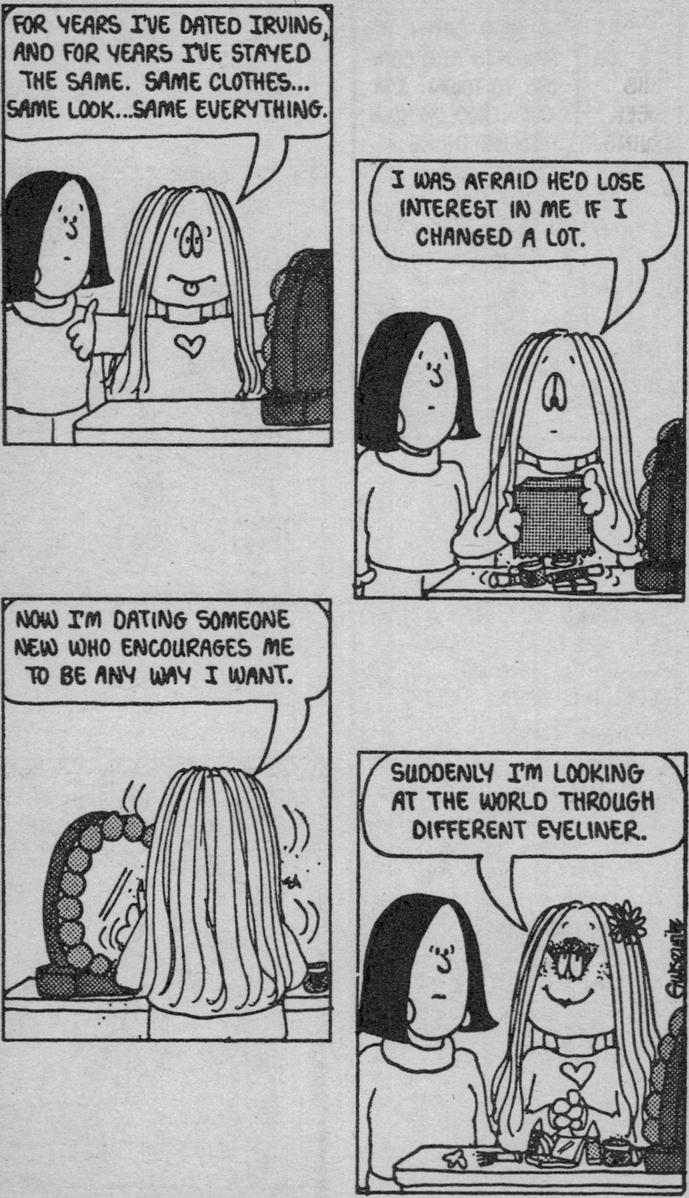
FOR YEARS I'VE DATED IRVING, AND FOR YEARS I'VE STAYED THE SAME. SAME CLOTHES... SAME LOOK...SAME EVERYTHING.
I WAS AFRAID HE'D LOSE INTEREST IN ME IF I CHANGED A LOT.
NOW I'M DATING SOMEONE NEW WHO ENCOURAGES ME TO BE ANY WAY I WANT.
SUDDENLY I'M LOOKING AT THE WORLD THROUGH DIFFERENT EYELINER.

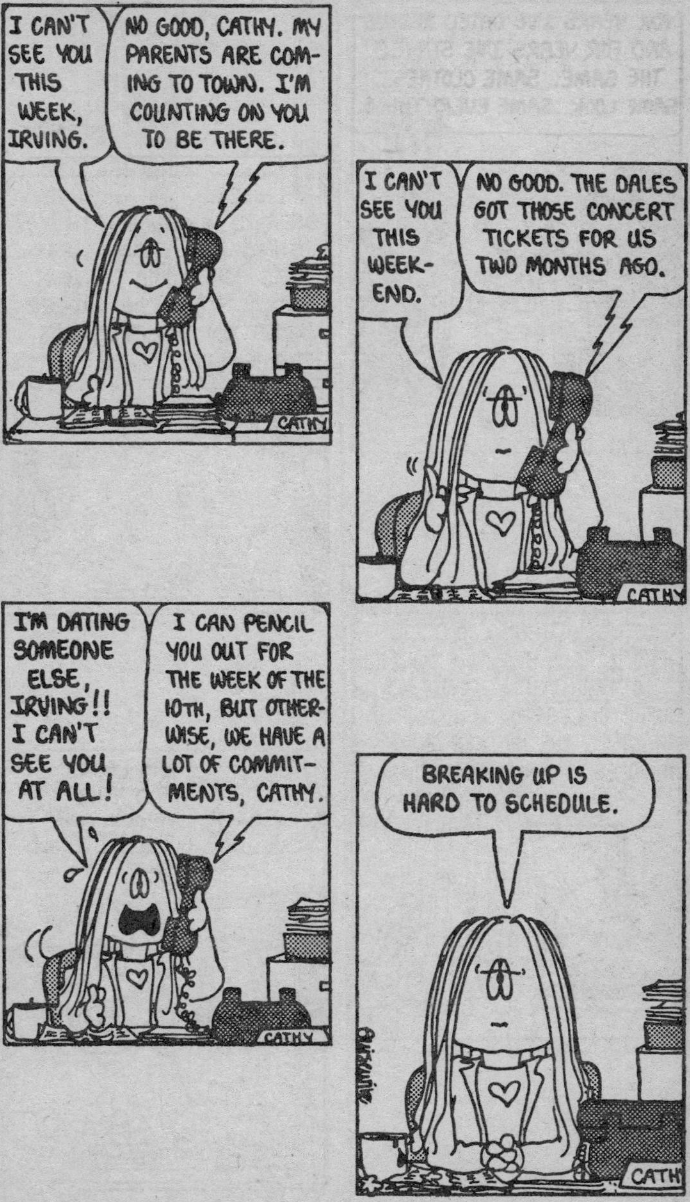
I CAN'T SEE YOU THIS WEEK, IRVING.
NO GOOD, CATHY. MY PARENTS ARE COMING TO TOWN. I'M COUNTING ON YOU TO BE THERE.
CATHY
I CAN'T SEE YOU THIS WEEK-END.
NO GOOD. THE DALES GOT THOSE CONCERT TICKETS FOR US TWO MONTHS AGO.
CATHY
I'M DATING SOMEONE ELSE, IRVING!! I CAN'T SEE YOU AT ALL!
I CAN PENCIL YOU OUT FOR THE WEEK OF THE 10TH, BUT OTHERWISE, WE HAVE A LOT OF COMMITMENTS, CATHY.
CATHY
BREAKING UP IS HARD TO SCHEDULE.
CATHY

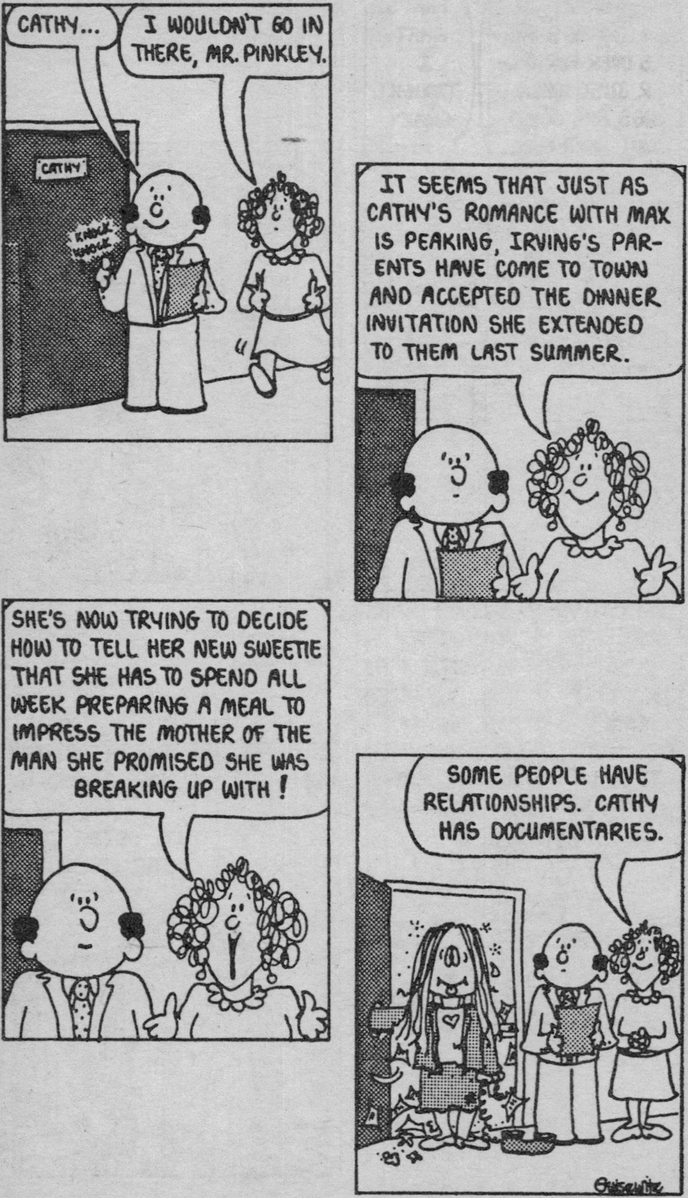
CATHY...
I WOULDN'T GO IN THERE, MR. PINKLEY.
CATHY
KNOCK KNOCK
IT SEEMS THAT JUST AS CATHY'S ROMANCE WITH MAX IS PEAKING, IRVING'S PARENTS HAVE COME TO TOWN AND ACCEPTED THE DINNER INVITATION SHE EXTENDED TO THEM LAST SUMMER.
SHE'S NOW TRYING TO DECIDE HOW TO TELL HER NEW SWEETIE THAT SHE HAS TO SPEND ALL WEEK PREPARING A MEAL TO IMPRESS THE MOTHER OF THE MAN SHE PROMISED SHE WAS BREAKING UP WITH!
SOME PEOPLE HAVE RELATIONSHIPS. CATHY HAS DOCUMENTARIES.
Guisewite

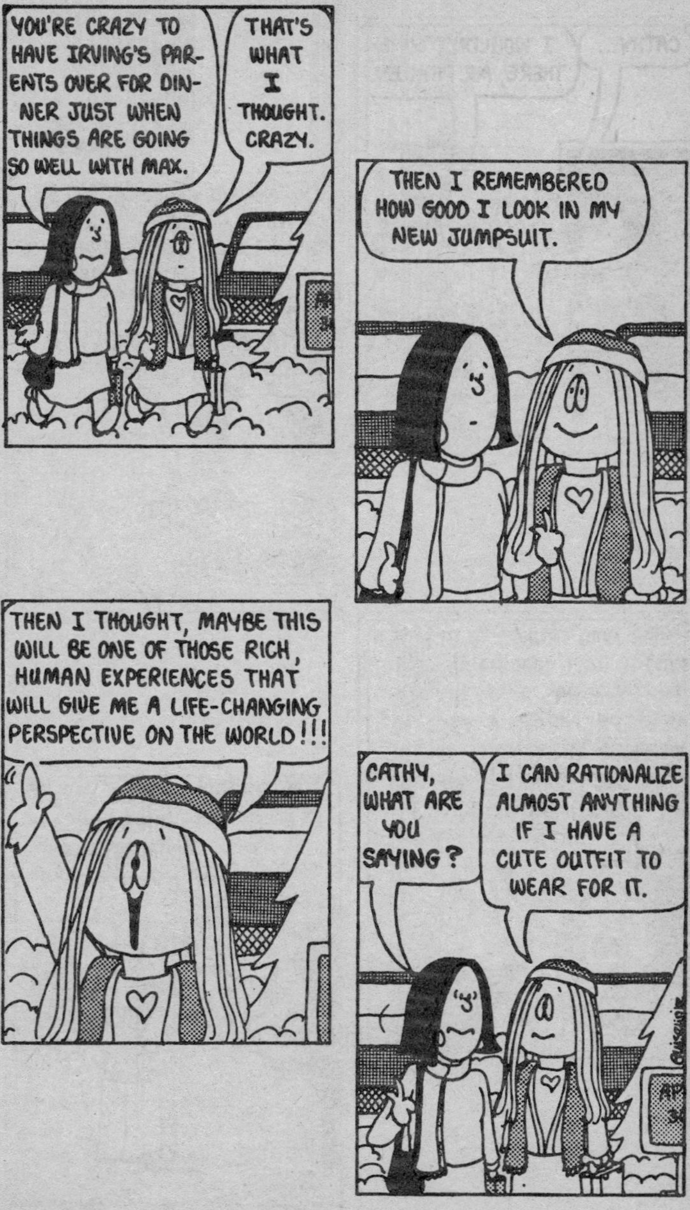
YOU'RE CRAZY TO HAVE IRVING'S PARENTS OVER FOR DINNER JUST WHEN THINGS ARE GOING SO WELL WITH MAX.
THAT'S WHAT I THOUGHT. CRAZY.
THEN I REMEMBERED HOW GOOD I LOOK IN MY NEW JUMPSUIT.
THEN I THOUGHT, MAYBE THIS WILL BE ONE OF THOSE RICH, HUMAN EXPERIENCES THAT WILL GIVE ME A LIFE-CHANGING PERSPECTIVE ON THE WORLD!!!
CATHY, WHAT ARE YOU SAYING?
I CAN RATIONALIZE ALMOST ANYTHING IF I HAVE A CUTE OUTFIT TO WEAR FOR IT.

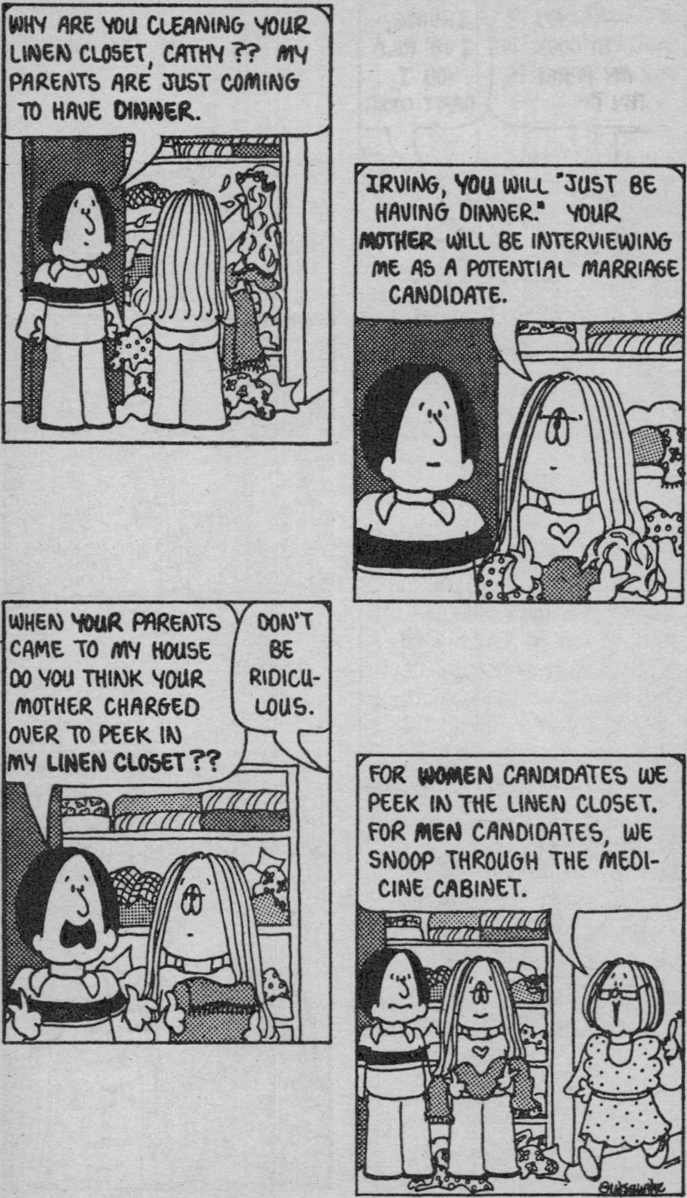
WHY ARE YOU CLEANING YOUR LINEN CLOSET, CATHY ?? MY PARENTS ARE JUST COMING TO HAVE DINNER.
IRVING, YOU WILL "JUST BE HAVING DINNER." YOUR MOTHER WILL BE INTERVIEWING ME AS A POTENTIAL MARRIAGE CANDIDATE.
WHEN YOUR PARENTS CAME TO MY HOUSE DO YOU THINK YOUR MOTHER CHARGED OVER TO PEEK IN MY LINEN CLOSET ??
DON'T BE RIDICU-LOUS.
FOR WOMEN CANDIDATES WE PEEK IN THE LINEN CLOSET. FOR MEN CANDIDATES, WE SNOOP THROUGH THE MEDI-CINE CABINET.

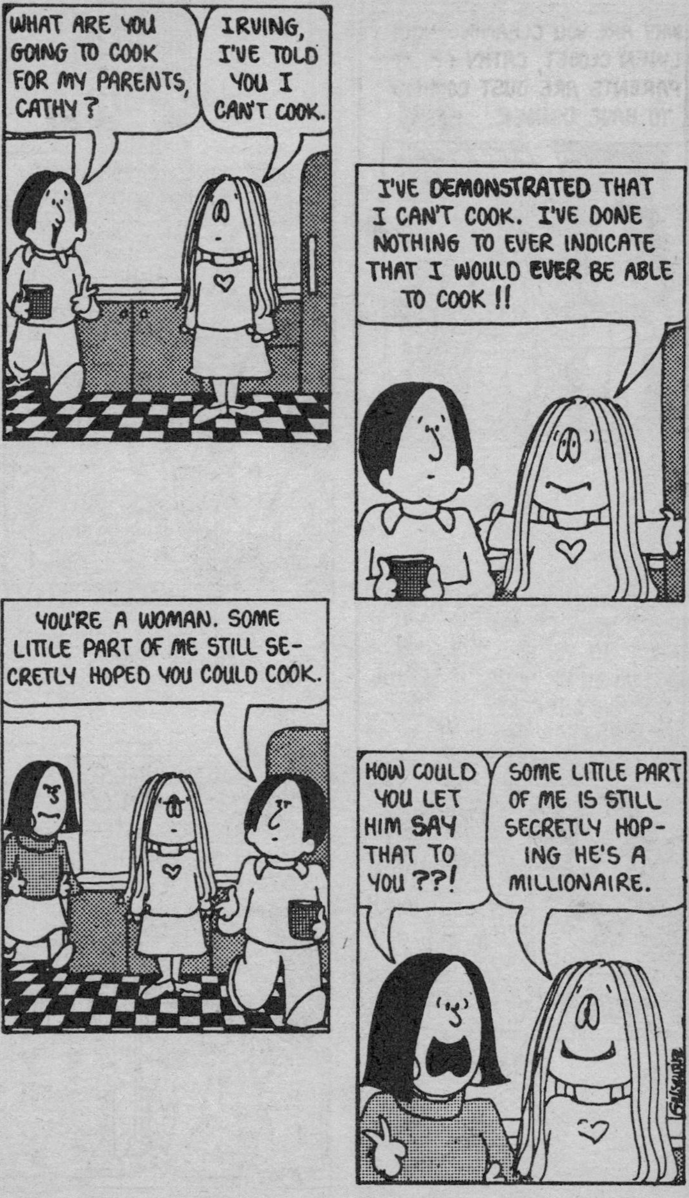
WHAT ARE YOU GOING TO COOK FOR MY PARENTS, CATHY?
IRVING, I'VE TOLD YOU I CAN'T COOK.
I'VE DEMONSTRATED THAT I CAN'T COOK. I'VE DONE NOTHING TO EVER INDICATE THAT I WOULD EVER BE ABLE TO COOK!!
YOU'RE A WOMAN. SOME LITTLE PART OF ME STILL SECRETLY HOPED YOU COULD COOK.
HOW COULD YOU LET HIM SAY THAT TO YOU??!
SOME LITTLE PART OF ME IS STILL SECRETLY HOPING HE'S A MILLIONAIRE.

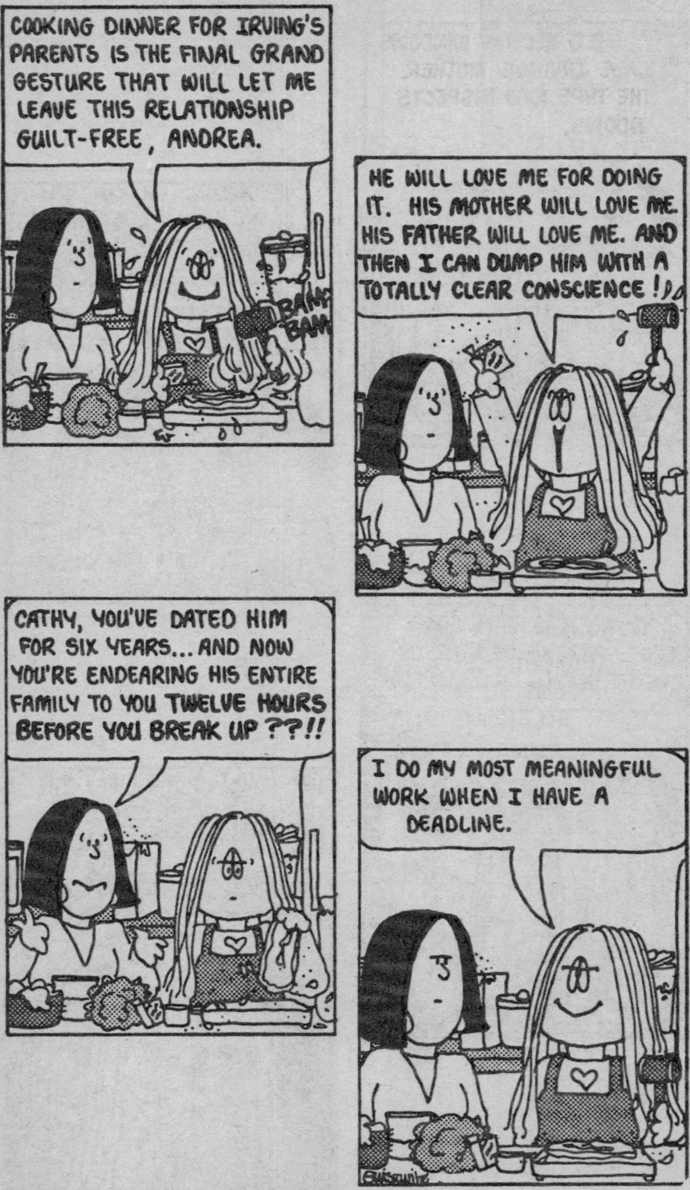
COOKING DINNER FOR IRVING'S PARENTS IS THE FINAL GRAND GESTURE THAT WILL LET ME LEAVE THIS RELATIONSHIP GUILT-FREE, ANDREA.
BAM BAM
HE WILL LOVE ME FOR DOING IT. HIS MOTHER WILL LOVE ME. HIS FATHER WILL LOVE ME. AND THEN I CAN DUMP HIM WITH A TOTALLY CLEAR CONSCIENCE!
CATHY, YOU'VE DATED HIM FOR SIX YEARS... AND NOW YOU'RE ENDEARING HIS ENTIRE FAMILY TO YOU TWELVE HOURS BEFORE YOU BREAK UP??!!
I DO MY MOST MEANINGFUL WORK WHEN I HAVE A DEADLINE.

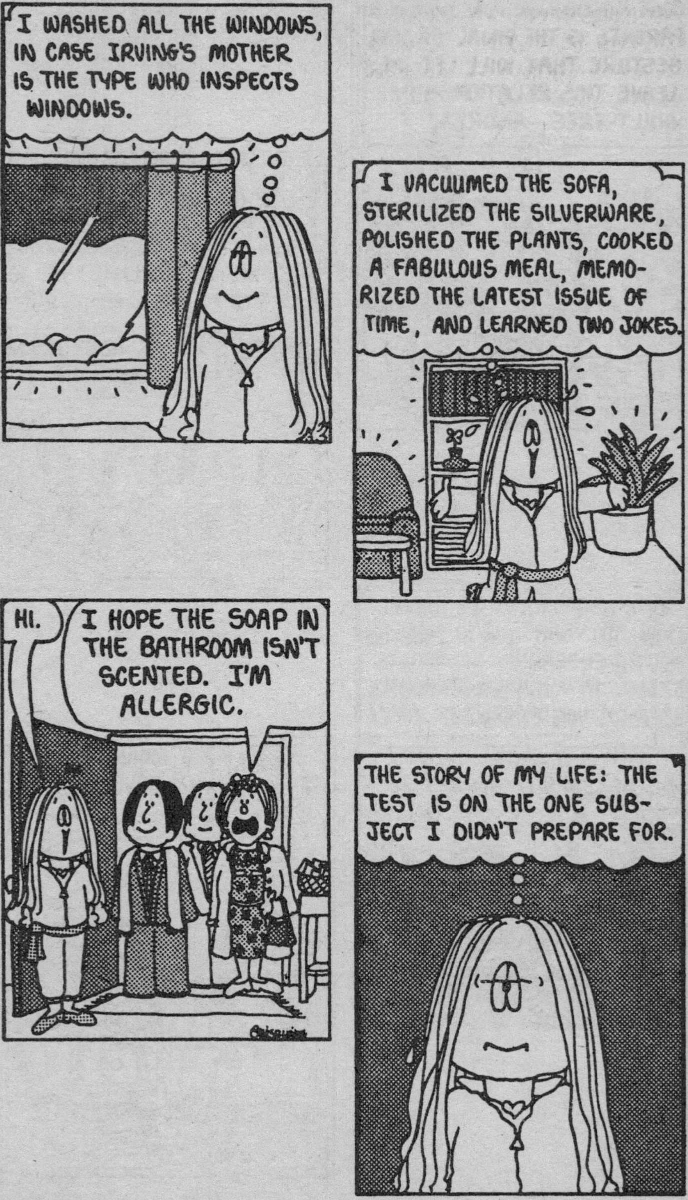
I WASHED ALL THE WINDOWS, IN CASE IRVING'S MOTHER IS THE TYPE WHO INSPECTS WINDOWS.
I VACUUMED THE SOFA, STERILIZED THE SILVERWARE, POLISHED THE PLANTS, COOKED A FABULOUS MEAL, MEMORIZED THE LATEST ISSUE OF TIME, AND LEARNED TWO JOKES.
HI.
I HOPE THE SOAP IN THE BATHROOM ISN'T SCENTED. I'M ALLERGIC.
THE STORY OF MY LIFE: THE TEST IS ON THE ONE SUBJECT I DIDN'T PREPARE FOR.

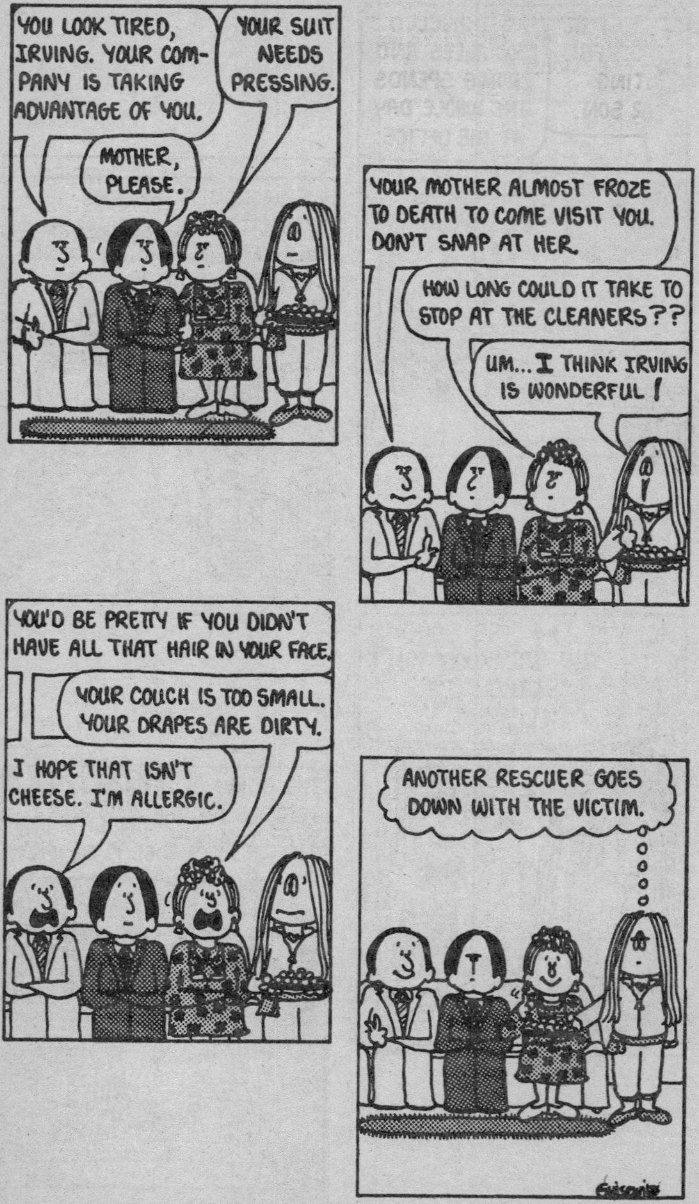
YOU LOOK TIRED, IRVING. YOUR COMPANY IS TAKING ADVANTAGE OF YOU.
YOUR SUIT NEEDS PRESSING.
MOTHER, PLEASE.
YOUR MOTHER ALMOST FROZE TO DEATH TO COME VISIT YOU. DON'T SNAP AT HER.
HOW LONG COULD IT TAKE TO STOP AT THE CLEANERS??
UM... I THINK IRVING IS WONDERFUL!
YOU'D BE PRETTY IF YOU DIDN'T HAVE ALL THAT HAIR IN YOUR FACE.
YOUR COUCH IS TOO SMALL. YOUR DRAPES ARE DIRTY.
I HOPE THAT ISN'T CHEESE. I'M ALLERGIC.
ANOTHER RESCUER GOES DOWN WITH THE VICTIM.

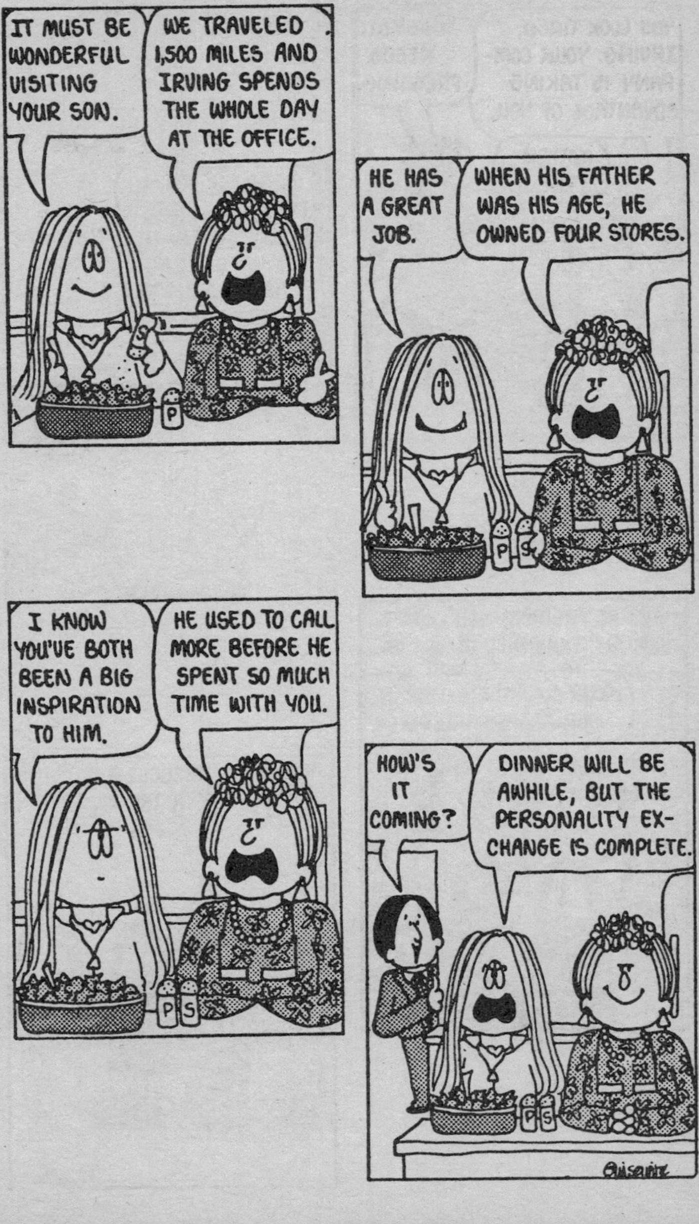
IT MUST BE WONDERFUL VISITING YOUR SON.
WE TRAVELED 1,500 MILES AND IRVING SPENDS THE WHOLE DAY AT THE OFFICE.
HE HAS A GREAT JOB.
WHEN HIS FATHER WAS HIS AGE, HE OWNED FOUR STORES.
I KNOW YOU'VE BOTH BEEN A BIG INSPIRATION TO HIM.
HE USED TO CALL MORE BEFORE HE SPENT SO MUCH TIME WITH YOU.
HOW'S IT COMING?
DINNER WILL BE AWHILE, BUT THE PERSONALITY EX-CHANGE IS COMPLETE.

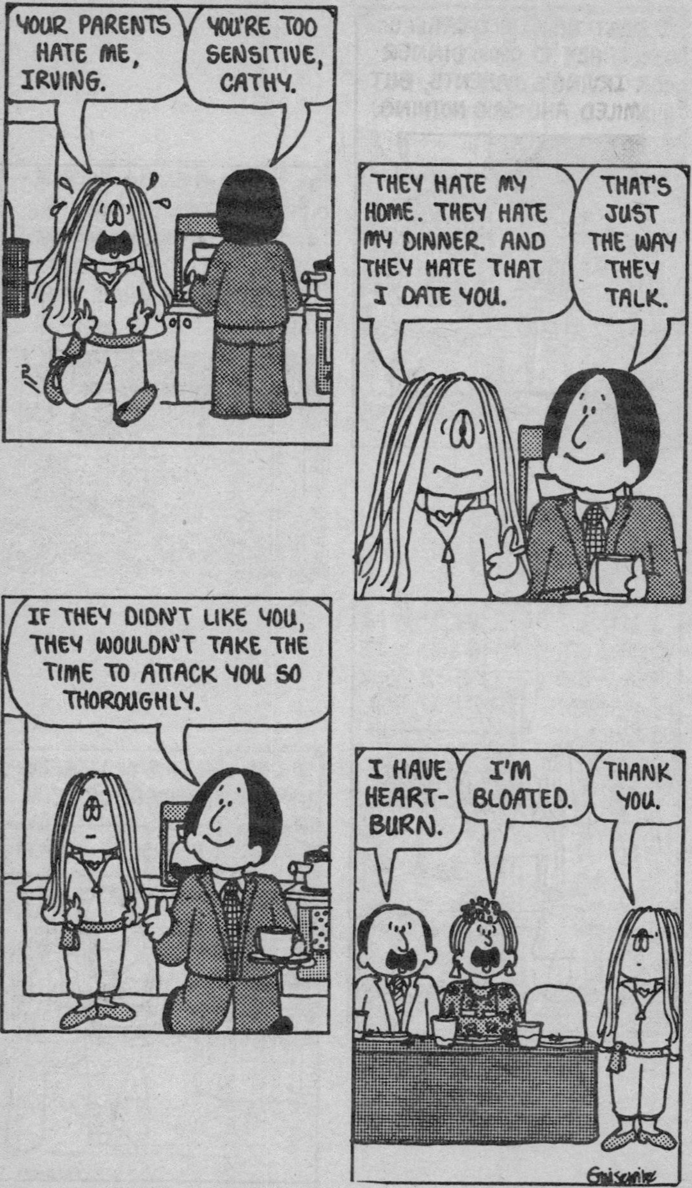
YOUR PARENTS HATE ME, IRVING.
YOU'RE TOO SENSITIVE, CATHY.
THEY HATE MY HOME. THEY HATE MY DINNER. AND THEY HATE THAT I DATE YOU.
THAT'S JUST THE WAY THEY TALK.
IF THEY DIDN'T LIKE YOU, THEY WOULDN'T TAKE THE TIME TO ATTACK YOU SO THOROUGHLY.
I HAVE HEART-BURN.
I'M BLOATED.
THANK YOU.
Guisewite

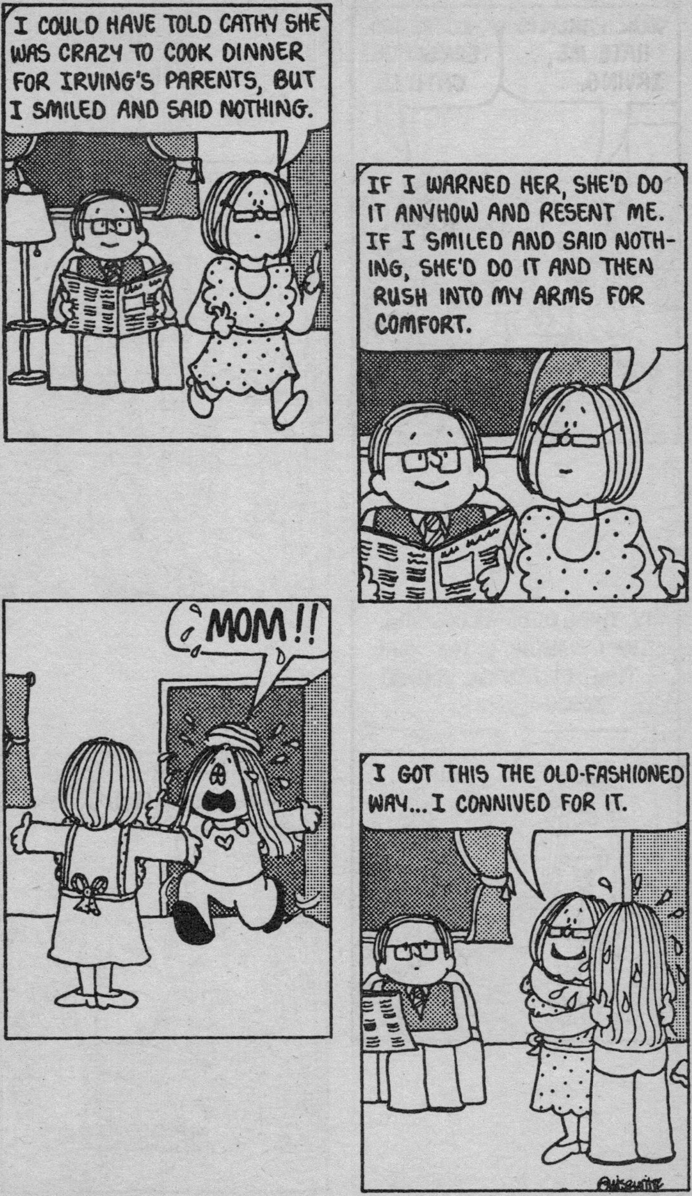
I COULD HAVE TOLD CATHY SHE WAS CRAZY TO COOK DINNER FOR IRVING'S PARENTS, BUT I SMILED AND SAID NOTHING.
IF I WARNED HER, SHE'D DO IT ANYHOW AND RESENT ME. IF I SMILED AND SAID NOTHING, SHE'D DO IT AND THEN RUSH INTO MY ARMS FOR COMFORT.
MOM!!
I GOT THIS THE OLD-FASHIONED WAY... I CONNIVED FOR IT.

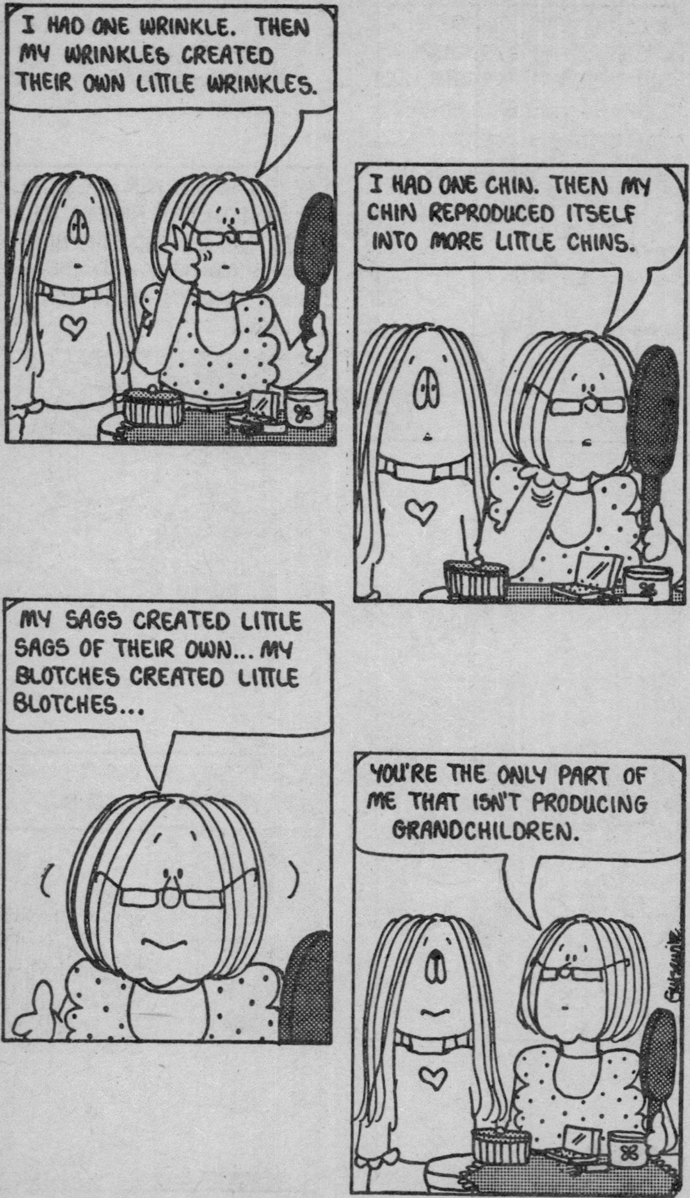
I HAD ONE WRINKLE. THEN MY WRINKLES CREATED THEIR OWN LITTLE WRINKLES.
I HAD ONE CHIN. THEN MY CHIN REPRODUCED ITSELF INTO MORE LITTLE CHINS.
MY SAGS CREATED LITTLE SAGS OF THEIR OWN... MY BLOTCHES CREATED LITTLE BLOTCHES...
YOU'RE THE ONLY PART OF ME THAT ISN'T PRODUCING GRANDCHILDREN.

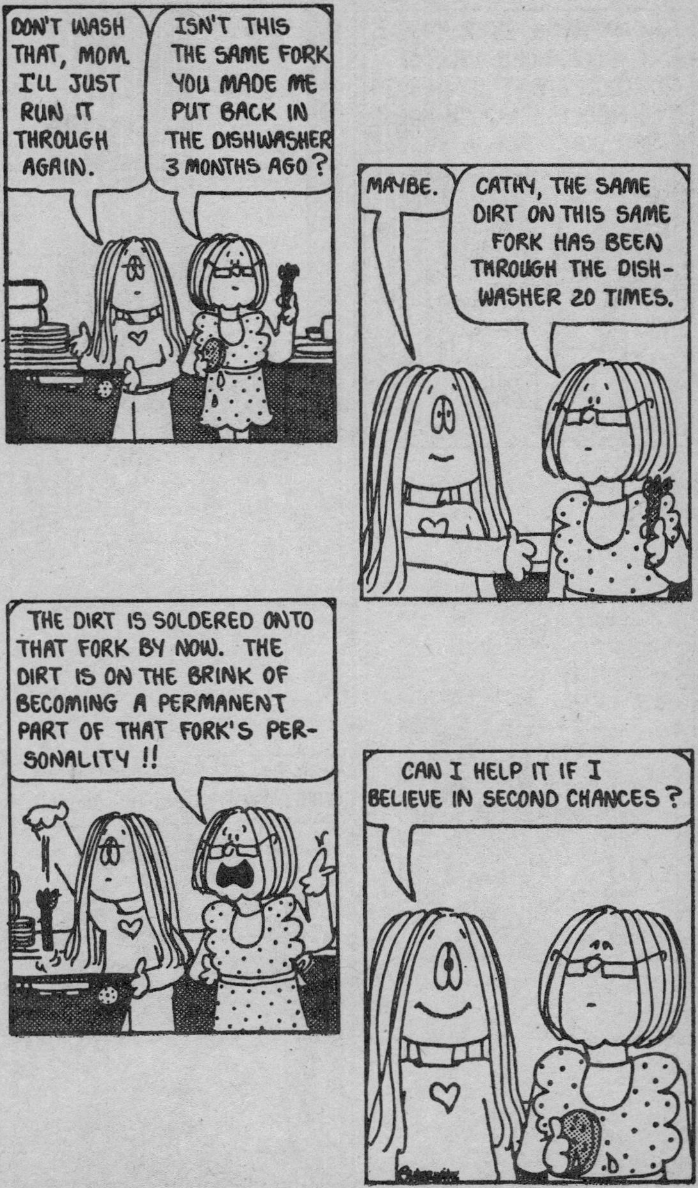
DON'T WASH THAT, MOM. I'LL JUST RUN IT THROUGH AGAIN.
ISN'T THIS THE SAME FORK YOU MADE ME PUT BACK IN THE DISHWASHER 3 MONTHS AGO?
MAYBE.
CATHY, THE SAME DIRT ON THIS SAME FORK HAS BEEN THROUGH THE DISH-WASHER 20 TIMES.
THE DIRT IS SOLDERED ONTO THAT FORK BY NOW. THE DIRT IS ON THE BRINK OF BECOMING A PERMANENT PART OF THAT FORK'S PER-SONALITY !!
CAN I HELP IT IF I BELIEVE IN SECOND CHANCES?

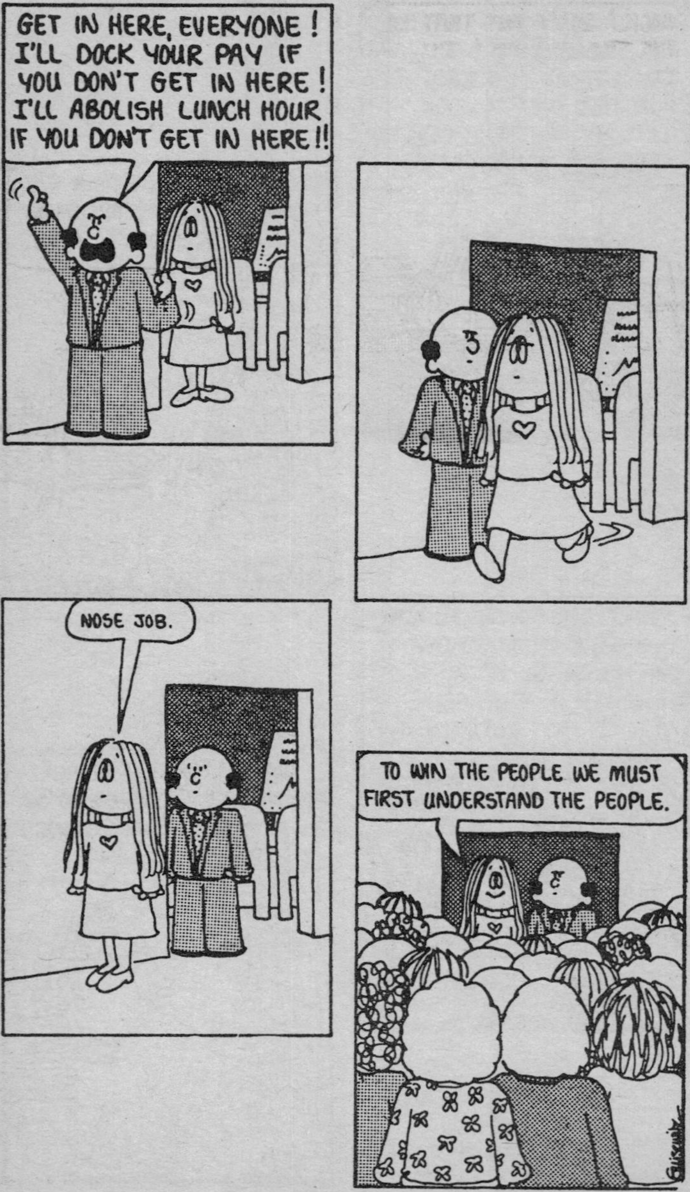
GET IN HERE, EVERYONE! I'LL DOCK YOUR PAY IF YOU DON'T GET IN HERE! I'LL ABOLISH LUNCH HOUR IF YOU DON'T GET IN HERE!!
NOSE JOB.
TO WIN THE PEOPLE WE MUST FIRST UNDERSTAND THE PEOPLE.

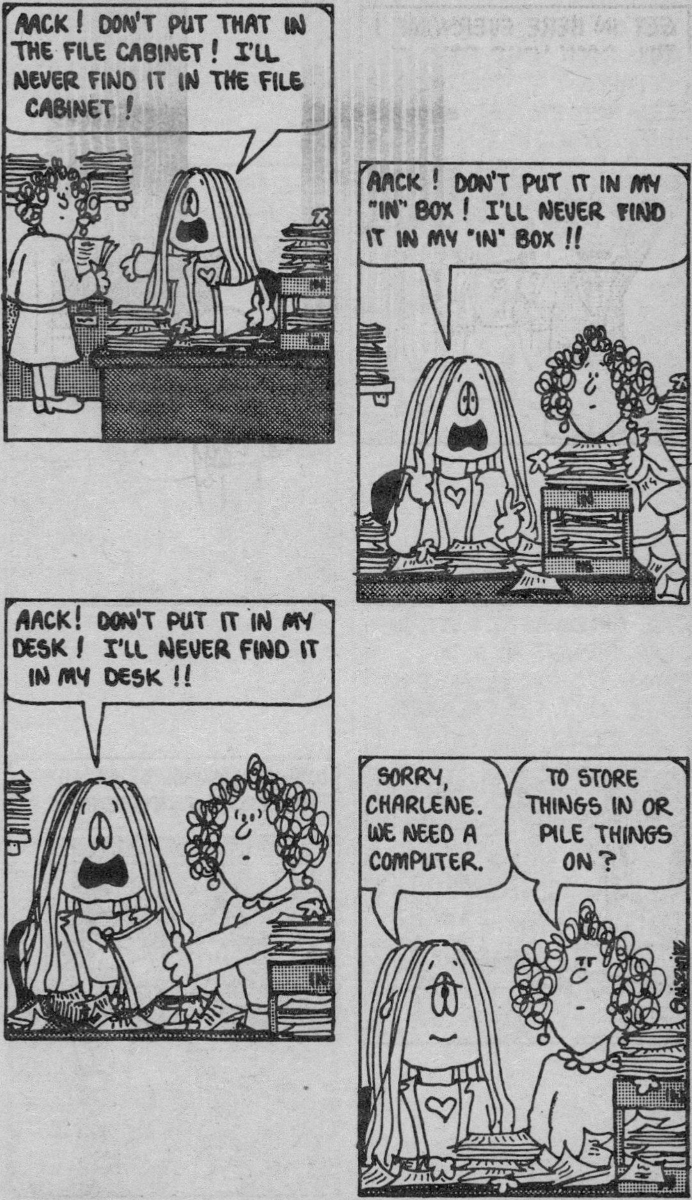
AACK! DON'T PUT THAT IN THE FILE CABINET! I'LL NEVER FIND IT IN THE FILE CABINET!
AACK! DON'T PUT IT IN MY "IN" BOX! I'LL NEVER FIND IT IN MY "IN" BOX!!
AACK! DON'T PUT IT IN MY DESK! I'LL NEVER FIND IT IN MY DESK!!
SORRY, CHARLENE. WE NEED A COMPUTER.
TO STORE THINGS IN OR PILE THINGS ON?

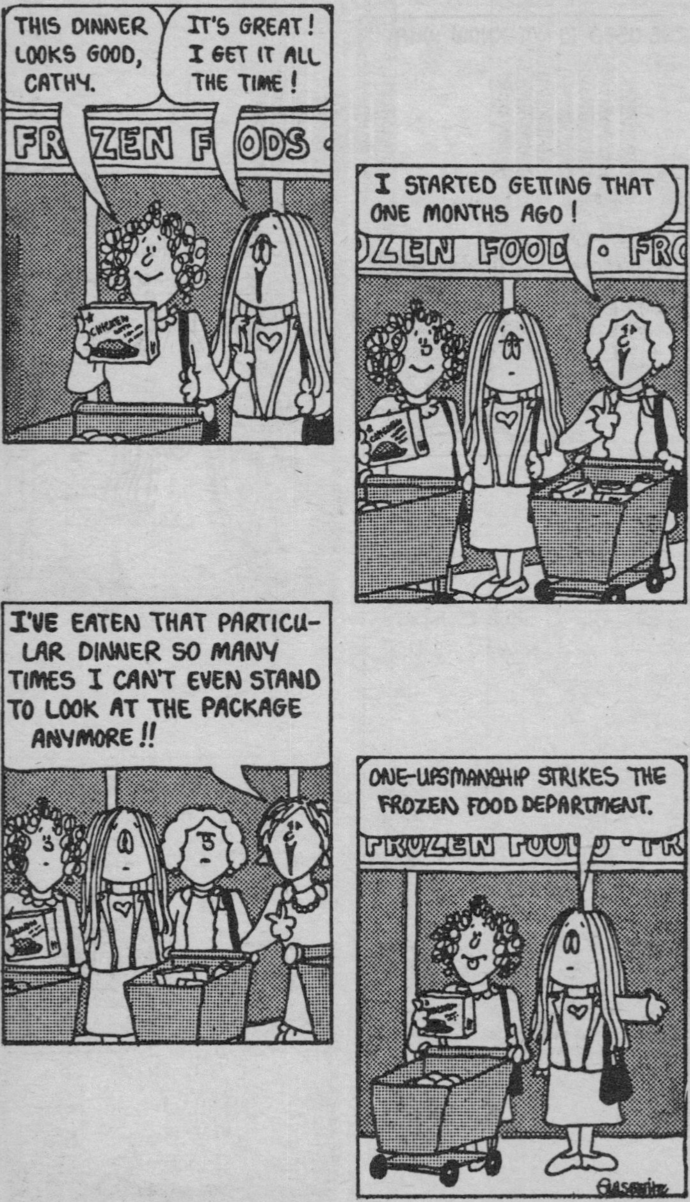
THIS DINNER LOOKS GOOD, CATHY.
IT'S GREAT! I GET IT ALL THE TIME!
FROZEN FOODS
I STARTED GETTING THAT ONE MONTHS AGO!
I'VE EATEN THAT PARTICULAR DINNER SO MANY TIMES I CAN'T EVEN STAND TO LOOK AT THE PACKAGE ANYMORE!!
ONE-UPSMANSHIP STRIKES THE FROZEN FOOD DEPARTMENT.

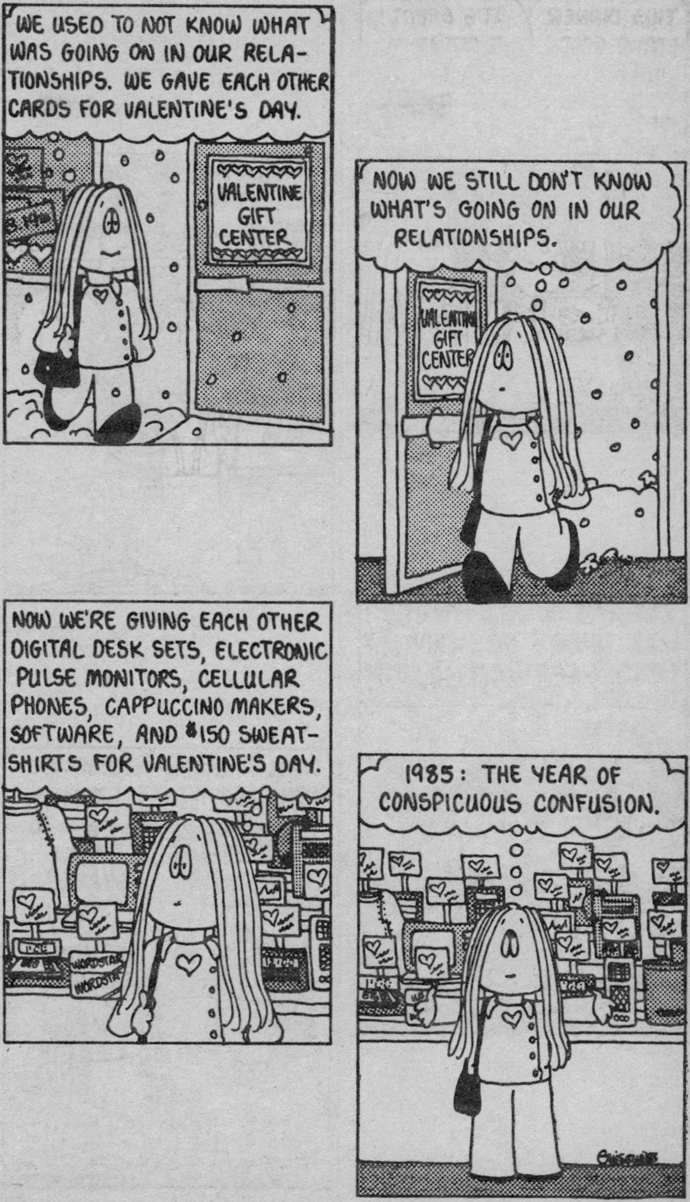
WE USED TO NOT KNOW WHAT WAS GOING ON IN OUR RELATIONSHIPS. WE GAVE EACH OTHER CARDS FOR VALENTINE'S DAY.
VALENTINE GIFT CENTER
NOW WE STILL DON'T KNOW WHAT'S GOING ON IN OUR RELATIONSHIPS.
VALENTINE GIFT CENTER
NOW WE'RE GIVING EACH OTHER DIGITAL DESK SETS, ELECTRONIC PULSE MONITORS, CELLULAR PHONES, CAPPUCCINO MAKERS, SOFTWARE, AND $150 SWEATSHIRTS FOR VALENTINE'S DAY.
WORDSTAR
WORDSTAR
1985: THE YEAR OF CONSPICUOUS CONFUSION.
Guisewite

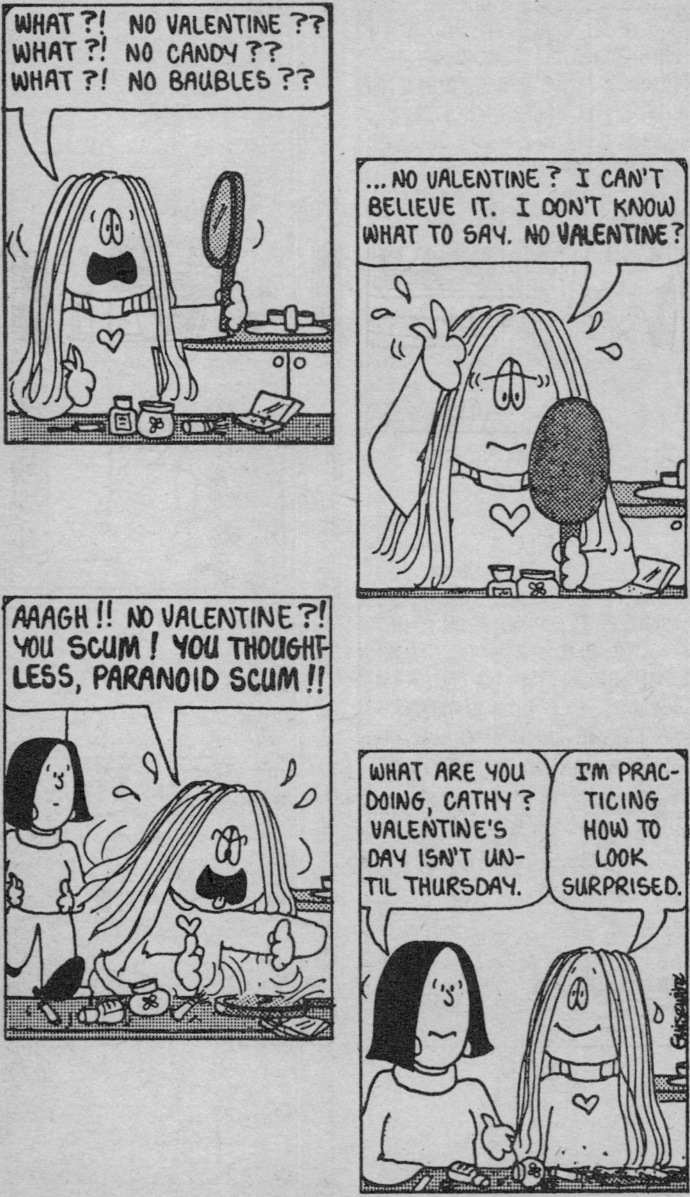

WHAT?! NO VALENTINE?? WHAT?! NO CANDY?? WHAT?! NO BAUBLES??
...NO VALENTINE? I CAN'T BELIEVE IT. I DON'T KNOW WHAT TO SAY. NO VALENTINE?
AAAGH!! NO VALENTINE?! YOU SCUM! YOU THOUGHTLESS, PARANOID SCUM!!
WHAT ARE YOU DOING, CATHY? VALENTINE'S DAY ISN'T UNTIL THURSDAY.
I'M PRACTICING HOW TO LOOK SURPRISED.
Guisewite

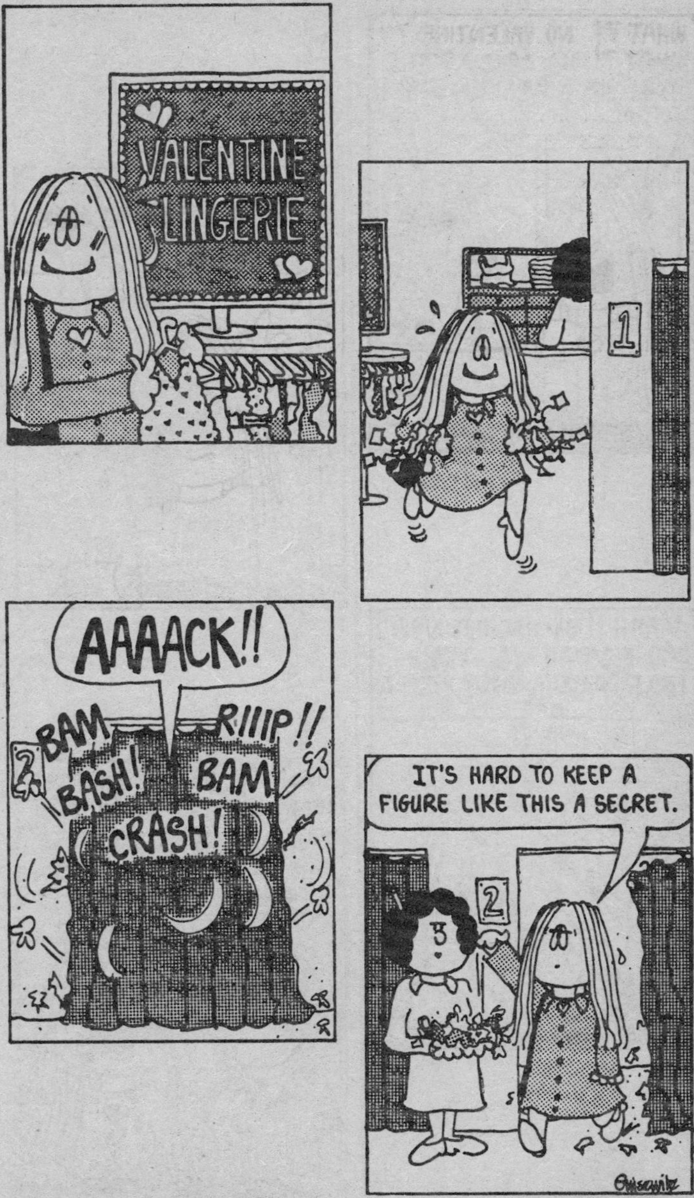
VALENTINE
LINGERIE
AAAACK!!
BAM
RIIIP!!
BASH!
BAM
CRASH!
IT'S HARD TO KEEP A FIGURE LIKE THIS A SECRET.
Guisewite

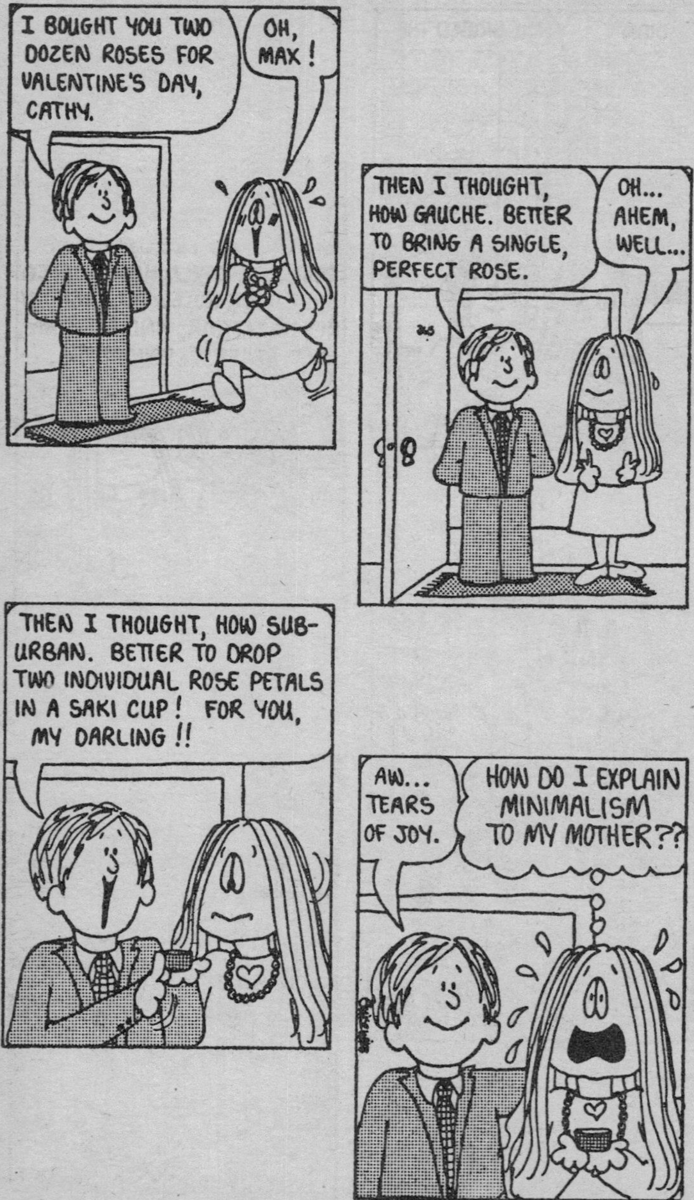

I BOUGHT YOU TWO DOZEN ROSES FOR VALENTINE'S DAY, CATHY.
OH, MAX!
THEN I THOUGHT, HOW GAUCHE. BETTER TO BRING A SINGLE, PERFECT ROSE.
OH... AHEM, WELL...
THEN I THOUGHT, HOW SUB-URBAN. BETTER TO DROP TWO INDIVIDUAL ROSE PETALS IN A SAKI CUP! FOR YOU, MY DARLING!!
AW... TEARS OF JOY.
HOW DO I EXPLAIN MINIMALISM TO MY MOTHER??

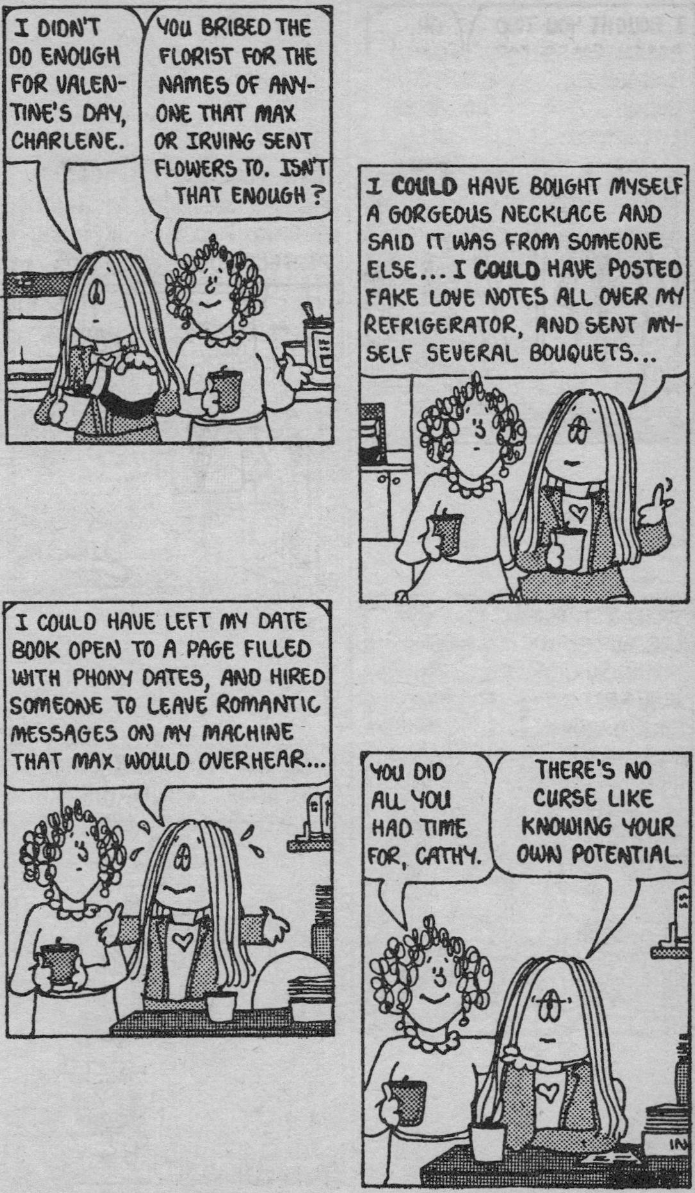
I DIDN'T DO ENOUGH FOR VALENTINE'S DAY, CHARLENE.
YOU BRIBED THE FLORIST FOR THE NAMES OF ANYONE THAT MAX OR IRVING SENT FLOWERS TO. ISN'T THAT ENOUGH?
I **COULD** HAVE BOUGHT MYSELF A GORGEOUS NECKLACE AND SAID IT WAS FROM SOMEONE ELSE... I **COULD** HAVE POSTED FAKE LOVE NOTES ALL OVER MY REFRIGERATOR, AND SENT MYSELF SEVERAL BOUQUETS...
I COULD HAVE LEFT MY DATE BOOK OPEN TO A PAGE FILLED WITH PHONY DATES, AND HIRED SOMEONE TO LEAVE ROMANTIC MESSAGES ON MY MACHINE THAT MAX WOULD OVERHEAR...
YOU DID ALL YOU HAD TIME FOR, CATHY.
THERE'S NO CURSE LIKE KNOWING YOUR OWN POTENTIAL.

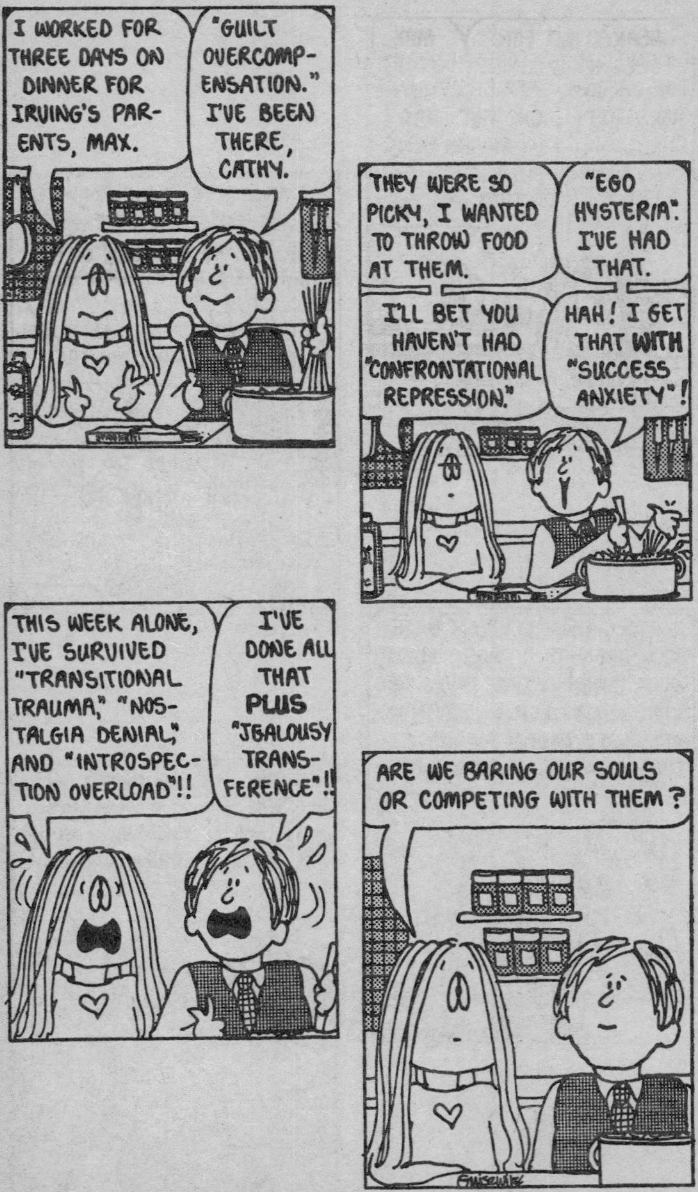
I WORKED FOR THREE DAYS ON DINNER FOR IRVING'S PARENTS, MAX.
"GUILT OVERCOMPENSATION." I'VE BEEN THERE, CATHY.
THEY WERE SO PICKY, I WANTED TO THROW FOOD AT THEM.
"EGO HYSTERIA". I'VE HAD THAT.
I'LL BET YOU HAVEN'T HAD "CONFRONTATIONAL REPRESSION."
HAH! I GET THAT WITH "SUCCESS ANXIETY"!
THIS WEEK ALONE, I'VE SURVIVED "TRANSITIONAL TRAUMA," "NOSTALGIA DENIAL," AND "INTROSPECTION OVERLOAD"!!
I'VE DONE ALL THAT PLUS "JEALOUSY TRANSFERENCE"!!
ARE WE BARING OUR SOULS OR COMPETING WITH THEM?

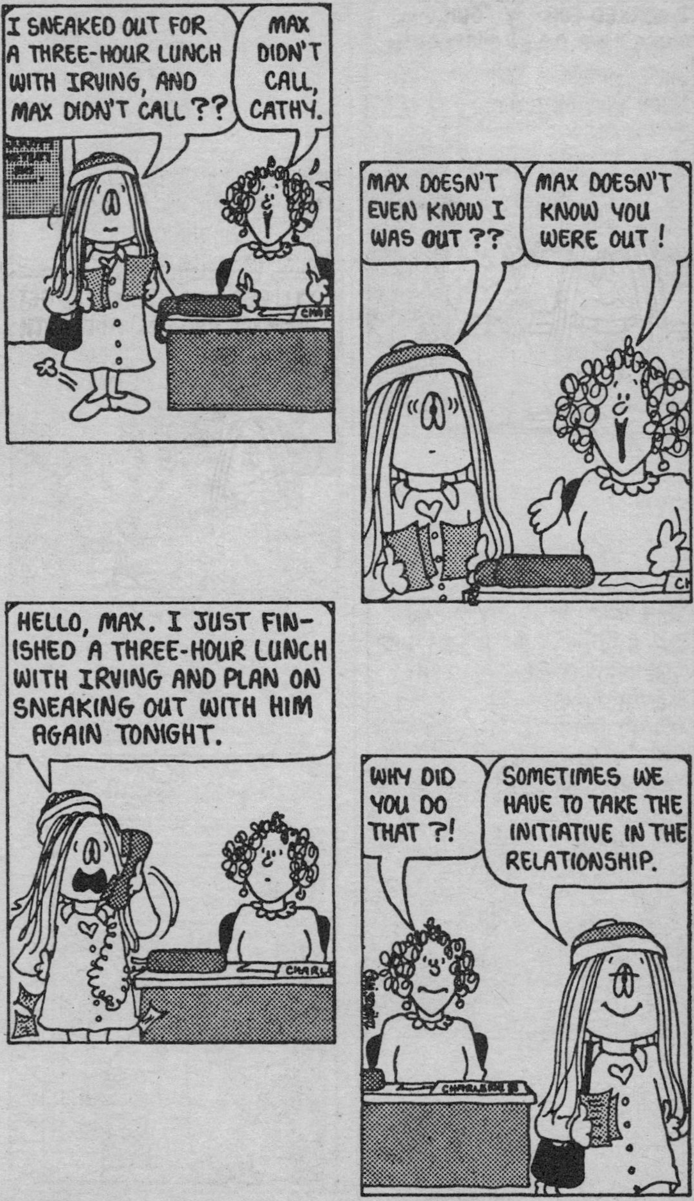
I SNEAKED OUT FOR A THREE-HOUR LUNCH WITH IRVING, AND MAX DIDN'T CALL ??
MAX DIDN'T CALL, CATHY.
MAX DOESN'T EVEN KNOW I WAS OUT ??
MAX DOESN'T KNOW YOU WERE OUT !
HELLO, MAX. I JUST FINISHED A THREE-HOUR LUNCH WITH IRVING AND PLAN ON SNEAKING OUT WITH HIM AGAIN TONIGHT.
WHY DID YOU DO THAT ?!
SOMETIMES WE HAVE TO TAKE THE INITIATIVE IN THE RELATIONSHIP.

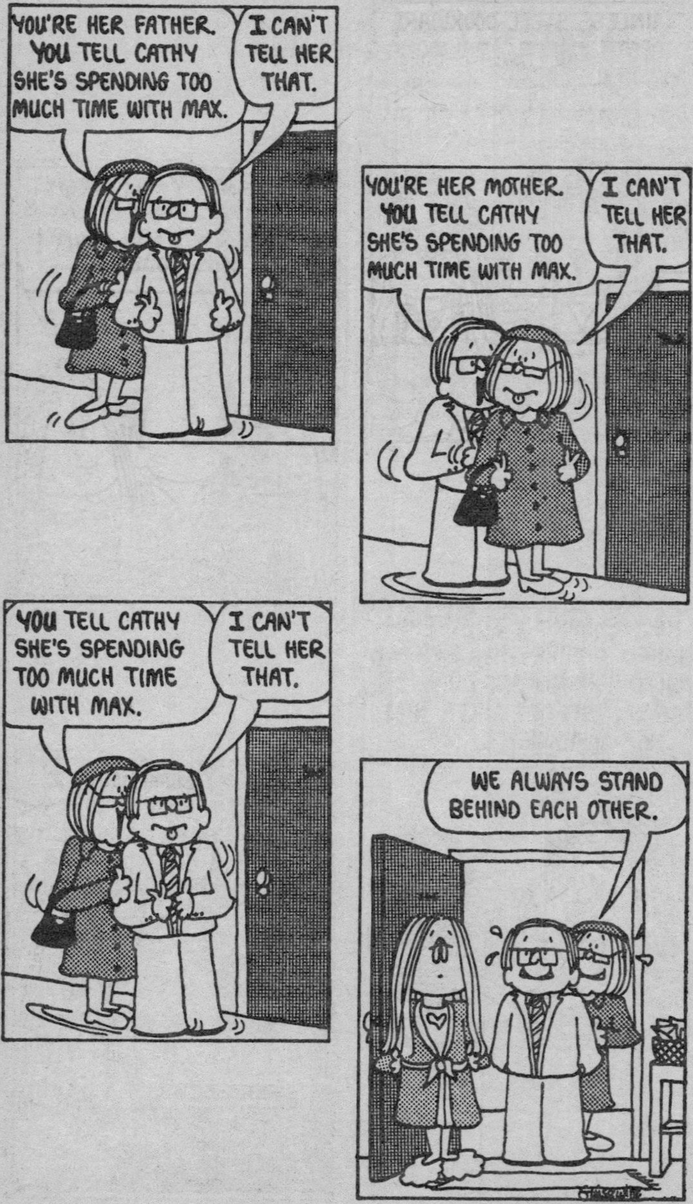

YOU'RE HER FATHER. YOU TELL CATHY SHE'S SPENDING TOO MUCH TIME WITH MAX.
I CAN'T TELL HER THAT.
YOU'RE HER MOTHER. YOU TELL CATHY SHE'S SPENDING TOO MUCH TIME WITH MAX.
I CAN'T TELL HER THAT.
YOU TELL CATHY SHE'S SPENDING TOO MUCH TIME WITH MAX.
I CAN'T TELL HER THAT.
WE ALWAYS STAND BEHIND EACH OTHER.

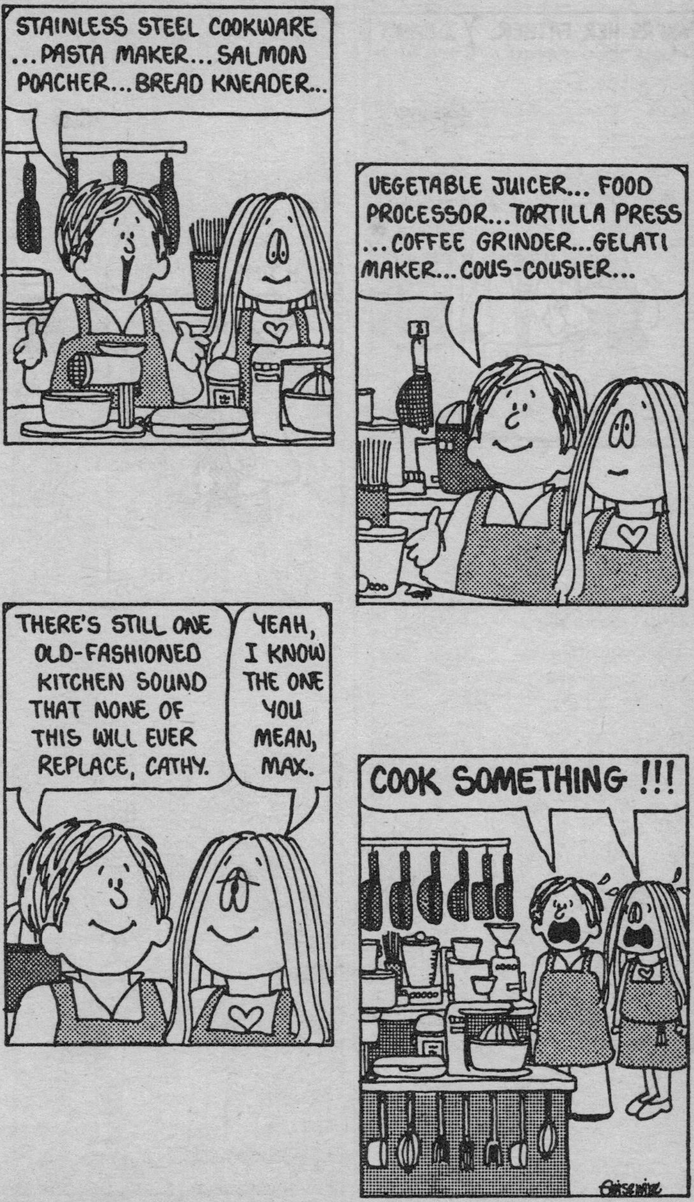
STAINLESS STEEL COOKWARE ...PASTA MAKER...SALMON POACHER...BREAD KNEADER...
VEGETABLE JUICER... FOOD PROCESSOR...TORTILLA PRESS ...COFFEE GRINDER...GELATI MAKER...COUS-COUSIER...
THERE'S STILL ONE OLD-FASHIONED KITCHEN SOUND THAT NONE OF THIS WILL EVER REPLACE, CATHY.
YEAH, I KNOW THE ONE YOU MEAN, MAX.
COOK SOMETHING !!!

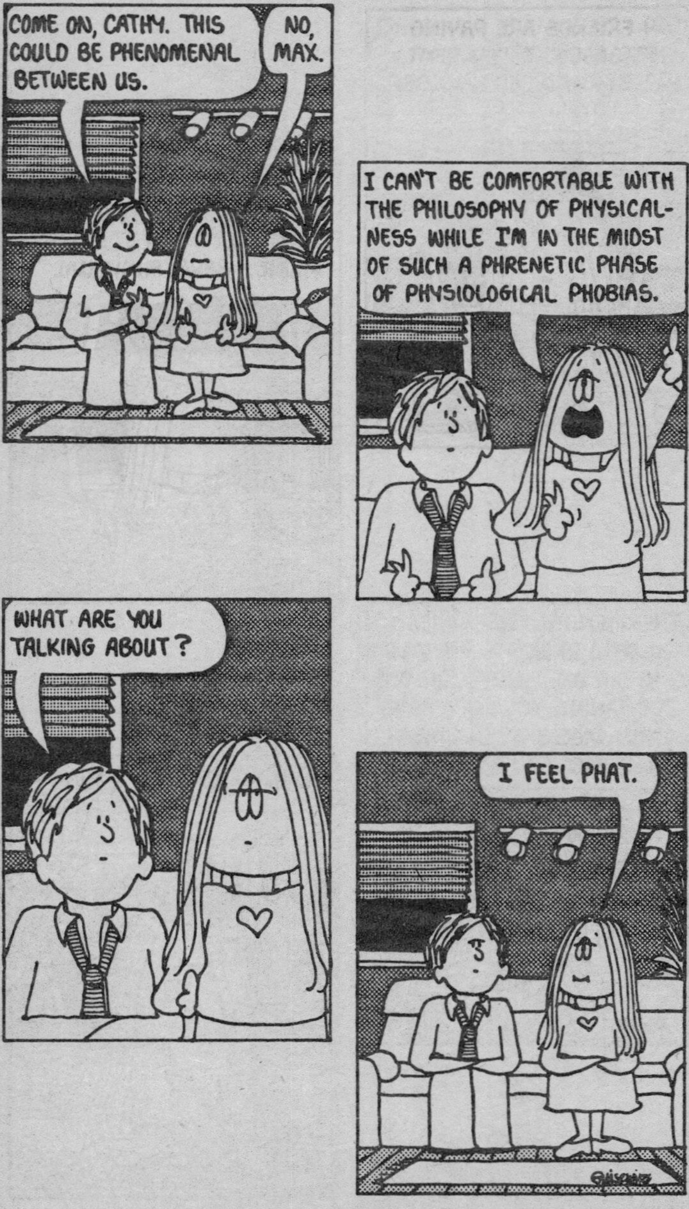
COME ON, CATHY. THIS COULD BE PHENOMENAL BETWEEN US.
NO, MAX.
I CAN'T BE COMFORTABLE WITH THE PHILOSOPHY OF PHYSICAL-NESS WHILE I'M IN THE MIDST OF SUCH A PHRENETIC PHASE OF PHYSIOLOGICAL PHOBIAS.
WHAT ARE YOU TALKING ABOUT?
I FEEL PHAT.

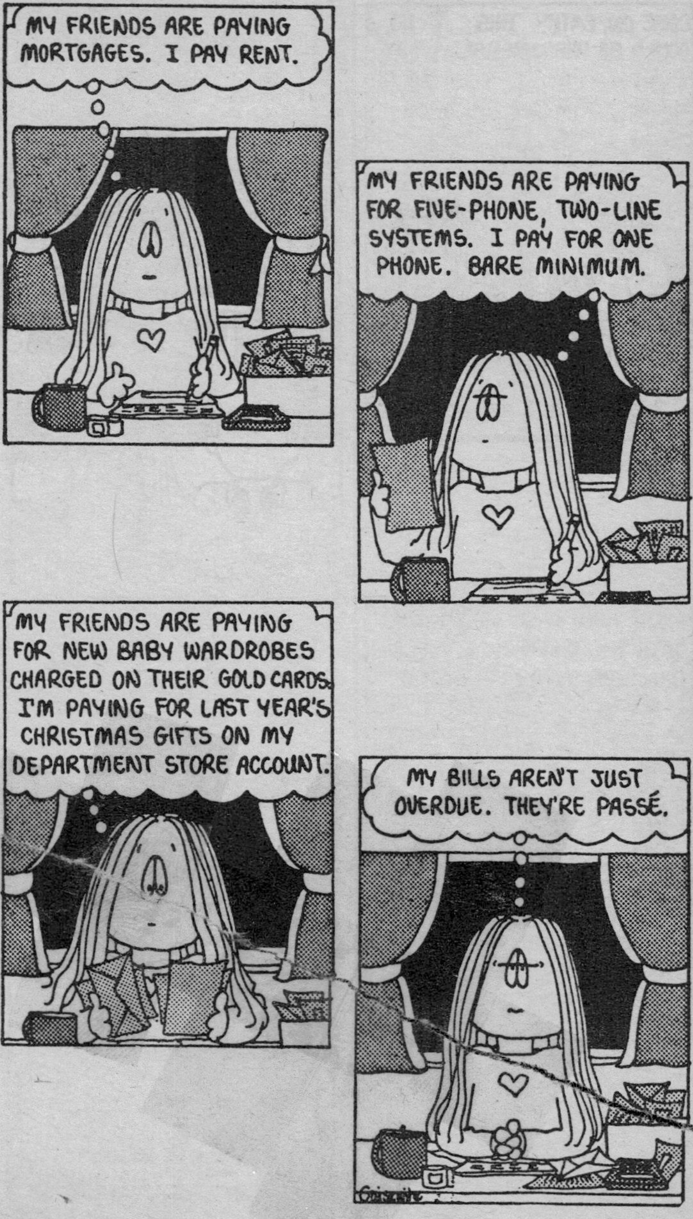
MY FRIENDS ARE PAYING MORTGAGES. I PAY RENT.
MY FRIENDS ARE PAYING FOR FIVE-PHONE, TWO-LINE SYSTEMS. I PAY FOR ONE PHONE. BARE MINIMUM.
MY FRIENDS ARE PAYING FOR NEW BABY WARDROBES CHARGED ON THEIR GOLD CARDS. I'M PAYING FOR LAST YEAR'S CHRISTMAS GIFTS ON MY DEPARTMENT STORE ACCOUNT.
MY BILLS AREN'T JUST OVERDUE. THEY'RE PASSÉ.

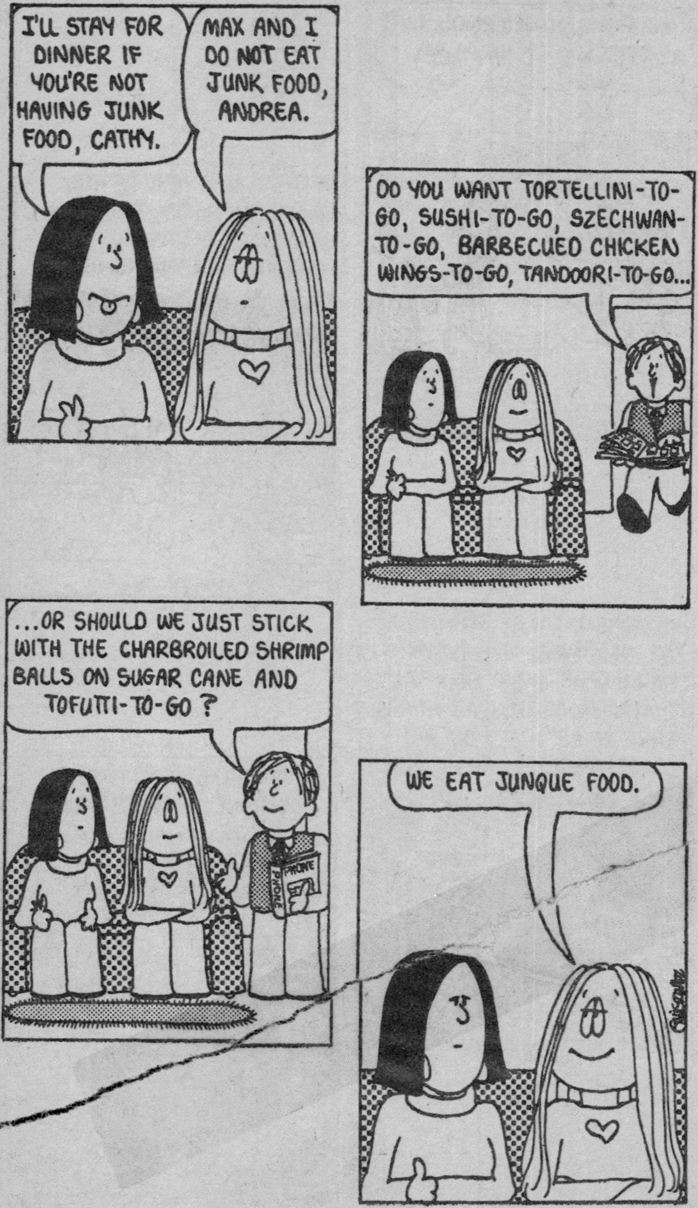
I'LL STAY FOR DINNER IF YOU'RE NOT HAVING JUNK FOOD, CATHY.
MAX AND I DO NOT EAT JUNK FOOD, ANDREA.
DO YOU WANT TORTELLINI-TO-GO, SUSHI-TO-GO, SZECHWAN-TO-GO, BARBECUED CHICKEN WINGS-TO-GO, TANDOORI-TO-GO...
...OR SHOULD WE JUST STICK WITH THE CHARBROILED SHRIMP BALLS ON SUGAR CANE AND TOFUTTI-TO-GO?
PHONE
WE EAT JUNQUE FOOD.

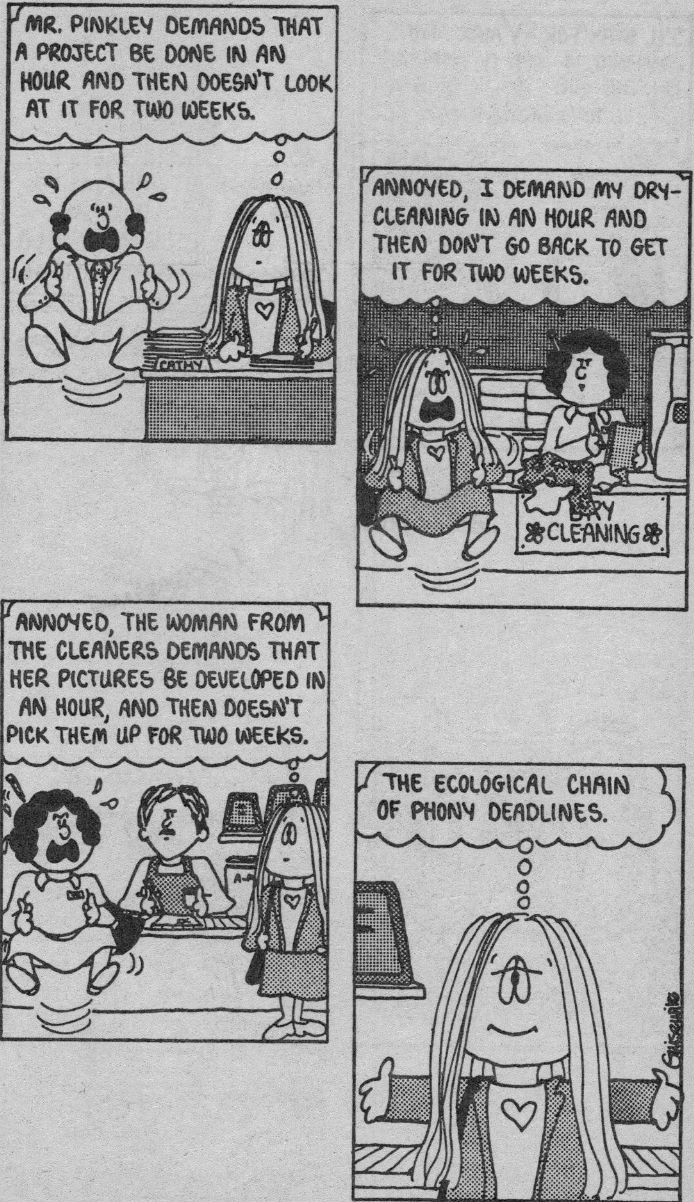
MR. PINKLEY DEMANDS THAT A PROJECT BE DONE IN AN HOUR AND THEN DOESN'T LOOK AT IT FOR TWO WEEKS.
CATHY
ANNOYED, I DEMAND MY DRY-CLEANING IN AN HOUR AND THEN DON'T GO BACK TO GET IT FOR TWO WEEKS.
CLEANING
ANNOYED, THE WOMAN FROM THE CLEANERS DEMANDS THAT HER PICTURES BE DEVELOPED IN AN HOUR, AND THEN DOESN'T PICK THEM UP FOR TWO WEEKS.
THE ECOLOGICAL CHAIN OF PHONY DEADLINES.
Guisewite

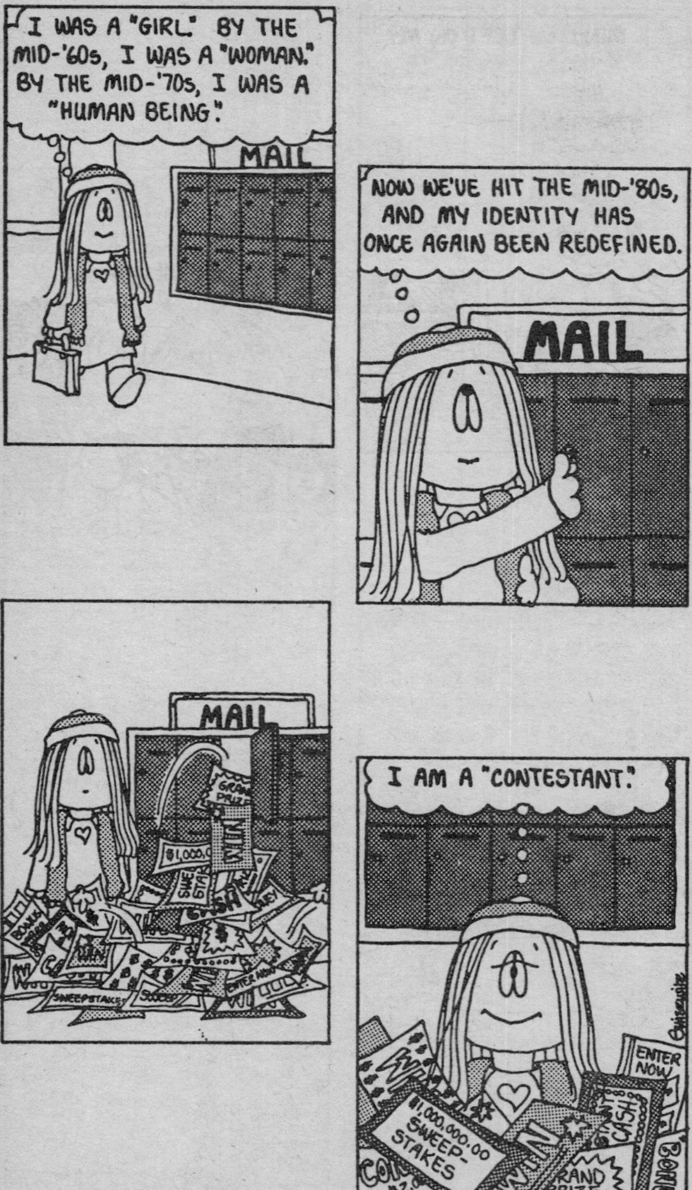
I WAS A "GIRL." BY THE MID-'60s, I WAS A "WOMAN." BY THE MID-'70s, I WAS A "HUMAN BEING."
MAIL
NOW WE'VE HIT THE MID-'80s, AND MY IDENTITY HAS ONCE AGAIN BEEN REDEFINED.
MAIL
MAIL
SWEEPSTAKES
ENTER NOW
I AM A "CONTESTANT."
ENTER NOW
$1,000,000.00 SWEEP-STAKES
GRAND PRIZE
CASH

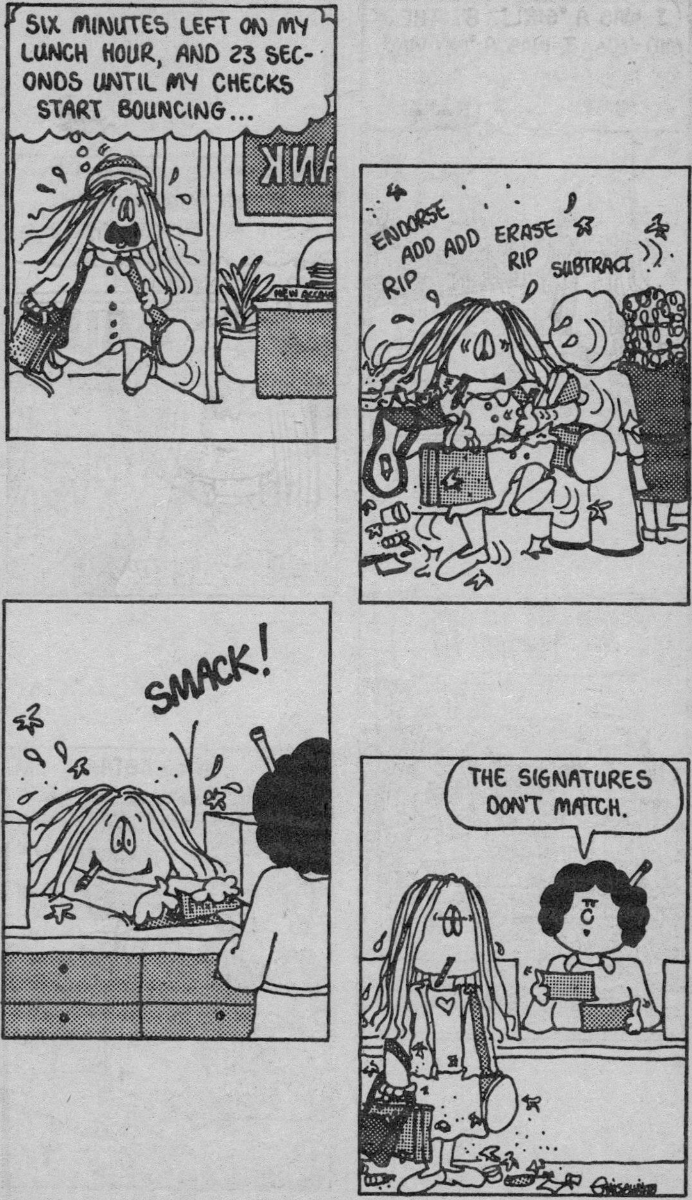
SIX MINUTES LEFT ON MY LUNCH HOUR, AND 23 SECONDS UNTIL MY CHECKS START BOUNCING...
ENDORSE
ADD ADD ERASE
RIP
RIP
SUBTRACT
SMACK!
THE SIGNATURES DON'T MATCH.

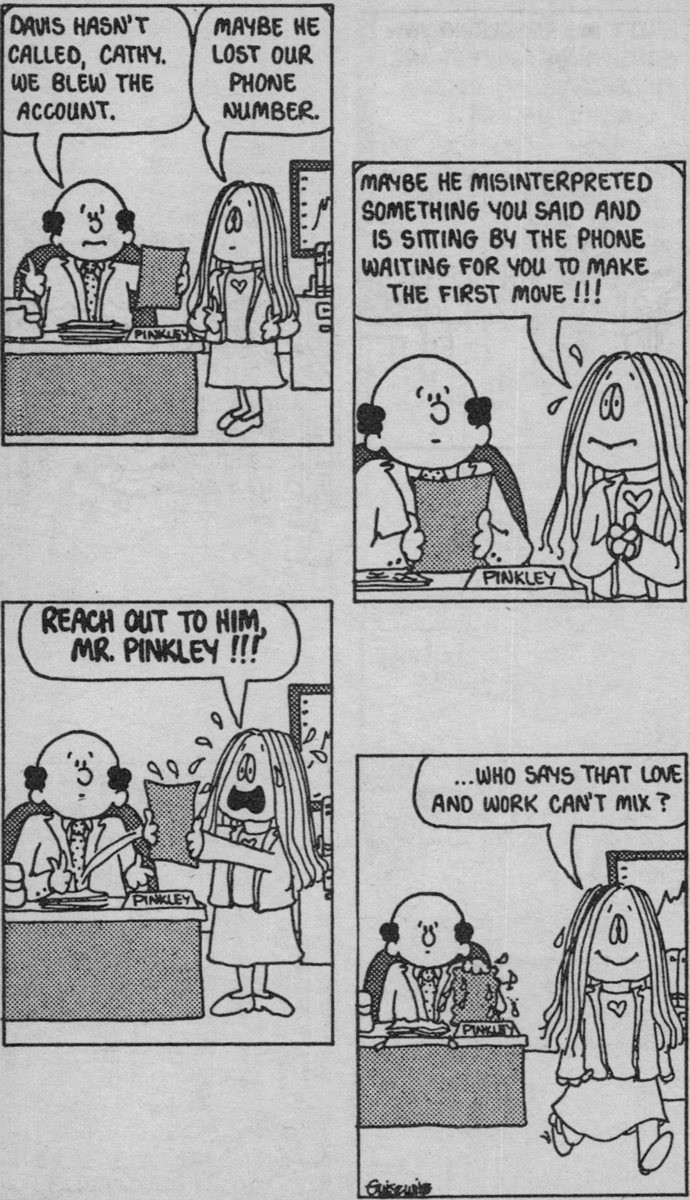
DAVIS HASN'T CALLED, CATHY. WE BLEW THE ACCOUNT.
MAYBE HE LOST OUR PHONE NUMBER.
PINKLEY
MAYBE HE MISINTERPRETED SOMETHING YOU SAID AND IS SITTING BY THE PHONE WAITING FOR YOU TO MAKE THE FIRST MOVE !!!
PINKLEY
REACH OUT TO HIM, MR. PINKLEY !!!
PINKLEY
...WHO SAYS THAT LOVE AND WORK CAN'T MIX ?
PINKLEY
Guisewite

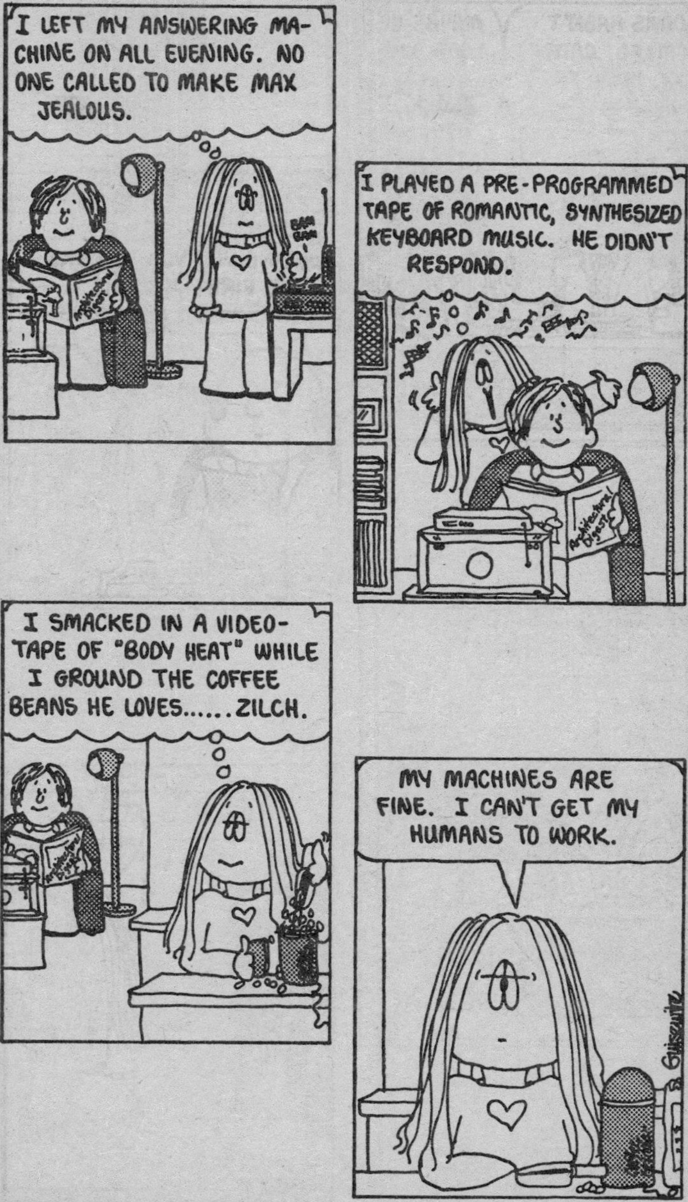
I LEFT MY ANSWERING MACHINE ON ALL EVENING. NO ONE CALLED TO MAKE MAX JEALOUS.
I PLAYED A PRE-PROGRAMMED TAPE OF ROMANTIC, SYNTHESIZED KEYBOARD MUSIC. HE DIDN'T RESPOND.
I SMACKED IN A VIDEOTAPE OF "BODY HEAT" WHILE I GROUND THE COFFEE BEANS HE LOVES...... ZILCH.
MY MACHINES ARE FINE. I CAN'T GET MY HUMANS TO WORK.
GUISEWITE

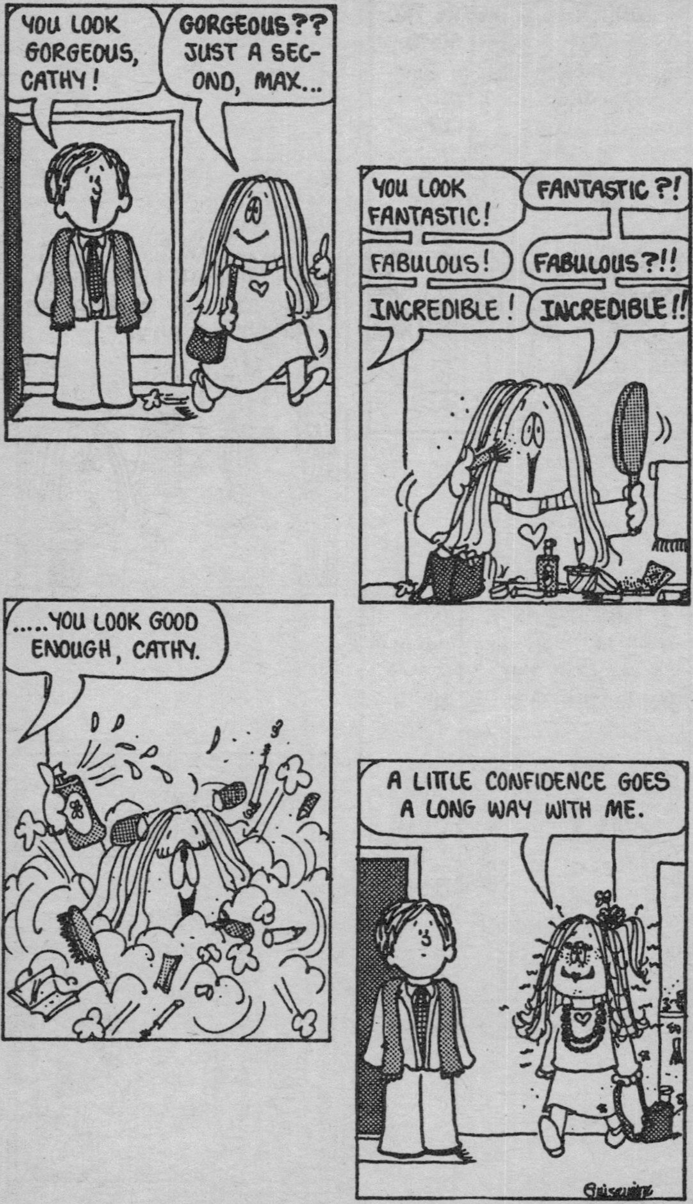
YOU LOOK GORGEOUS, CATHY!
GORGEOUS?? JUST A SECOND, MAX...
YOU LOOK FANTASTIC!
FANTASTIC?!
FABULOUS!
FABULOUS?!!
INCREDIBLE!
INCREDIBLE!!
.....YOU LOOK GOOD ENOUGH, CATHY.
A LITTLE CONFIDENCE GOES A LONG WAY WITH ME.

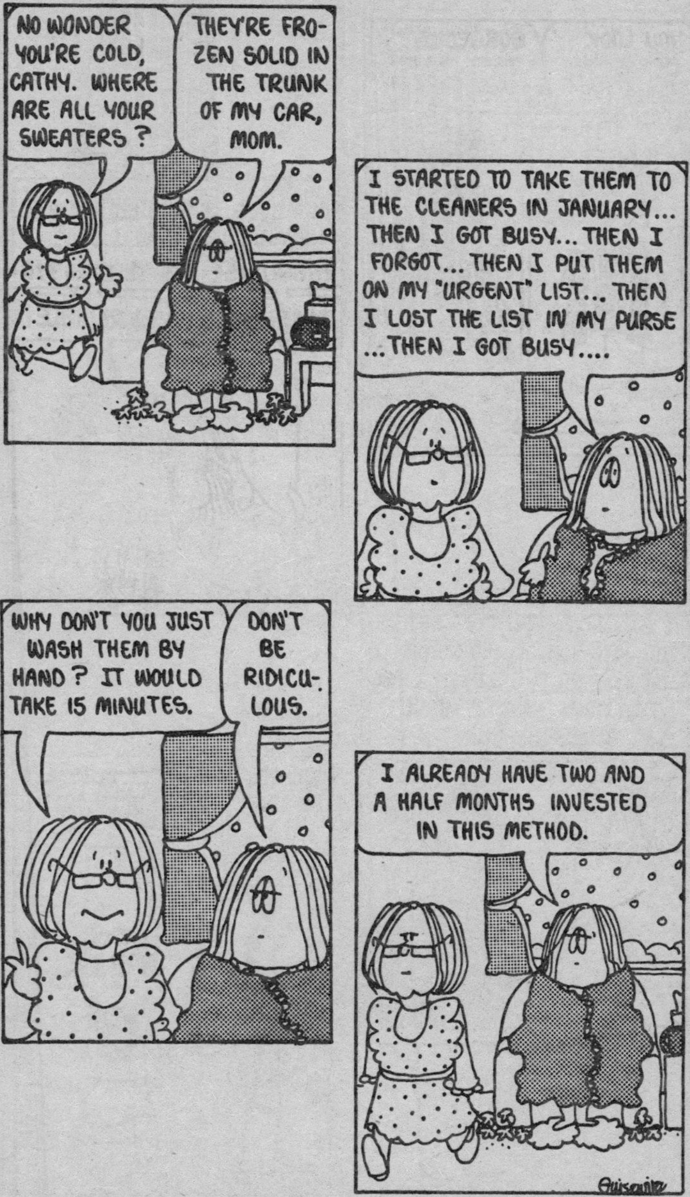
NO WONDER YOU'RE COLD, CATHY. WHERE ARE ALL YOUR SWEATERS?
THEY'RE FROZEN SOLID IN THE TRUNK OF MY CAR, MOM.
I STARTED TO TAKE THEM TO THE CLEANERS IN JANUARY... THEN I GOT BUSY... THEN I FORGOT... THEN I PUT THEM ON MY "URGENT" LIST... THEN I LOST THE LIST IN MY PURSE ...THEN I GOT BUSY....
WHY DON'T YOU JUST WASH THEM BY HAND? IT WOULD TAKE 15 MINUTES.
DON'T BE RIDICULOUS.
I ALREADY HAVE TWO AND A HALF MONTHS INVESTED IN THIS METHOD.
Guisewite

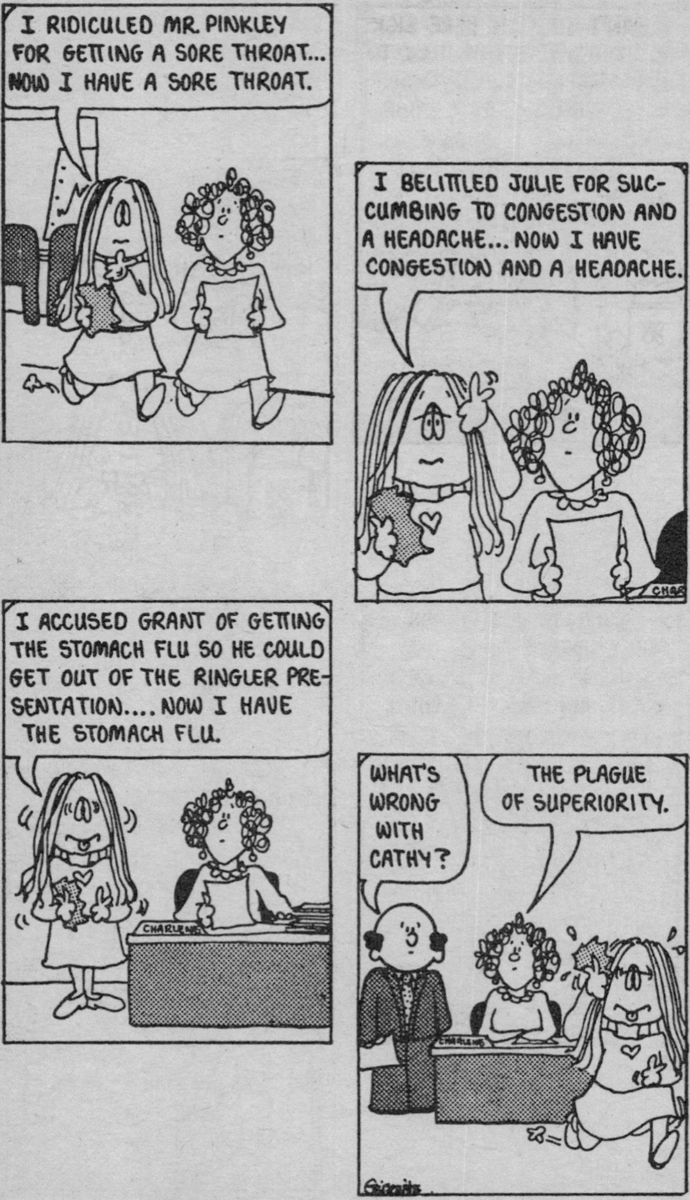
I RIDICULED MR. PINKLEY FOR GETTING A SORE THROAT... NOW I HAVE A SORE THROAT.
I BELITTLED JULIE FOR SUCCUMBING TO CONGESTION AND A HEADACHE... NOW I HAVE CONGESTION AND A HEADACHE.
I ACCUSED GRANT OF GETTING THE STOMACH FLU SO HE COULD GET OUT OF THE RINGLER PRESENTATION.... NOW I HAVE THE STOMACH FLU.
WHAT'S WRONG WITH CATHY?
THE PLAGUE OF SUPERIORITY.

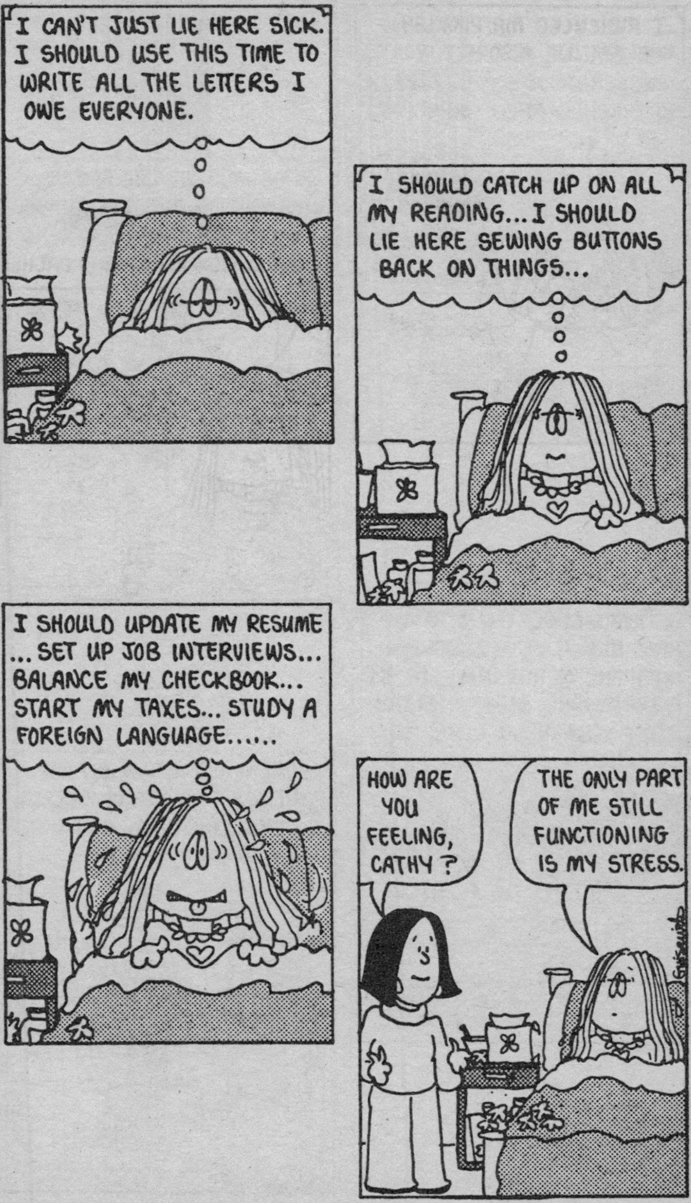
I CAN'T JUST LIE HERE SICK. I SHOULD USE THIS TIME TO WRITE ALL THE LETTERS I OWE EVERYONE.
I SHOULD CATCH UP ON ALL MY READING... I SHOULD LIE HERE SEWING BUTTONS BACK ON THINGS...
I SHOULD UPDATE MY RESUME ... SET UP JOB INTERVIEWS... BALANCE MY CHECKBOOK... START MY TAXES... STUDY A FOREIGN LANGUAGE......
HOW ARE YOU FEELING, CATHY?
THE ONLY PART OF ME STILL FUNCTIONING IS MY STRESS.
GUISEWITE

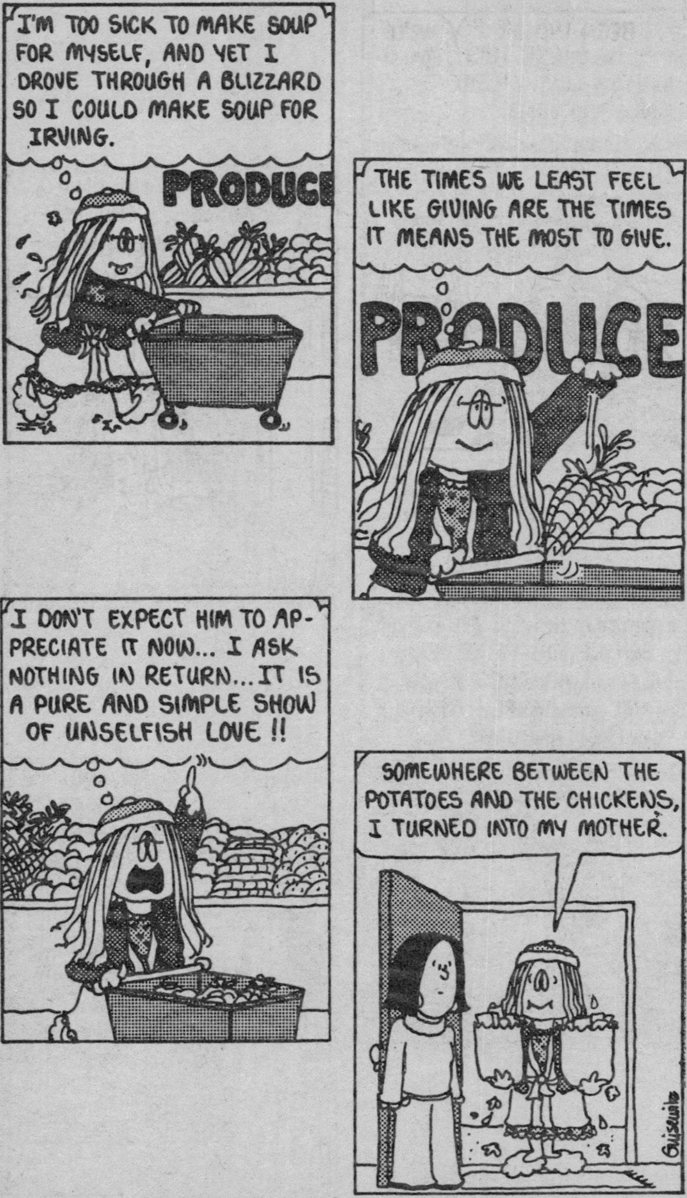
I'M TOO SICK TO MAKE SOUP FOR MYSELF, AND YET I DROVE THROUGH A BLIZZARD SO I COULD MAKE SOUP FOR IRVING.
PRODUCE
THE TIMES WE LEAST FEEL LIKE GIVING ARE THE TIMES IT MEANS THE MOST TO GIVE.
PRODUCE
I DON'T EXPECT HIM TO APPRECIATE IT NOW... I ASK NOTHING IN RETURN... IT IS A PURE AND SIMPLE SHOW OF UNSELFISH LOVE !!
SOMEWHERE BETWEEN THE POTATOES AND THE CHICKENS, I TURNED INTO MY MOTHER.
Guisewite

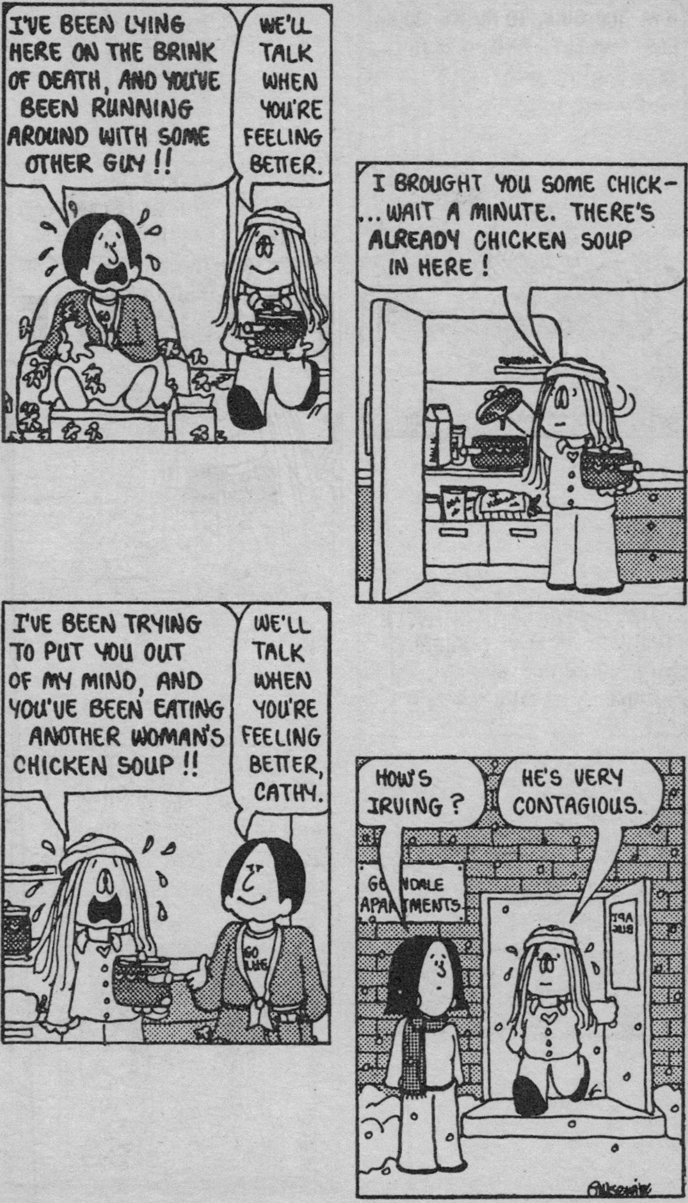
I'VE BEEN LYING HERE ON THE BRINK OF DEATH, AND YOU'VE BEEN RUNNING AROUND WITH SOME OTHER GUY !!
WE'LL TALK WHEN YOU'RE FEELING BETTER.
I BROUGHT YOU SOME CHICK- ...WAIT A MINUTE. THERE'S ALREADY CHICKEN SOUP IN HERE !
I'VE BEEN TRYING TO PUT YOU OUT OF MY MIND, AND YOU'VE BEEN EATING ANOTHER WOMAN'S CHICKEN SOUP !!
WE'LL TALK WHEN YOU'RE FEELING BETTER, CATHY.
HOW'S IRVING ?
HE'S VERY CONTAGIOUS.

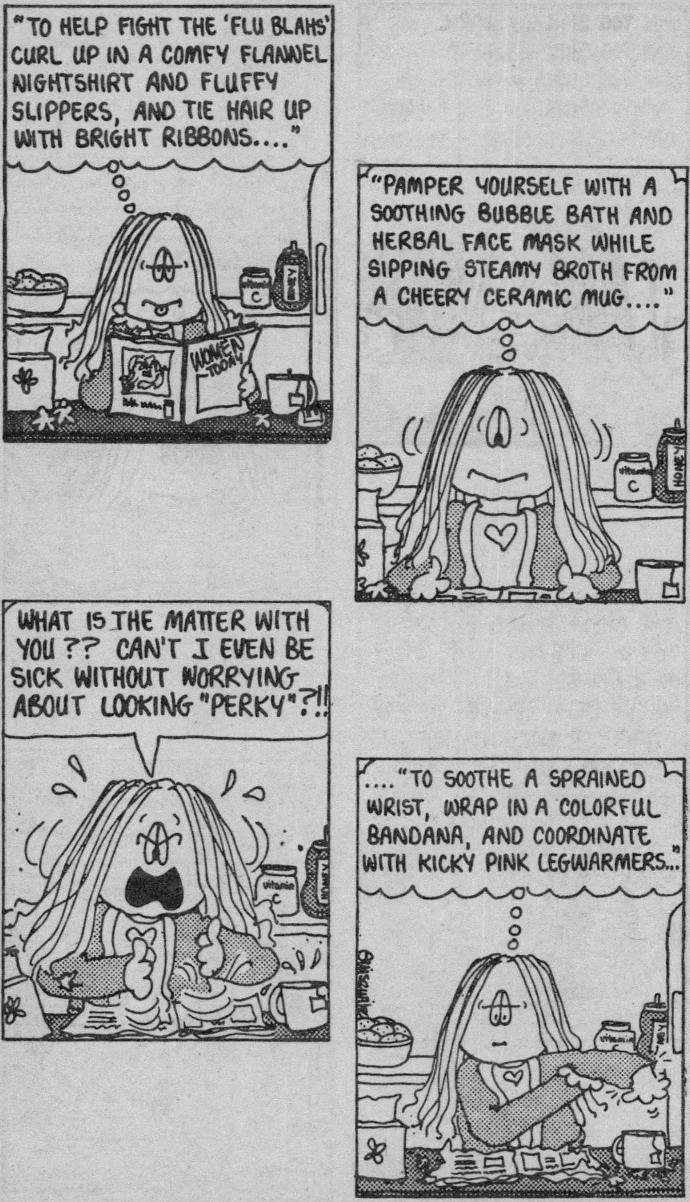
"TO HELP FIGHT THE 'FLU BLAHS' CURL UP IN A COMFY FLANNEL NIGHTSHIRT AND FLUFFY SLIPPERS, AND TIE HAIR UP WITH BRIGHT RIBBONS...."
WOMEN TODAY
"PAMPER YOURSELF WITH A SOOTHING BUBBLE BATH AND HERBAL FACE MASK WHILE SIPPING STEAMY BROTH FROM A CHEERY CERAMIC MUG...."
WHAT IS THE MATTER WITH YOU?? CAN'T I EVEN BE SICK WITHOUT WORRYING ABOUT LOOKING "PERKY"?!!
...."TO SOOTHE A SPRAINED WRIST, WRAP IN A COLORFUL BANDANA, AND COORDINATE WITH KICKY PINK LEGWARMERS..."

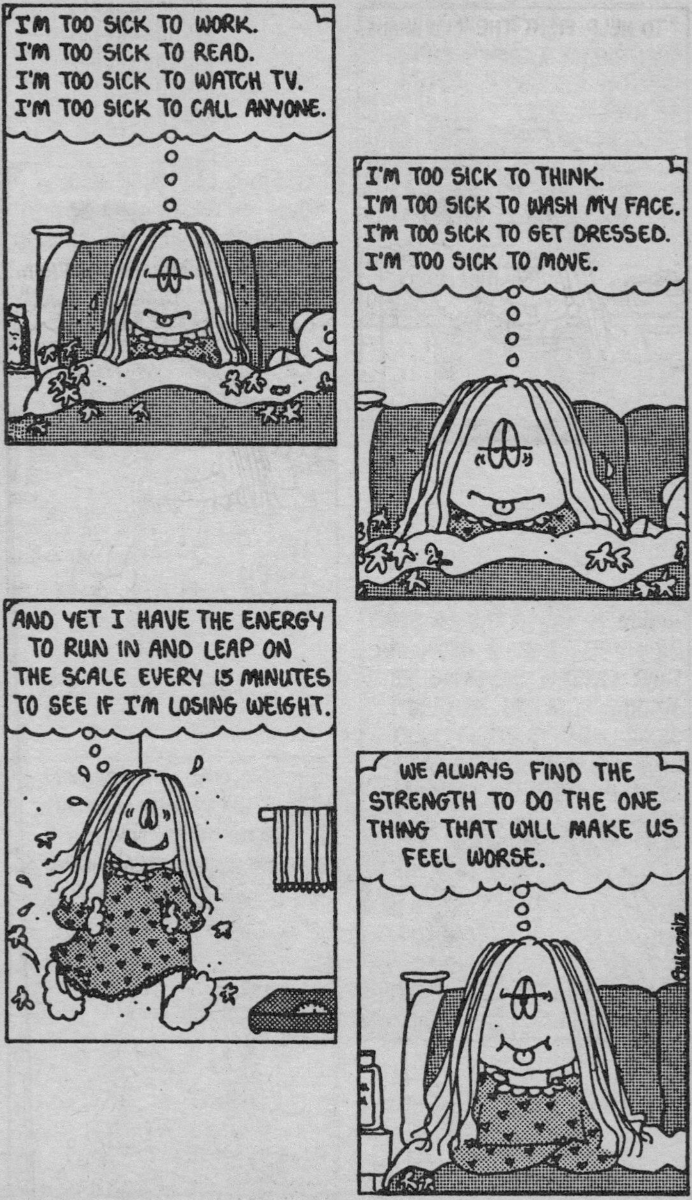
I'M TOO SICK TO WORK.
I'M TOO SICK TO READ.
I'M TOO SICK TO WATCH TV.
I'M TOO SICK TO CALL ANYONE.
I'M TOO SICK TO THINK.
I'M TOO SICK TO WASH MY FACE.
I'M TOO SICK TO GET DRESSED.
I'M TOO SICK TO MOVE.
AND YET I HAVE THE ENERGY TO RUN IN AND LEAP ON THE SCALE EVERY 15 MINUTES TO SEE IF I'M LOSING WEIGHT.
WE ALWAYS FIND THE STRENGTH TO DO THE ONE THING THAT WILL MAKE US FEEL WORSE.

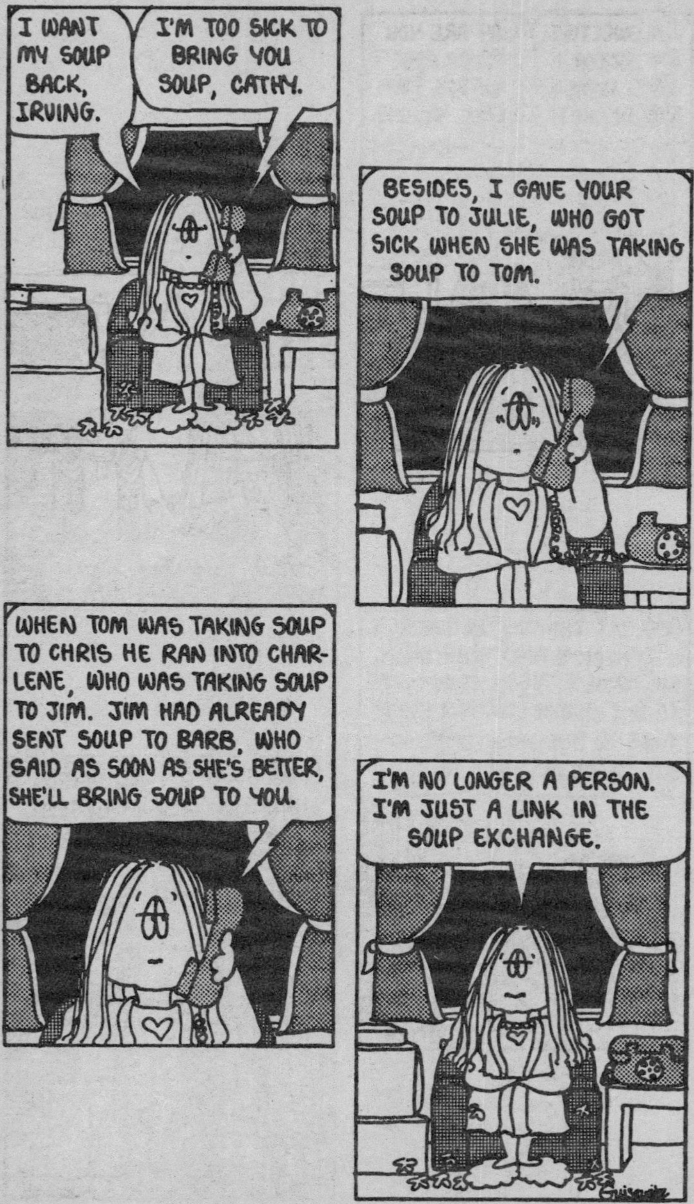
I WANT MY SOUP BACK, IRVING.
I'M TOO SICK TO BRING YOU SOUP, CATHY.
BESIDES, I GAVE YOUR SOUP TO JULIE, WHO GOT SICK WHEN SHE WAS TAKING SOUP TO TOM.
WHEN TOM WAS TAKING SOUP TO CHRIS HE RAN INTO CHAR-LENE, WHO WAS TAKING SOUP TO JIM. JIM HAD ALREADY SENT SOUP TO BARB, WHO SAID AS SOON AS SHE'S BETTER, SHE'LL BRING SOUP TO YOU.
I'M NO LONGER A PERSON. I'M JUST A LINK IN THE SOUP EXCHANGE.
Guisewite

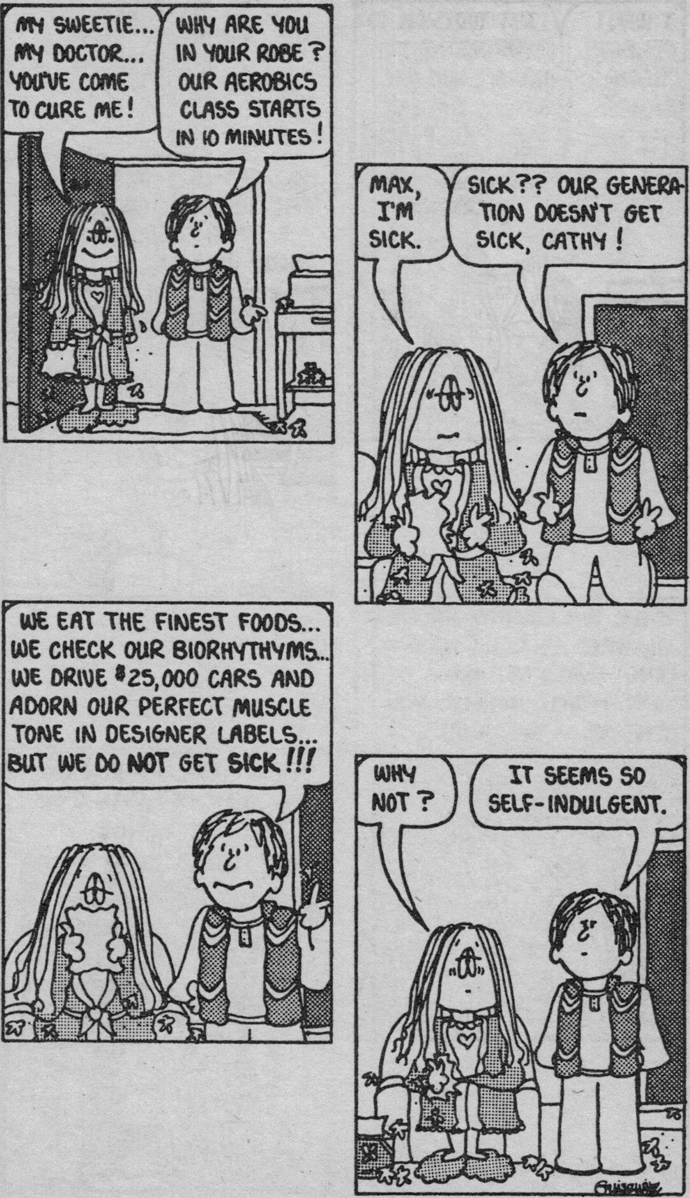
MY SWEETIE... MY DOCTOR... YOU'VE COME TO CURE ME!
WHY ARE YOU IN YOUR ROBE? OUR AEROBICS CLASS STARTS IN 10 MINUTES!
MAX, I'M SICK.
SICK?? OUR GENERATION DOESN'T GET SICK, CATHY!
WE EAT THE FINEST FOODS... WE CHECK OUR BIORHYTHYMS... WE DRIVE $25,000 CARS AND ADORN OUR PERFECT MUSCLE TONE IN DESIGNER LABELS... BUT WE DO NOT GET SICK!!!
WHY NOT?
IT SEEMS SO SELF-INDULGENT.
Guisewite

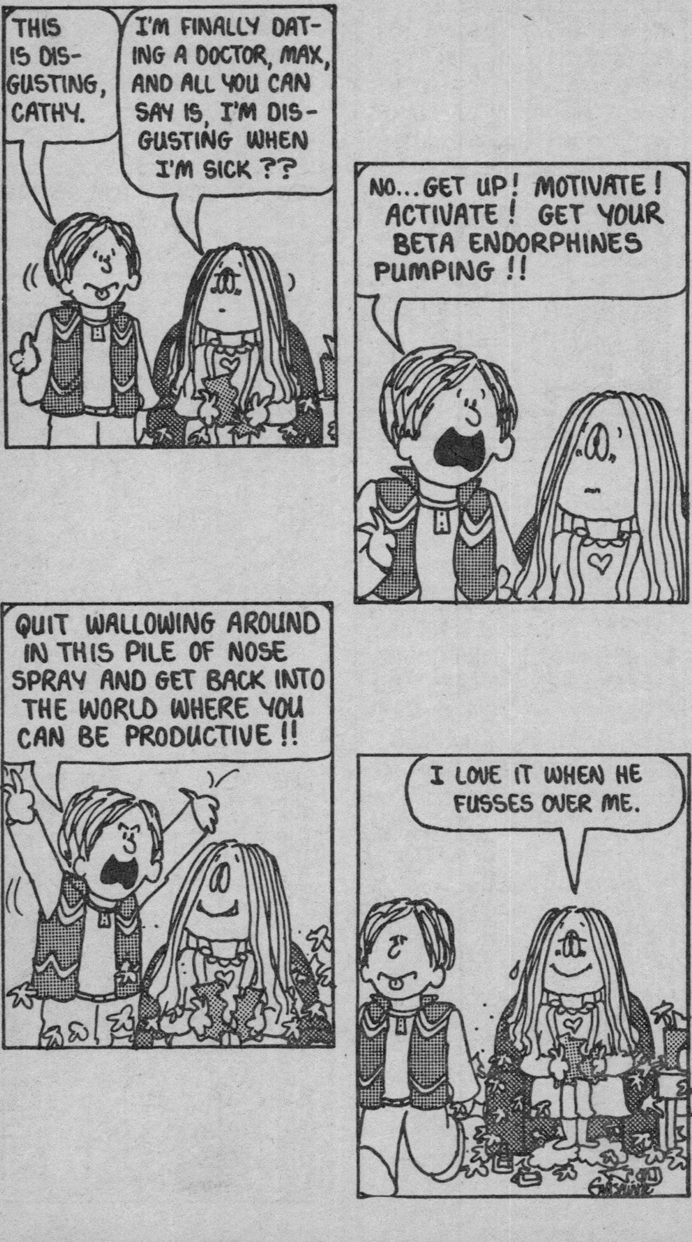
THIS IS DIS-GUSTING, CATHY.
I'M FINALLY DAT-ING A DOCTOR, MAX, AND ALL YOU CAN SAY IS, I'M DIS-GUSTING WHEN I'M SICK ??
NO...GET UP! MOTIVATE! ACTIVATE! GET YOUR BETA ENDORPHINES PUMPING !!
QUIT WALLOWING AROUND IN THIS PILE OF NOSE SPRAY AND GET BACK INTO THE WORLD WHERE YOU CAN BE PRODUCTIVE !!
I LOVE IT WHEN HE FUSSES OVER ME.

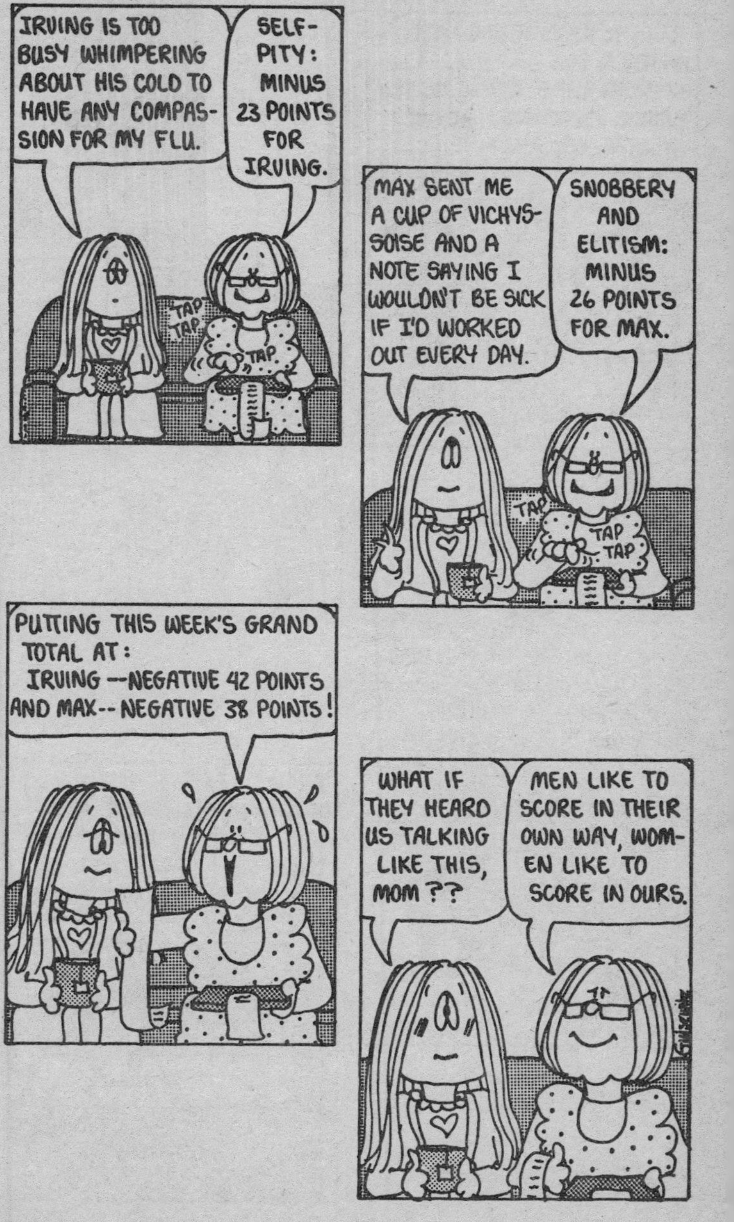
IRVING IS TOO BUSY WHIMPERING ABOUT HIS COLD TO HAVE ANY COMPASSION FOR MY FLU.
SELF-PITY: MINUS 23 POINTS FOR IRVING.
TAP TAP
TAP
MAX SENT ME A CUP OF VICHYSSOISE AND A NOTE SAYING I WOULDN'T BE SICK IF I'D WORKED OUT EVERY DAY.
SNOBBERY AND ELITISM: MINUS 26 POINTS FOR MAX.
TAP
TAP TAP
PUTTING THIS WEEK'S GRAND TOTAL AT:
IRVING --NEGATIVE 42 POINTS
AND MAX-- NEGATIVE 38 POINTS!
WHAT IF THEY HEARD US TALKING LIKE THIS, MOM??
MEN LIKE TO SCORE IN THEIR OWN WAY, WOMEN LIKE TO SCORE IN OURS.

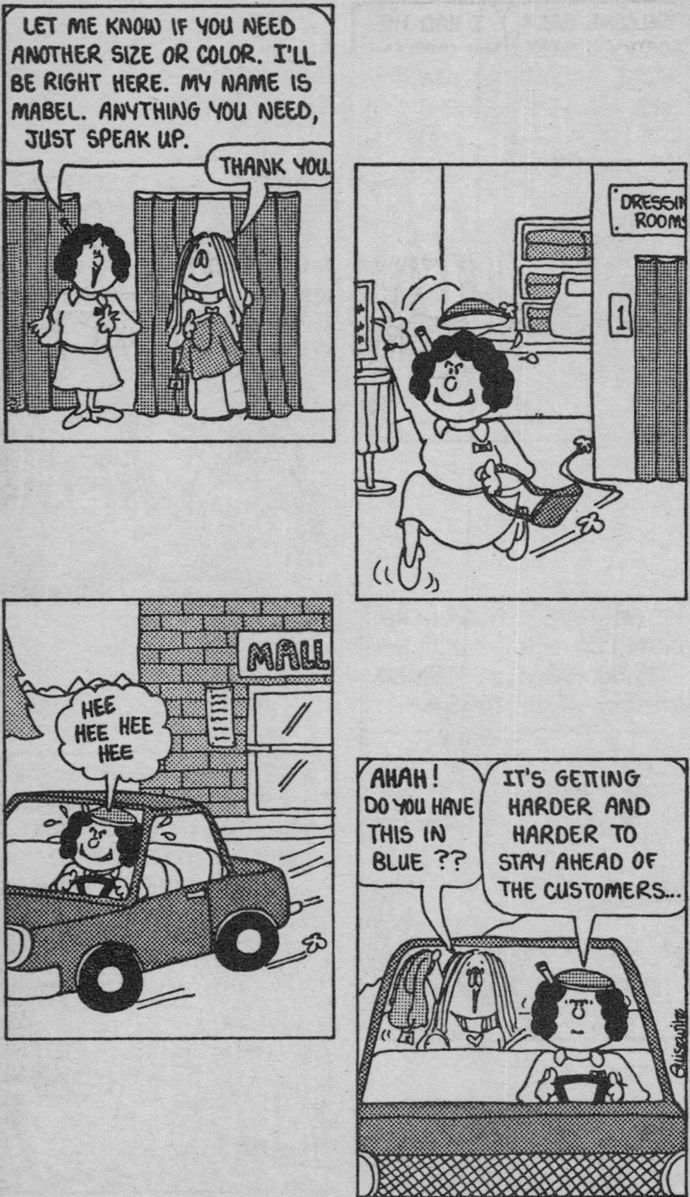
LET ME KNOW IF YOU NEED ANOTHER SIZE OR COLOR. I'LL BE RIGHT HERE. MY NAME IS MABEL. ANYTHING YOU NEED, JUST SPEAK UP.
THANK YOU
DRESSIN ROOMS
1
MALL
HEE HEE HEE HEE
AHAH! DO YOU HAVE THIS IN BLUE ??
IT'S GETTING HARDER AND HARDER TO STAY AHEAD OF THE CUSTOMERS...

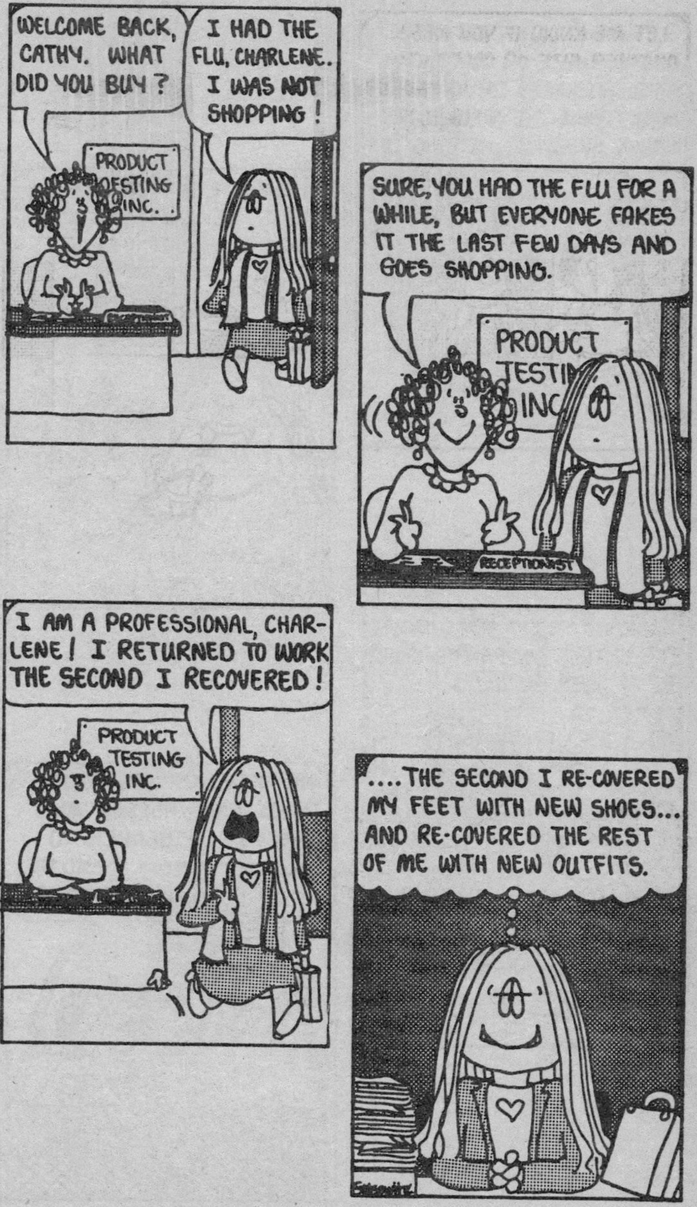
WELCOME BACK, CATHY. WHAT DID YOU BUY ?
I HAD THE FLU, CHARLENE. I WAS NOT SHOPPING !
PRODUCT TESTING INC.
SURE, YOU HAD THE FLU FOR A WHILE, BUT EVERYONE FAKES IT THE LAST FEW DAYS AND GOES SHOPPING.
RECEPTIONIST
I AM A PROFESSIONAL, CHARLENE! I RETURNED TO WORK THE SECOND I RECOVERED !
PRODUCT TESTING INC.
....THE SECOND I RE-COVERED MY FEET WITH NEW SHOES... AND RE-COVERED THE REST OF ME WITH NEW OUTFITS.

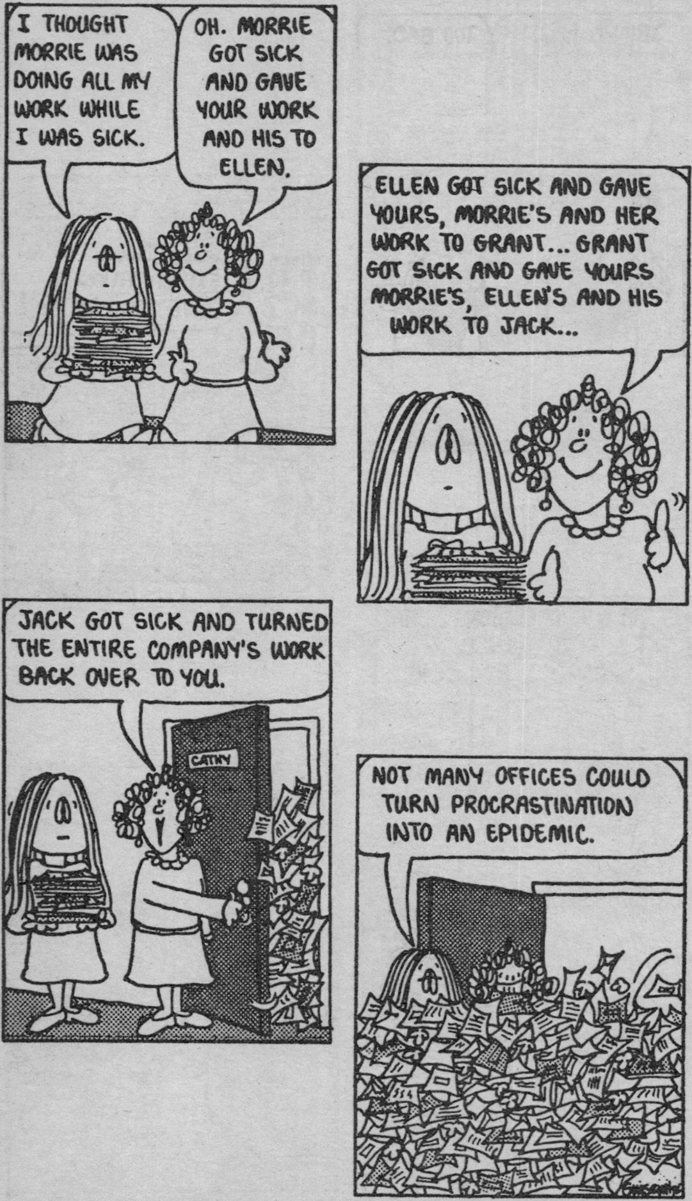
I THOUGHT MORRIE WAS DOING ALL MY WORK WHILE I WAS SICK.
OH. MORRIE GOT SICK AND GAVE YOUR WORK AND HIS TO ELLEN.
ELLEN GOT SICK AND GAVE YOURS, MORRIE'S AND HER WORK TO GRANT... GRANT GOT SICK AND GAVE YOURS MORRIE'S, ELLEN'S AND HIS WORK TO JACK...
JACK GOT SICK AND TURNED THE ENTIRE COMPANY'S WORK BACK OVER TO YOU.
CATHY
NOT MANY OFFICES COULD TURN PROCRASTINATION INTO AN EPIDEMIC.

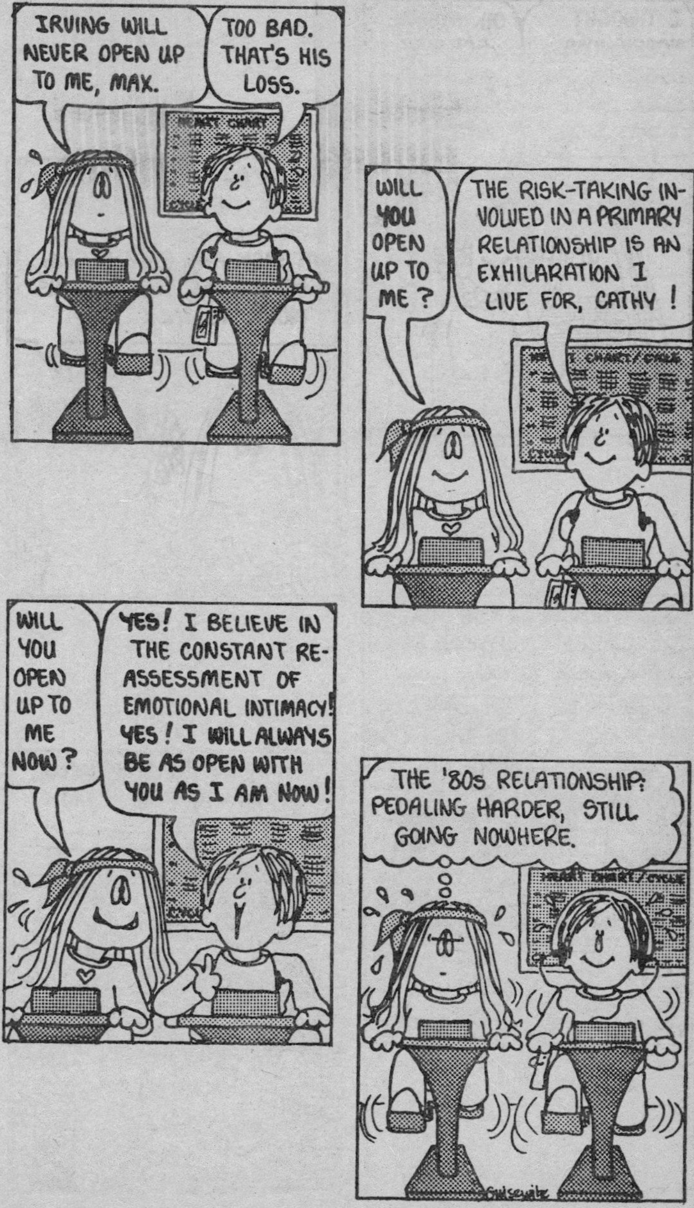
IRVING WILL NEVER OPEN UP TO ME, MAX.
TOO BAD. THAT'S HIS LOSS.
WILL YOU OPEN UP TO ME?
THE RISK-TAKING INVOLVED IN A PRIMARY RELATIONSHIP IS AN EXHILARATION I LIVE FOR, CATHY!
WILL YOU OPEN UP TO ME NOW?
YES! I BELIEVE IN THE CONSTANT RE-ASSESSMENT OF EMOTIONAL INTIMACY! YES! I WILL ALWAYS BE AS OPEN WITH YOU AS I AM NOW!
THE '80s RELATIONSHIP: PEDALING HARDER, STILL GOING NOWHERE.
Guisewite

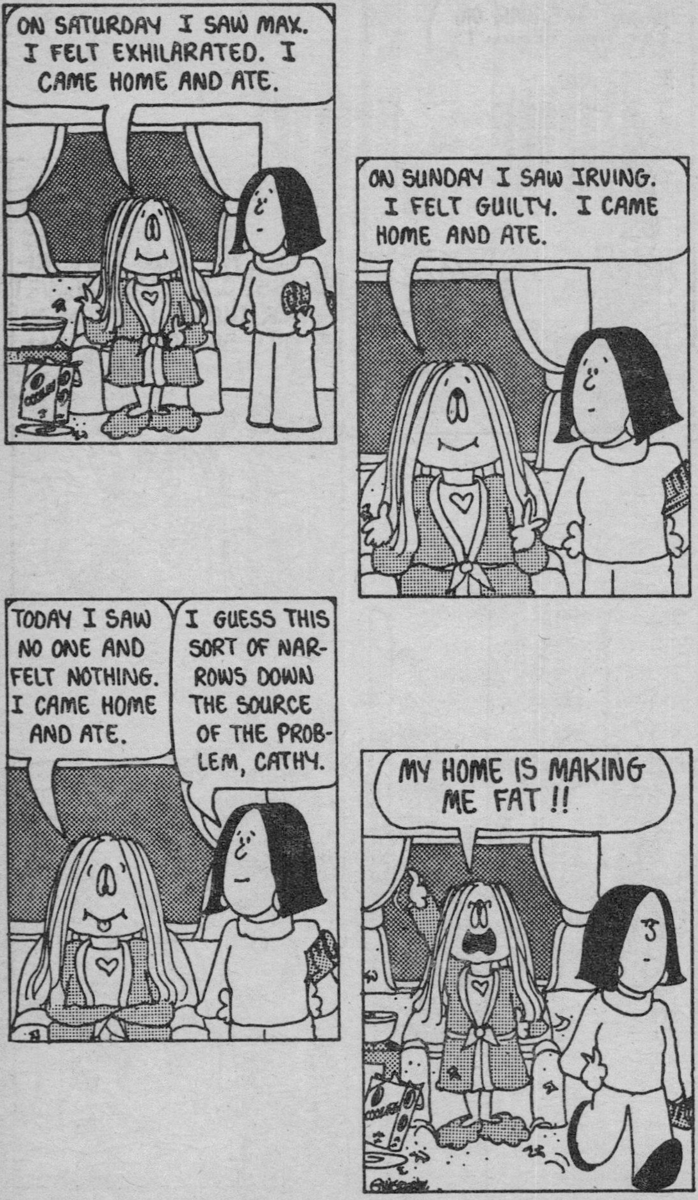
ON SATURDAY I SAW MAX. I FELT EXHILARATED. I CAME HOME AND ATE.
ON SUNDAY I SAW IRVING. I FELT GUILTY. I CAME HOME AND ATE.
TODAY I SAW NO ONE AND FELT NOTHING. I CAME HOME AND ATE.
I GUESS THIS SORT OF NARROWS DOWN THE SOURCE OF THE PROBLEM, CATHY.
MY HOME IS MAKING ME FAT !!

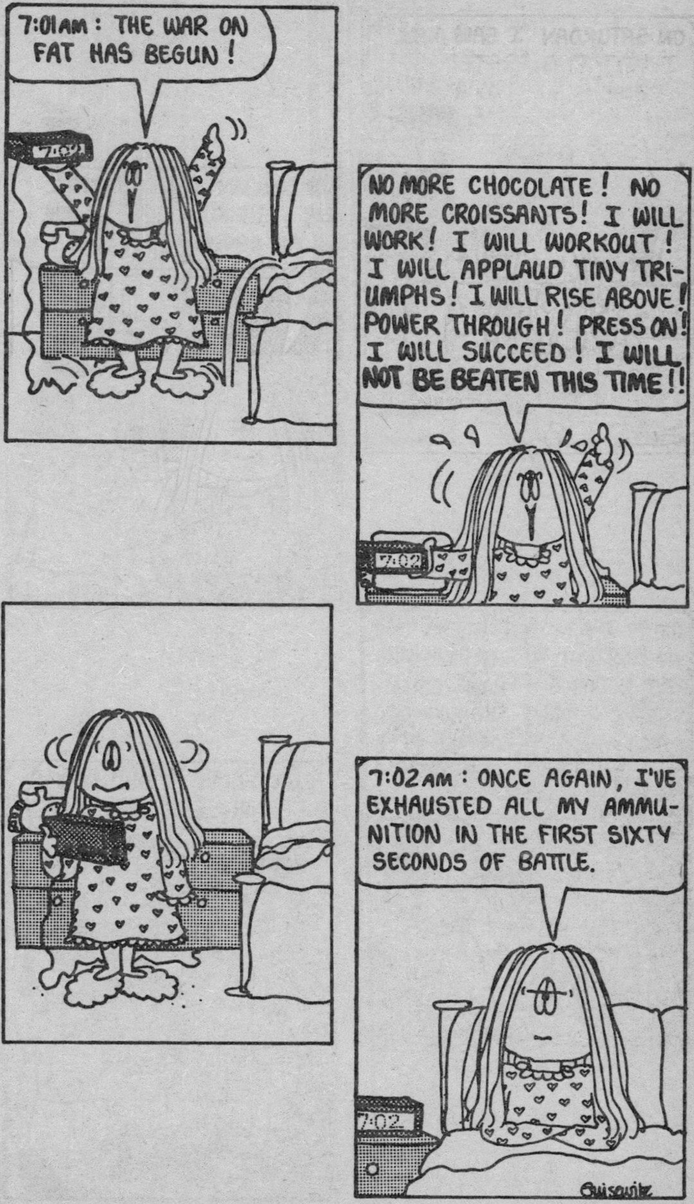
7:01AM: THE WAR ON FAT HAS BEGUN!
NO MORE CHOCOLATE! NO MORE CROISSANTS! I WILL WORK! I WILL WORKOUT! I WILL APPLAUD TINY TRIUMPHS! I WILL RISE ABOVE! POWER THROUGH! PRESS ON! I WILL SUCCEED! I WILL NOT BE BEATEN THIS TIME!!
7:02AM: ONCE AGAIN, I'VE EXHAUSTED ALL MY AMMUNITION IN THE FIRST SIXTY SECONDS OF BATTLE.
Guisewite

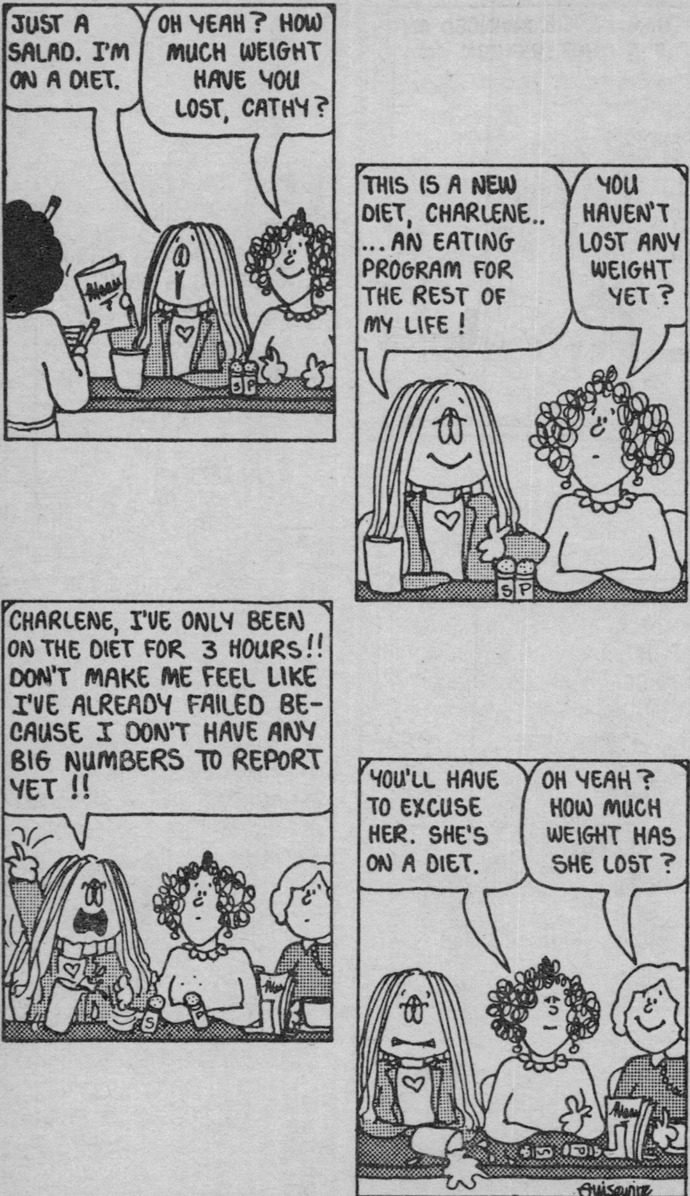
JUST A SALAD. I'M ON A DIET.
OH YEAH? HOW MUCH WEIGHT HAVE YOU LOST, CATHY?
THIS IS A NEW DIET, CHARLENE.. ...AN EATING PROGRAM FOR THE REST OF MY LIFE!
YOU HAVEN'T LOST ANY WEIGHT YET?
CHARLENE, I'VE ONLY BEEN ON THE DIET FOR 3 HOURS!! DON'T MAKE ME FEEL LIKE I'VE ALREADY FAILED BE-CAUSE I DON'T HAVE ANY BIG NUMBERS TO REPORT YET!!
YOU'LL HAVE TO EXCUSE HER. SHE'S ON A DIET.
OH YEAH? HOW MUCH WEIGHT HAS SHE LOST?

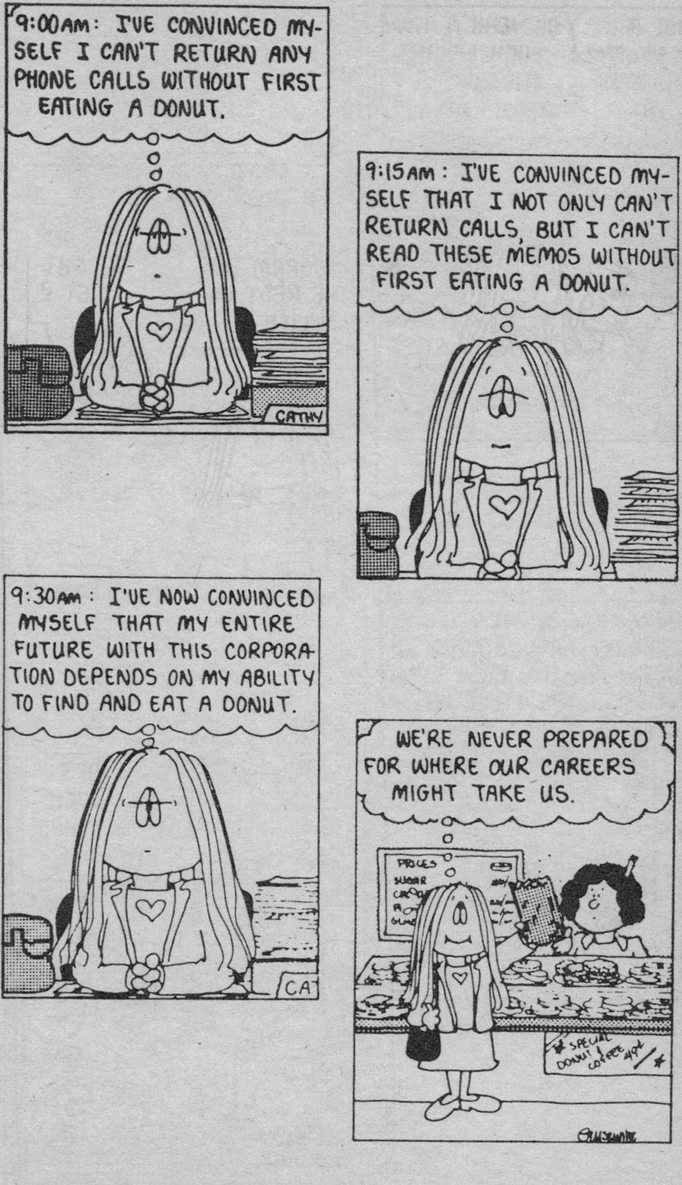
9:00AM: I'VE CONVINCED MYSELF I CAN'T RETURN ANY PHONE CALLS WITHOUT FIRST EATING A DONUT.
CATHY
9:15AM: I'VE CONVINCED MYSELF THAT I NOT ONLY CAN'T RETURN CALLS, BUT I CAN'T READ THESE MEMOS WITHOUT FIRST EATING A DONUT.
9:30AM: I'VE NOW CONVINCED MYSELF THAT MY ENTIRE FUTURE WITH THIS CORPORATION DEPENDS ON MY ABILITY TO FIND AND EAT A DONUT.
WE'RE NEVER PREPARED FOR WHERE OUR CAREERS MIGHT TAKE US.
PRICES
SPECIAL DONUT & COFFEE

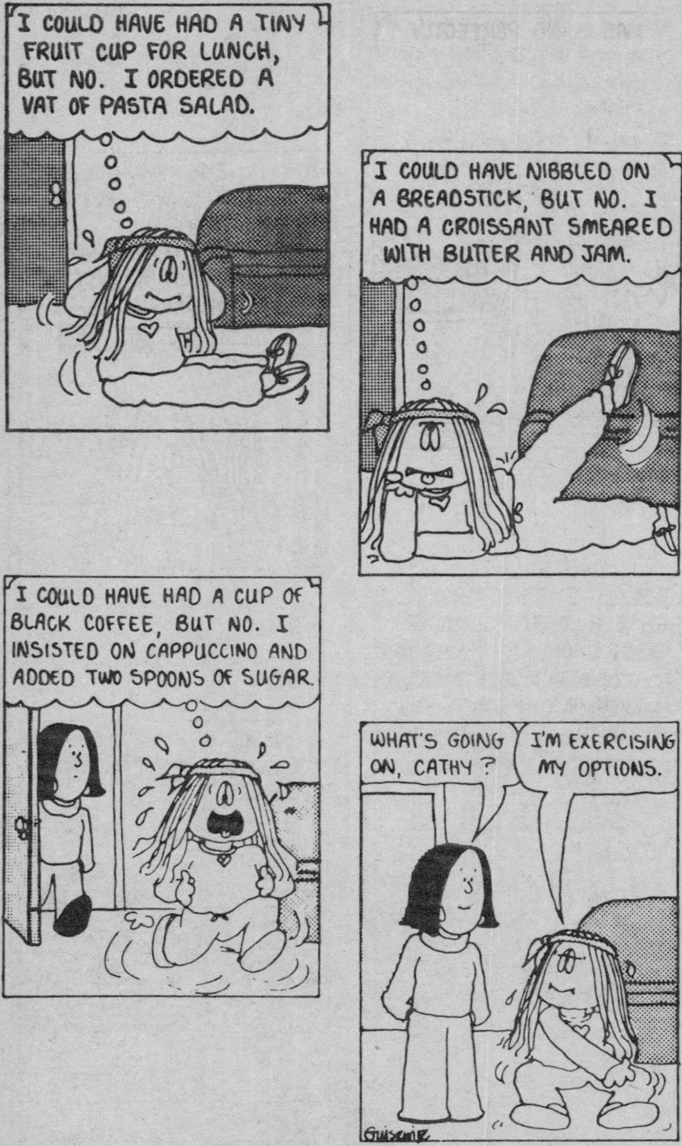
I COULD HAVE HAD A TINY FRUIT CUP FOR LUNCH, BUT NO. I ORDERED A VAT OF PASTA SALAD.
I COULD HAVE NIBBLED ON A BREADSTICK, BUT NO. I HAD A CROISSANT SMEARED WITH BUTTER AND JAM.
I COULD HAVE HAD A CUP OF BLACK COFFEE, BUT NO. I INSISTED ON CAPPUCCINO AND ADDED TWO SPOONS OF SUGAR.
WHAT'S GOING ON, CATHY?
I'M EXERCISING MY OPTIONS.
Guisewite

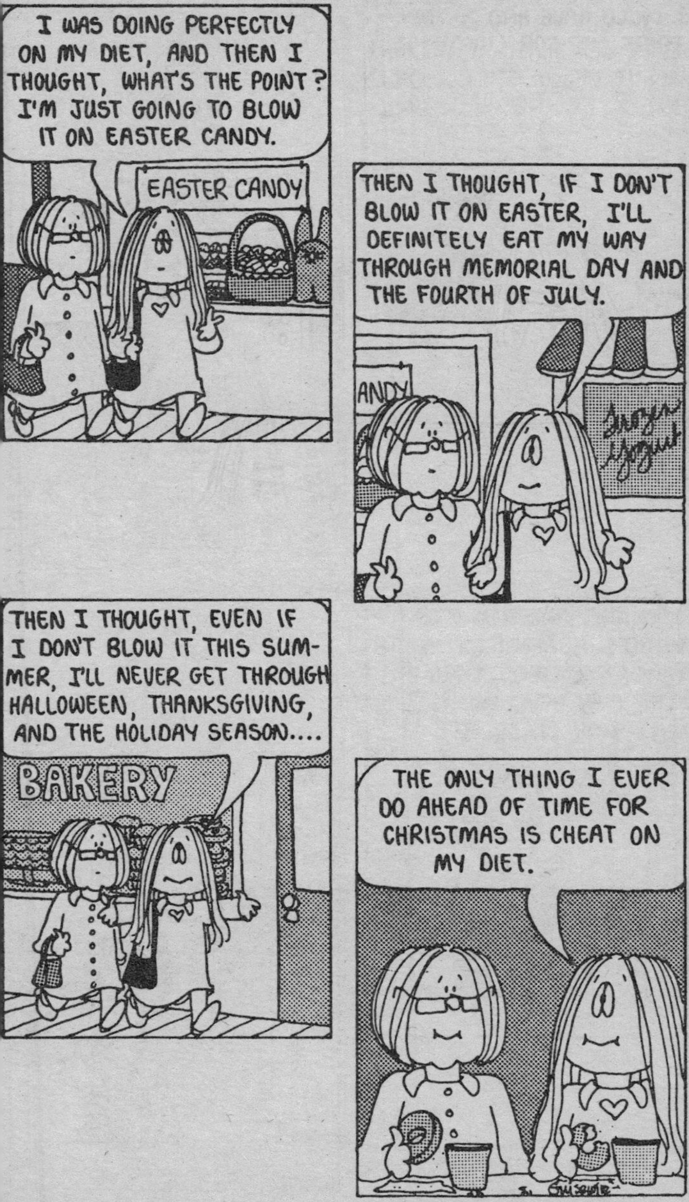
I WAS DOING PERFECTLY ON MY DIET, AND THEN I THOUGHT, WHAT'S THE POINT? I'M JUST GOING TO BLOW IT ON EASTER CANDY.
EASTER CANDY
THEN I THOUGHT, IF I DON'T BLOW IT ON EASTER, I'LL DEFINITELY EAT MY WAY THROUGH MEMORIAL DAY AND THE FOURTH OF JULY.
ANDY
Frozen Yogurt
THEN I THOUGHT, EVEN IF I DON'T BLOW IT THIS SUMMER, I'LL NEVER GET THROUGH HALLOWEEN, THANKSGIVING, AND THE HOLIDAY SEASON....
BAKERY
THE ONLY THING I EVER DO AHEAD OF TIME FOR CHRISTMAS IS CHEAT ON MY DIET.

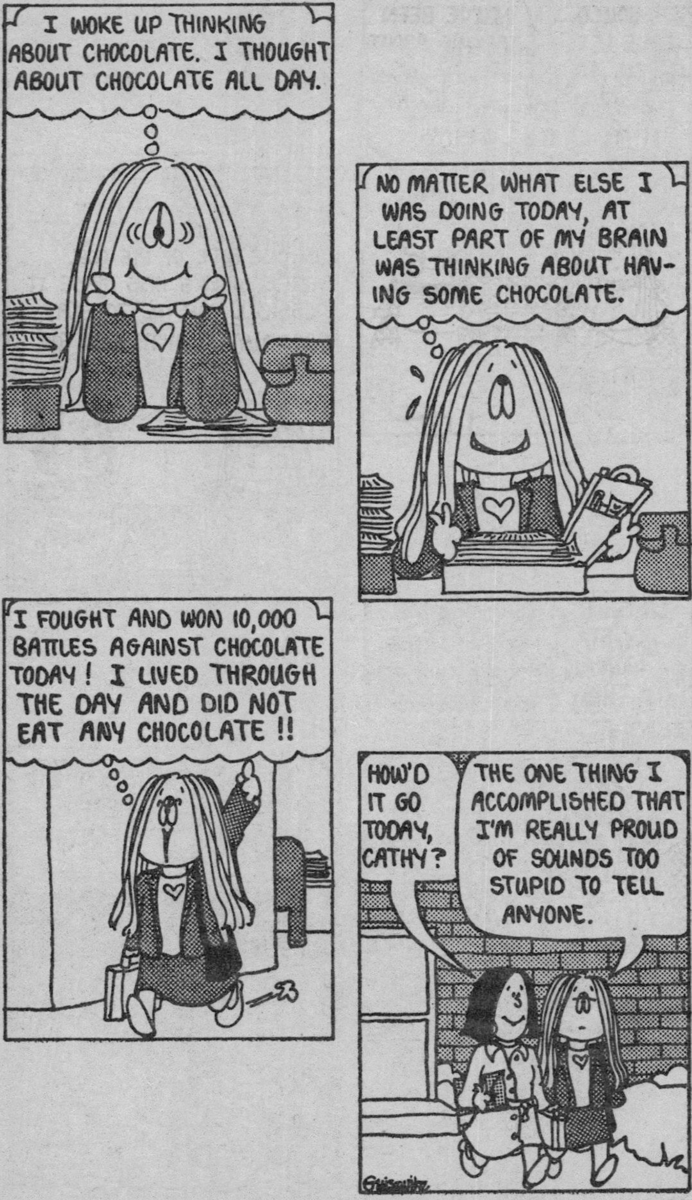
I WOKE UP THINKING ABOUT CHOCOLATE. I THOUGHT ABOUT CHOCOLATE ALL DAY.
NO MATTER WHAT ELSE I WAS DOING TODAY, AT LEAST PART OF MY BRAIN WAS THINKING ABOUT HAVING SOME CHOCOLATE.
I FOUGHT AND WON 10,000 BATTLES AGAINST CHOCOLATE TODAY! I LIVED THROUGH THE DAY AND DID NOT EAT ANY CHOCOLATE !!
HOW'D IT GO TODAY, CATHY?
THE ONE THING I ACCOMPLISHED THAT I'M REALLY PROUD OF SOUNDS TOO STUPID TO TELL ANYONE.
Guisewite

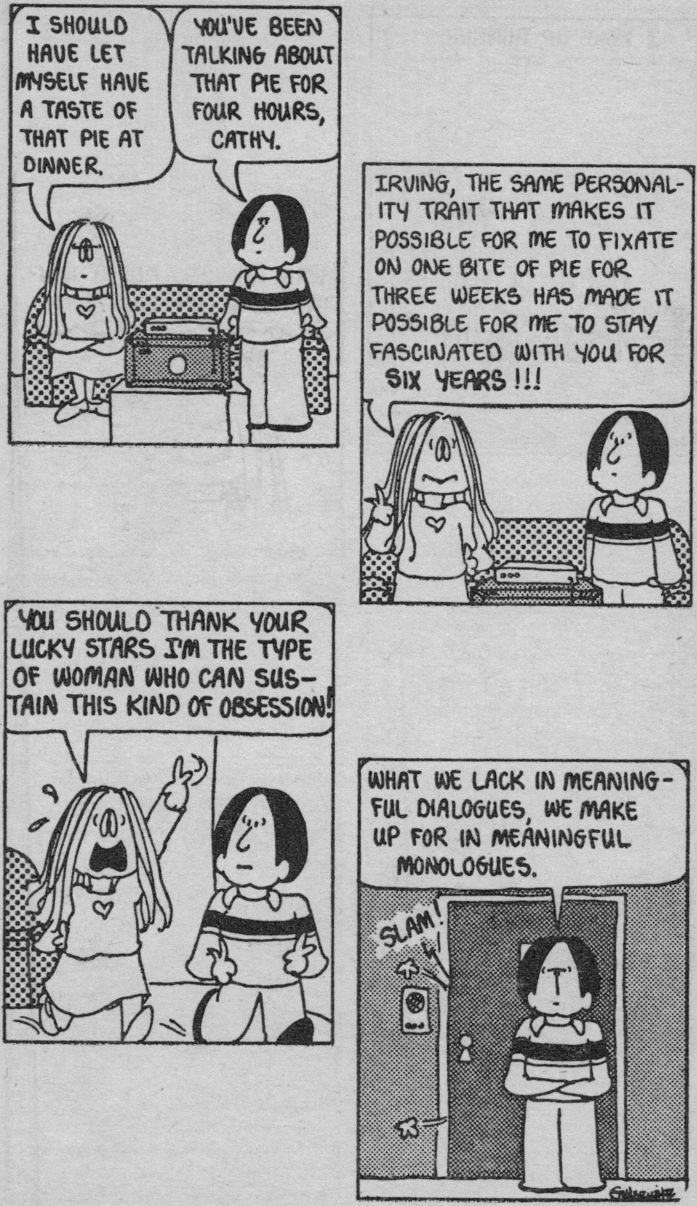
I SHOULD HAVE LET MYSELF HAVE A TASTE OF THAT PIE AT DINNER.
YOU'VE BEEN TALKING ABOUT THAT PIE FOR FOUR HOURS, CATHY.
IRVING, THE SAME PERSONALITY TRAIT THAT MAKES IT POSSIBLE FOR ME TO FIXATE ON ONE BITE OF PIE FOR THREE WEEKS HAS MADE IT POSSIBLE FOR ME TO STAY FASCINATED WITH YOU FOR SIX YEARS!!!
YOU SHOULD THANK YOUR LUCKY STARS I'M THE TYPE OF WOMAN WHO CAN SUSTAIN THIS KIND OF OBSESSION!
WHAT WE LACK IN MEANINGFUL DIALOGUES, WE MAKE UP FOR IN MEANINGFUL MONOLOGUES.
SLAM!

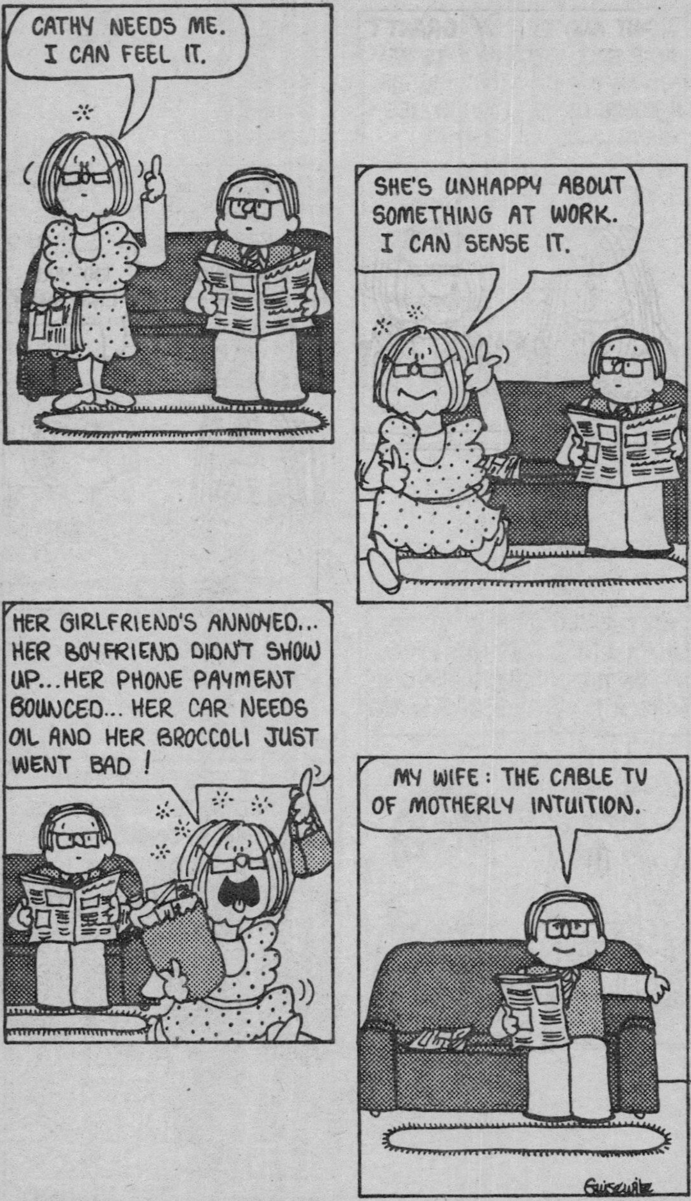
CATHY NEEDS ME. I CAN FEEL IT.
SHE'S UNHAPPY ABOUT SOMETHING AT WORK. I CAN SENSE IT.
HER GIRLFRIEND'S ANNOYED... HER BOYFRIEND DIDN'T SHOW UP... HER PHONE PAYMENT BOUNCED... HER CAR NEEDS OIL AND HER BROCCOLI JUST WENT BAD!
MY WIFE: THE CABLE TV OF MOTHERLY INTUITION.
Guisewite

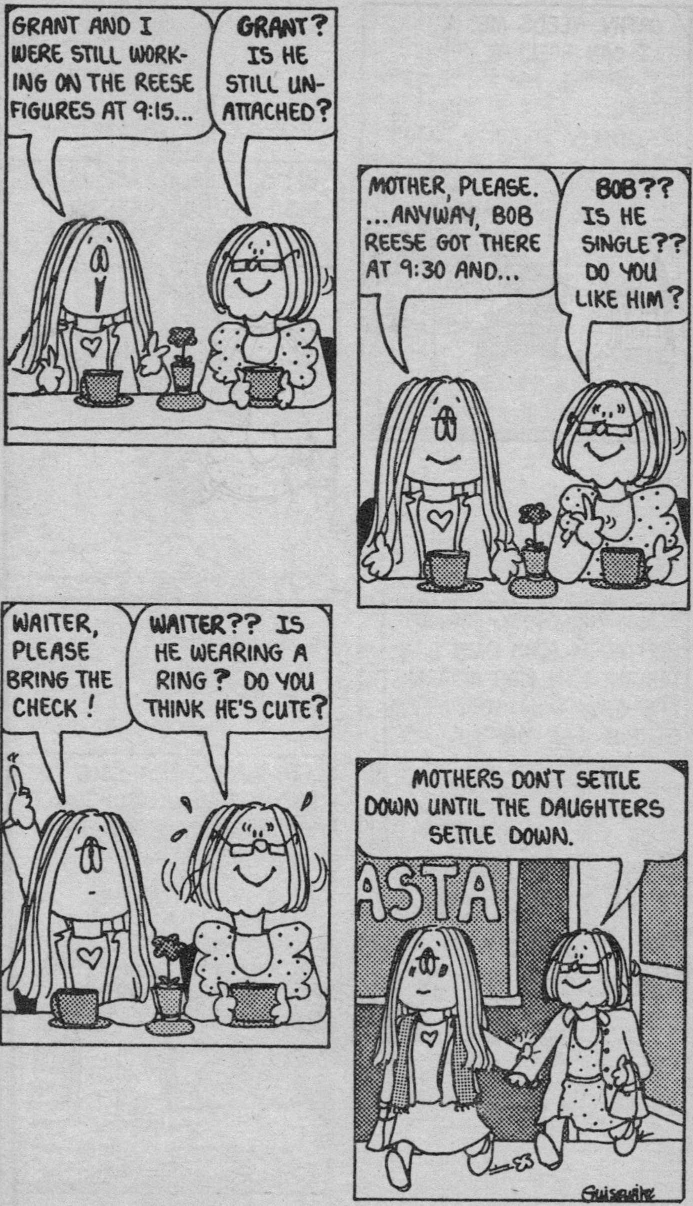
GRANT AND I WERE STILL WORKING ON THE REESE FIGURES AT 9:15...
GRANT? IS HE STILL UNATTACHED?
MOTHER, PLEASE. ...ANYWAY, BOB REESE GOT THERE AT 9:30 AND...
BOB?? IS HE SINGLE?? DO YOU LIKE HIM?
WAITER, PLEASE BRING THE CHECK!
WAITER?? IS HE WEARING A RING? DO YOU THINK HE'S CUTE?
MOTHERS DON'T SETTLE DOWN UNTIL THE DAUGHTERS SETTLE DOWN.
ASTA
Guisewite

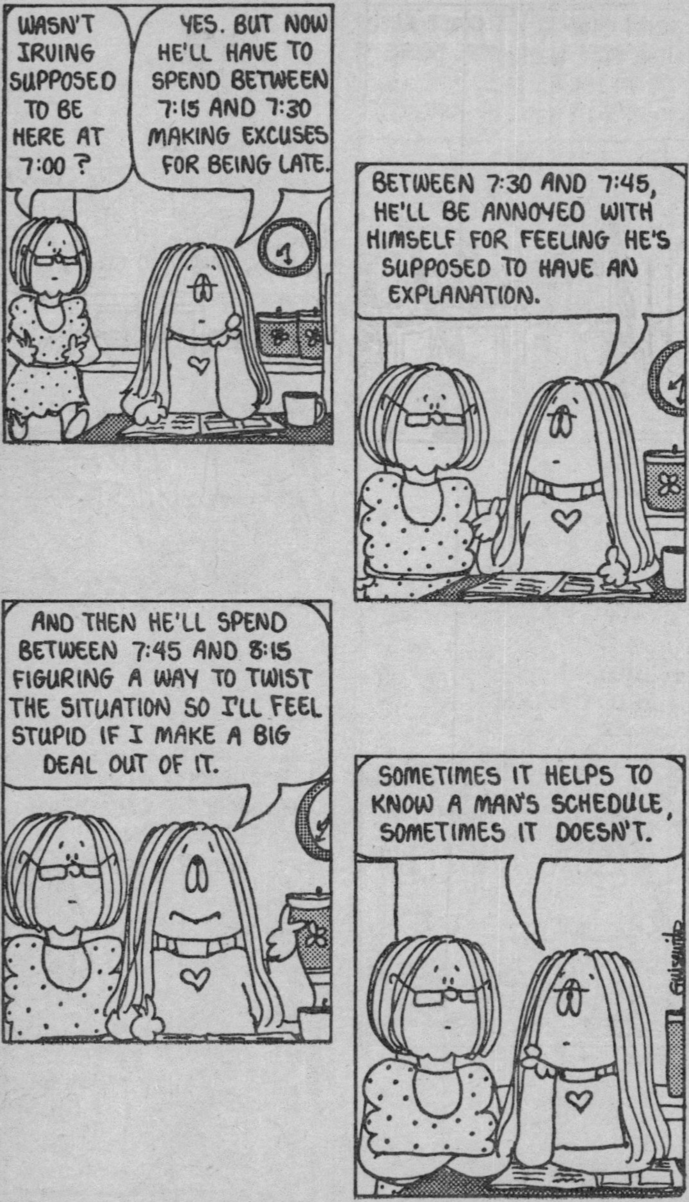
WASN'T IRVING SUPPOSED TO BE HERE AT 7:00 ?
YES. BUT NOW HE'LL HAVE TO SPEND BETWEEN 7:15 AND 7:30 MAKING EXCUSES FOR BEING LATE.
BETWEEN 7:30 AND 7:45, HE'LL BE ANNOYED WITH HIMSELF FOR FEELING HE'S SUPPOSED TO HAVE AN EXPLANATION.
AND THEN HE'LL SPEND BETWEEN 7:45 AND 8:15 FIGURING A WAY TO TWIST THE SITUATION SO I'LL FEEL STUPID IF I MAKE A BIG DEAL OUT OF IT.
SOMETIMES IT HELPS TO KNOW A MAN'S SCHEDULE, SOMETIMES IT DOESN'T.

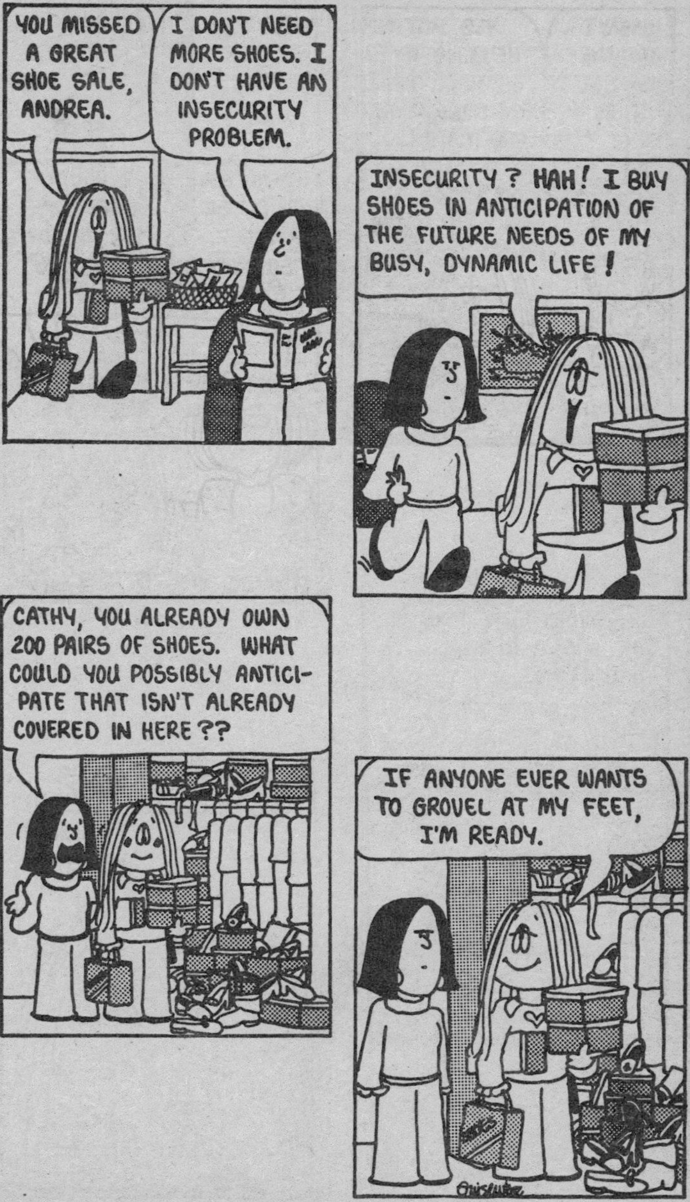
YOU MISSED A GREAT SHOE SALE, ANDREA.
I DON'T NEED MORE SHOES. I DON'T HAVE AN INSECURITY PROBLEM.
INSECURITY? HAH! I BUY SHOES IN ANTICIPATION OF THE FUTURE NEEDS OF MY BUSY, DYNAMIC LIFE!
CATHY, YOU ALREADY OWN 200 PAIRS OF SHOES. WHAT COULD YOU POSSIBLY ANTICI-PATE THAT ISN'T ALREADY COVERED IN HERE??
IF ANYONE EVER WANTS TO GROVEL AT MY FEET, I'M READY.

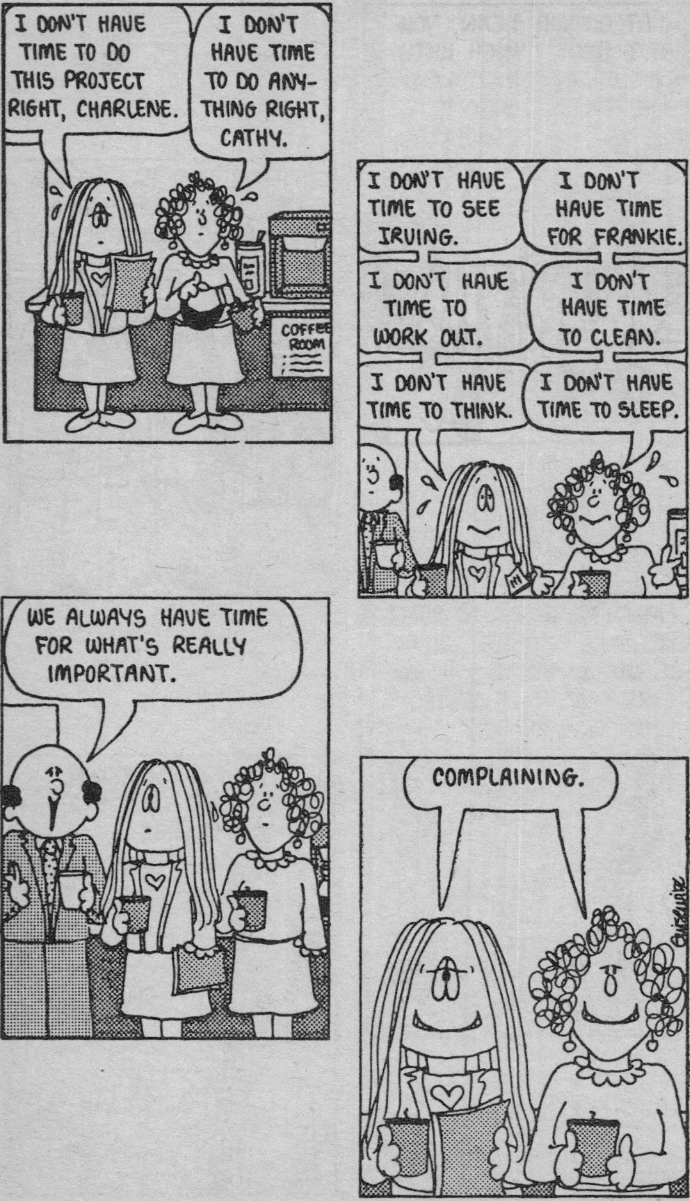
I DON'T HAVE TIME TO DO THIS PROJECT RIGHT, CHARLENE.
I DON'T HAVE TIME TO DO ANY-THING RIGHT, CATHY.
COFFEE ROOM
I DON'T HAVE TIME TO SEE IRVING.
I DON'T HAVE TIME FOR FRANKIE.
I DON'T HAVE TIME TO WORK OUT.
I DON'T HAVE TIME TO CLEAN.
I DON'T HAVE TIME TO THINK.
I DON'T HAVE TIME TO SLEEP.
WE ALWAYS HAVE TIME FOR WHAT'S REALLY IMPORTANT.
COMPLAINING.

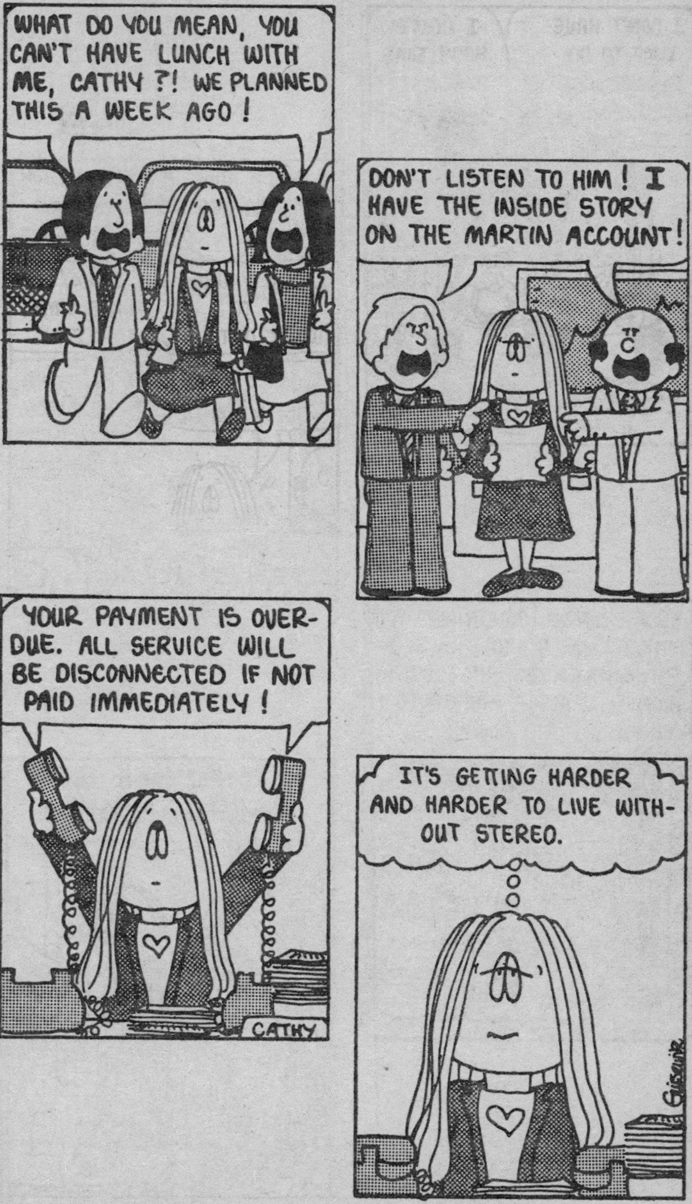
WHAT DO YOU MEAN, YOU CAN'T HAVE LUNCH WITH ME, CATHY ?! WE PLANNED THIS A WEEK AGO !
DON'T LISTEN TO HIM ! I HAVE THE INSIDE STORY ON THE MARTIN ACCOUNT !
YOUR PAYMENT IS OVER-DUE. ALL SERVICE WILL BE DISCONNECTED IF NOT PAID IMMEDIATELY !
CATHY
IT'S GETTING HARDER AND HARDER TO LIVE WITH-OUT STEREO.

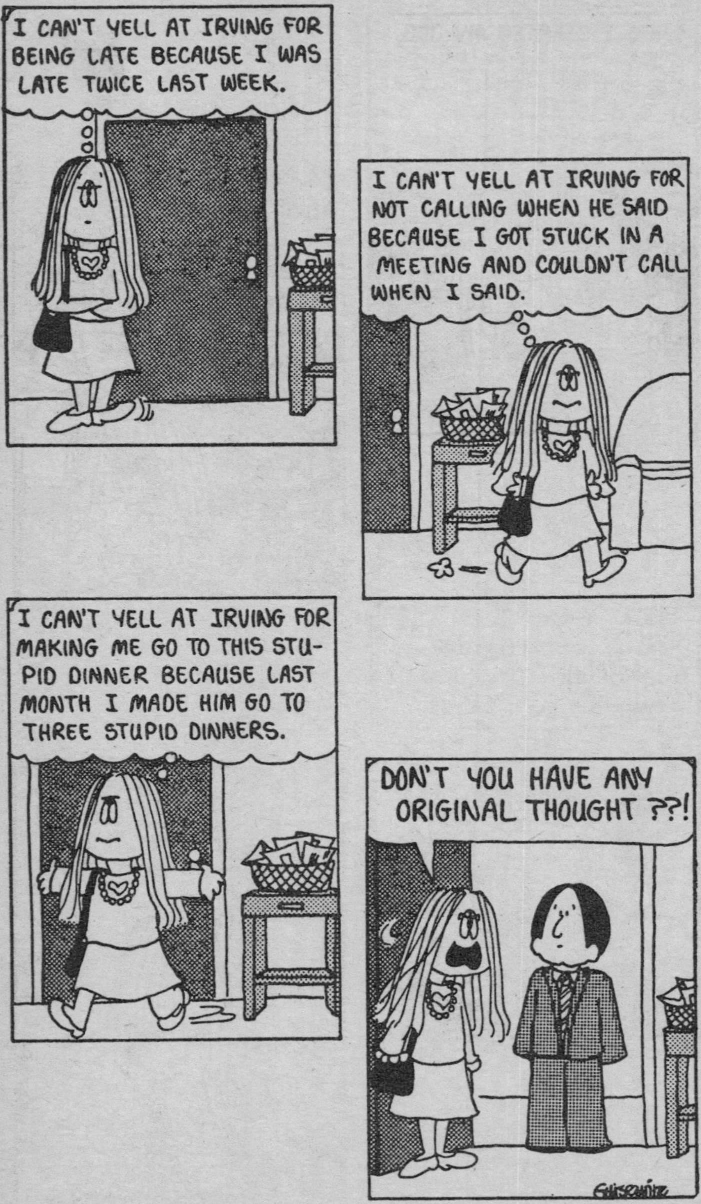
I CAN'T YELL AT IRVING FOR BEING LATE BECAUSE I WAS LATE TWICE LAST WEEK.
I CAN'T YELL AT IRVING FOR NOT CALLING WHEN HE SAID BECAUSE I GOT STUCK IN A MEETING AND COULDN'T CALL WHEN I SAID.
I CAN'T YELL AT IRVING FOR MAKING ME GO TO THIS STUPID DINNER BECAUSE LAST MONTH I MADE HIM GO TO THREE STUPID DINNERS.
DON'T YOU HAVE ANY ORIGINAL THOUGHT ??!

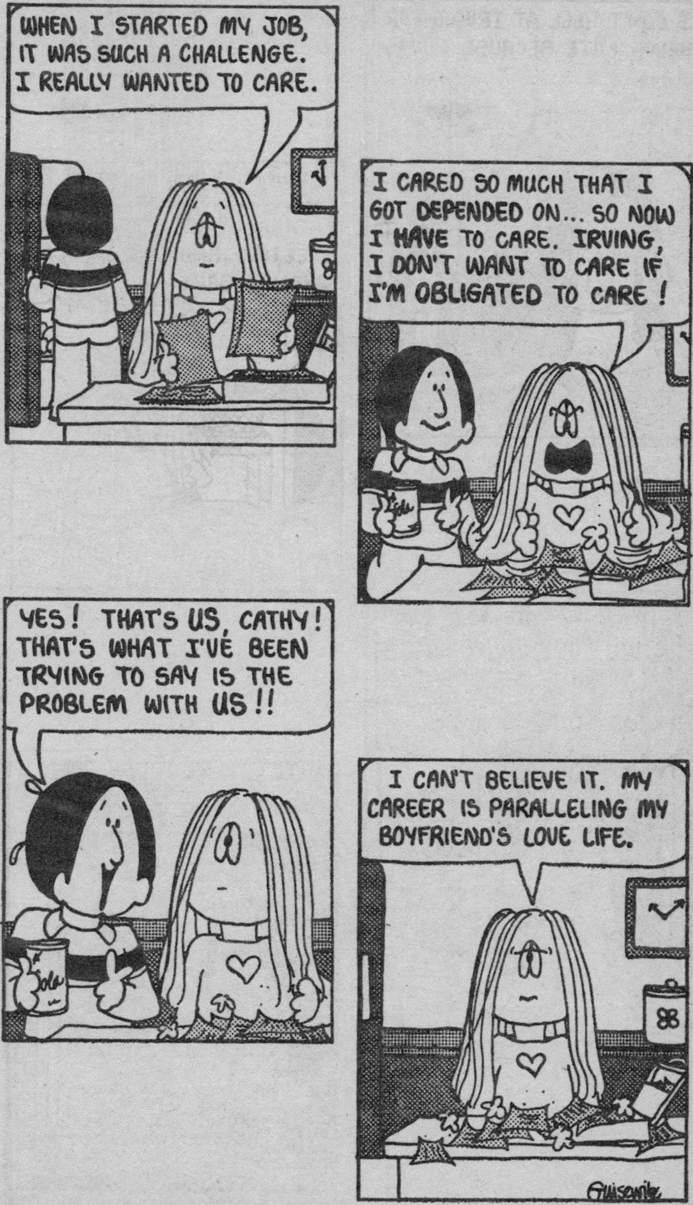

WHEN I STARTED MY JOB, IT WAS SUCH A CHALLENGE. I REALLY WANTED TO CARE.
I CARED SO MUCH THAT I GOT DEPENDED ON... SO NOW I HAVE TO CARE. IRVING, I DON'T WANT TO CARE IF I'M OBLIGATED TO CARE!
YES! THAT'S US, CATHY! THAT'S WHAT I'VE BEEN TRYING TO SAY IS THE PROBLEM WITH US!!
I CAN'T BELIEVE IT. MY CAREER IS PARALLELING MY BOYFRIEND'S LOVE LIFE.
Guisewite

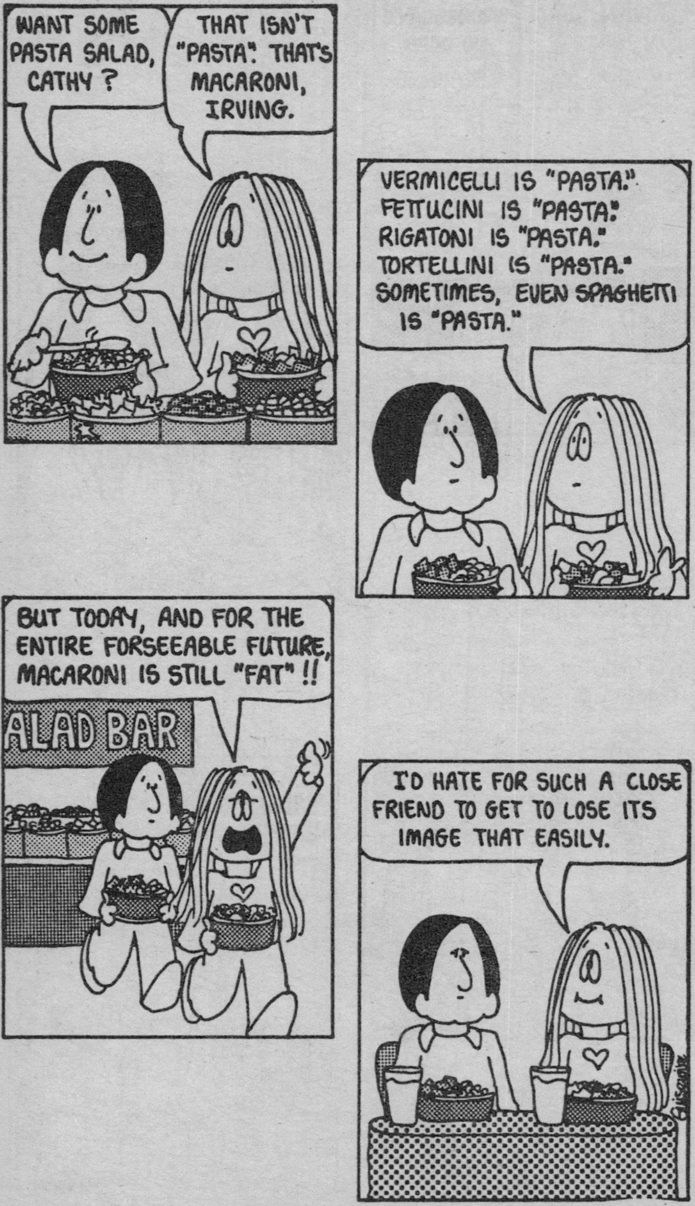
WANT SOME PASTA SALAD, CATHY ?
THAT ISN'T "PASTA". THAT'S MACARONI, IRVING.
VERMICELLI IS "PASTA." FETTUCINI IS "PASTA." RIGATONI IS "PASTA." TORTELLINI IS "PASTA." SOMETIMES, EVEN SPAGHETTI IS "PASTA."
BUT TODAY, AND FOR THE ENTIRE FORSEEABLE FUTURE, MACARONI IS STILL "FAT" !!
ALAD BAR
I'D HATE FOR SUCH A CLOSE FRIEND TO GET TO LOSE ITS IMAGE THAT EASILY.

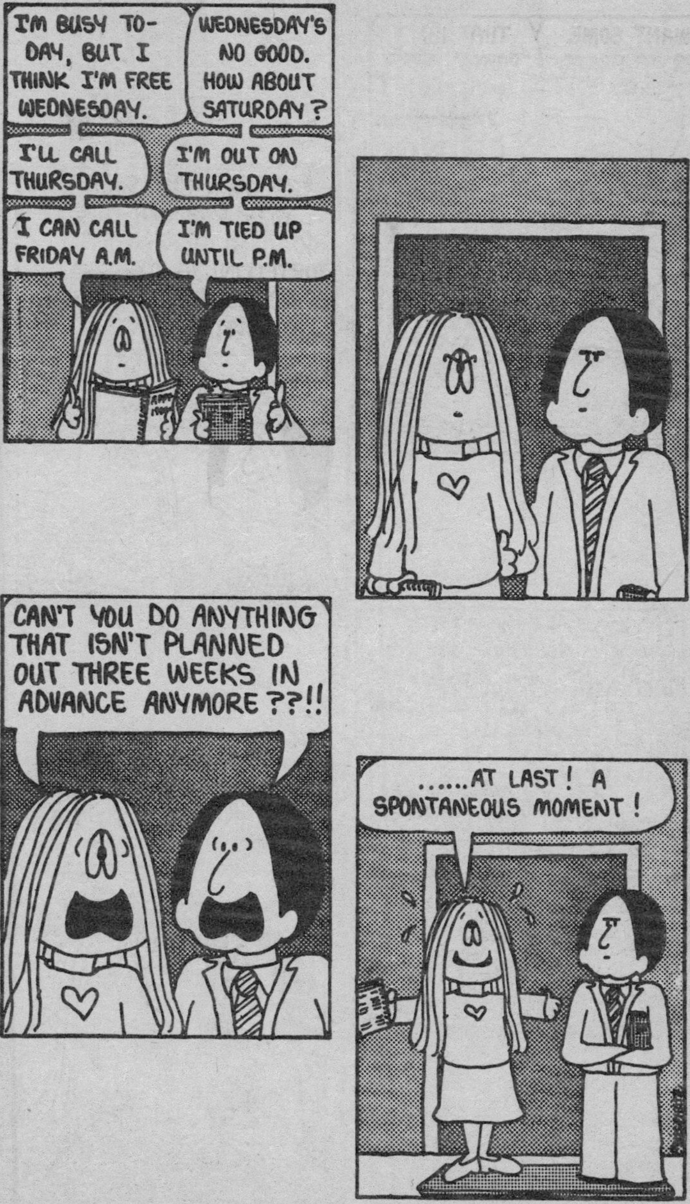
I'M BUSY TO-DAY, BUT I THINK I'M FREE WEDNESDAY.
WEDNESDAY'S NO GOOD. HOW ABOUT SATURDAY?
I'LL CALL THURSDAY.
I'M OUT ON THURSDAY.
I CAN CALL FRIDAY A.M.
I'M TIED UP UNTIL P.M.
CAN'T YOU DO ANYTHING THAT ISN'T PLANNED OUT THREE WEEKS IN ADVANCE ANYMORE??!!
......AT LAST! A SPONTANEOUS MOMENT!

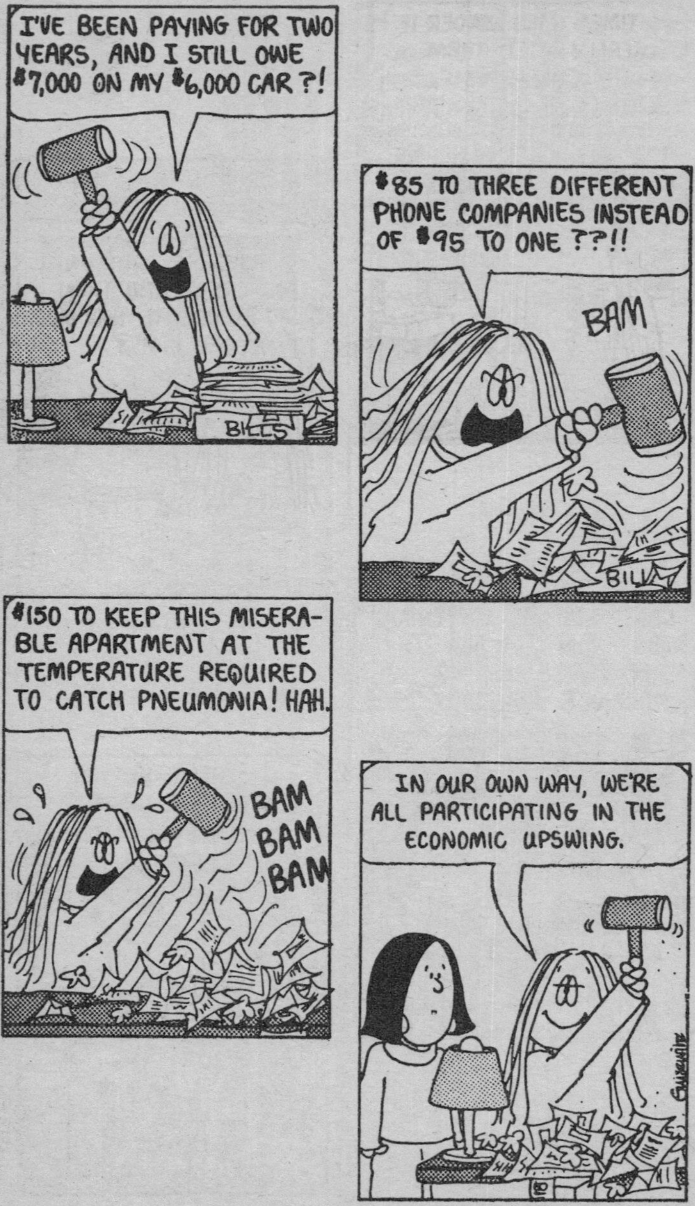
I'VE BEEN PAYING FOR TWO YEARS, AND I STILL OWE $7,000 ON MY $6,000 CAR ?!
BILLS
$85 TO THREE DIFFERENT PHONE COMPANIES INSTEAD OF $95 TO ONE ??!!
BAM
$150 TO KEEP THIS MISERA-BLE APARTMENT AT THE TEMPERATURE REQUIRED TO CATCH PNEUMONIA! HAH.
BAM
BAM
BAM
IN OUR OWN WAY, WE'RE ALL PARTICIPATING IN THE ECONOMIC UPSWING.

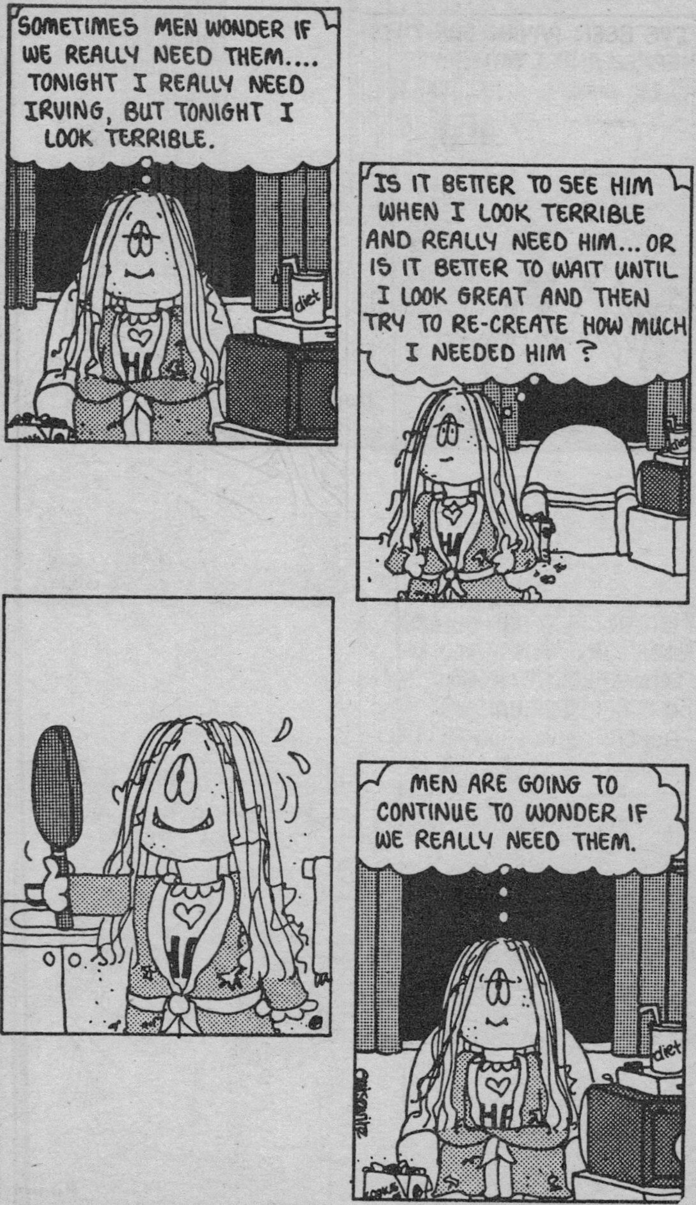
SOMETIMES MEN WONDER IF WE REALLY NEED THEM.... TONIGHT I REALLY NEED IRVING, BUT TONIGHT I LOOK TERRIBLE.
diet
IS IT BETTER TO SEE HIM WHEN I LOOK TERRIBLE AND REALLY NEED HIM... OR IS IT BETTER TO WAIT UNTIL I LOOK GREAT AND THEN TRY TO RE-CREATE HOW MUCH I NEEDED HIM?
MEN ARE GOING TO CONTINUE TO WONDER IF WE REALLY NEED THEM.
diet
Guisewite

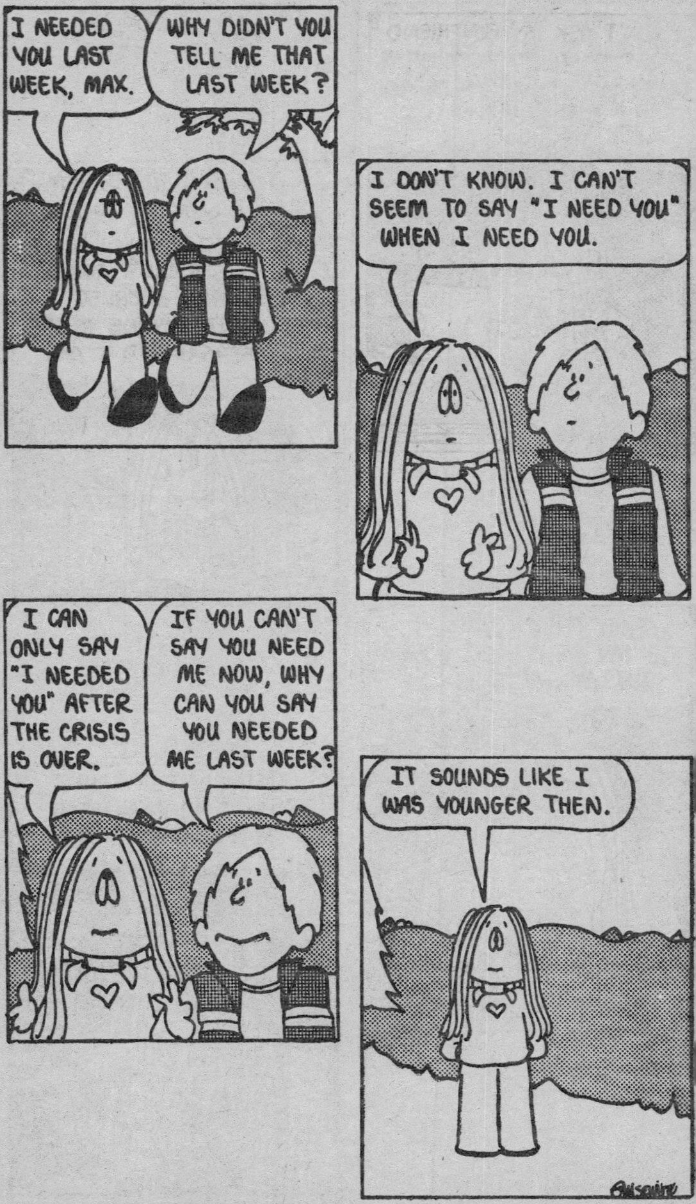
I NEEDED YOU LAST WEEK, MAX.
WHY DIDN'T YOU TELL ME THAT LAST WEEK?
I DON'T KNOW. I CAN'T SEEM TO SAY "I NEED YOU" WHEN I NEED YOU.
I CAN ONLY SAY "I NEEDED YOU" AFTER THE CRISIS IS OVER.
IF YOU CAN'T SAY YOU NEED ME NOW, WHY CAN YOU SAY YOU NEEDED ME LAST WEEK?
IT SOUNDS LIKE I WAS YOUNGER THEN.

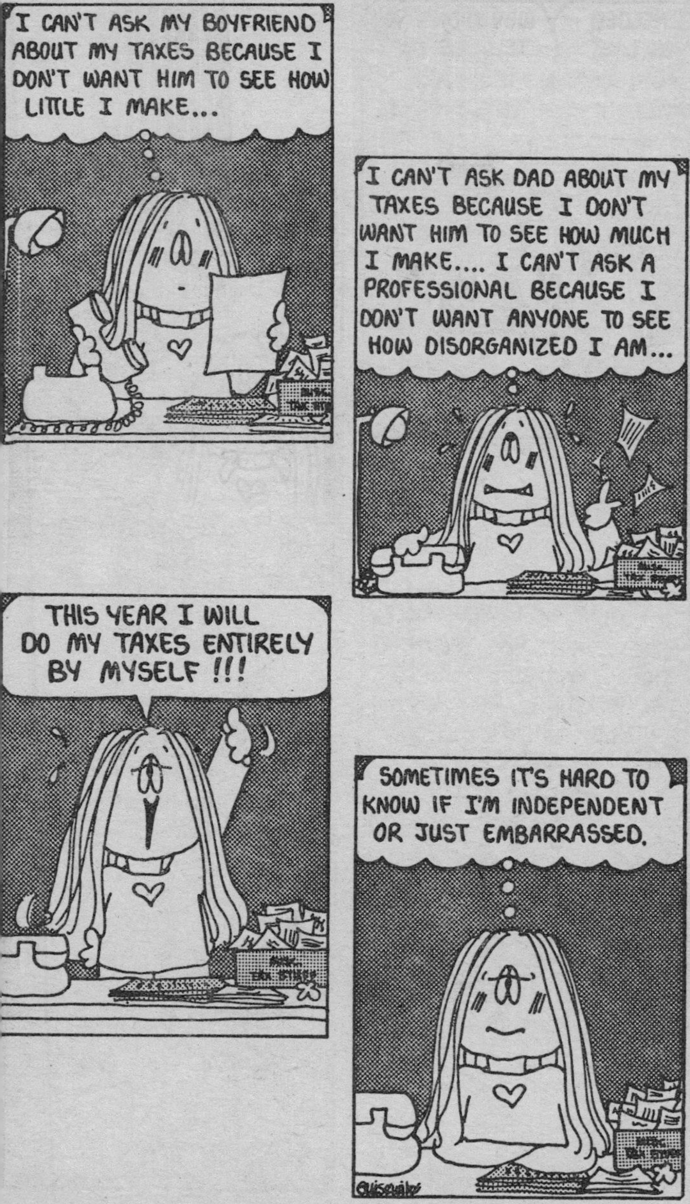
I CAN'T ASK MY BOYFRIEND ABOUT MY TAXES BECAUSE I DON'T WANT HIM TO SEE HOW LITTLE I MAKE...
I CAN'T ASK DAD ABOUT MY TAXES BECAUSE I DON'T WANT HIM TO SEE HOW MUCH I MAKE.... I CAN'T ASK A PROFESSIONAL BECAUSE I DON'T WANT ANYONE TO SEE HOW DISORGANIZED I AM...
THIS YEAR I WILL DO MY TAXES ENTIRELY BY MYSELF !!!
SOMETIMES IT'S HARD TO KNOW IF I'M INDEPENDENT OR JUST EMBARRASSED.
GUISEWITE

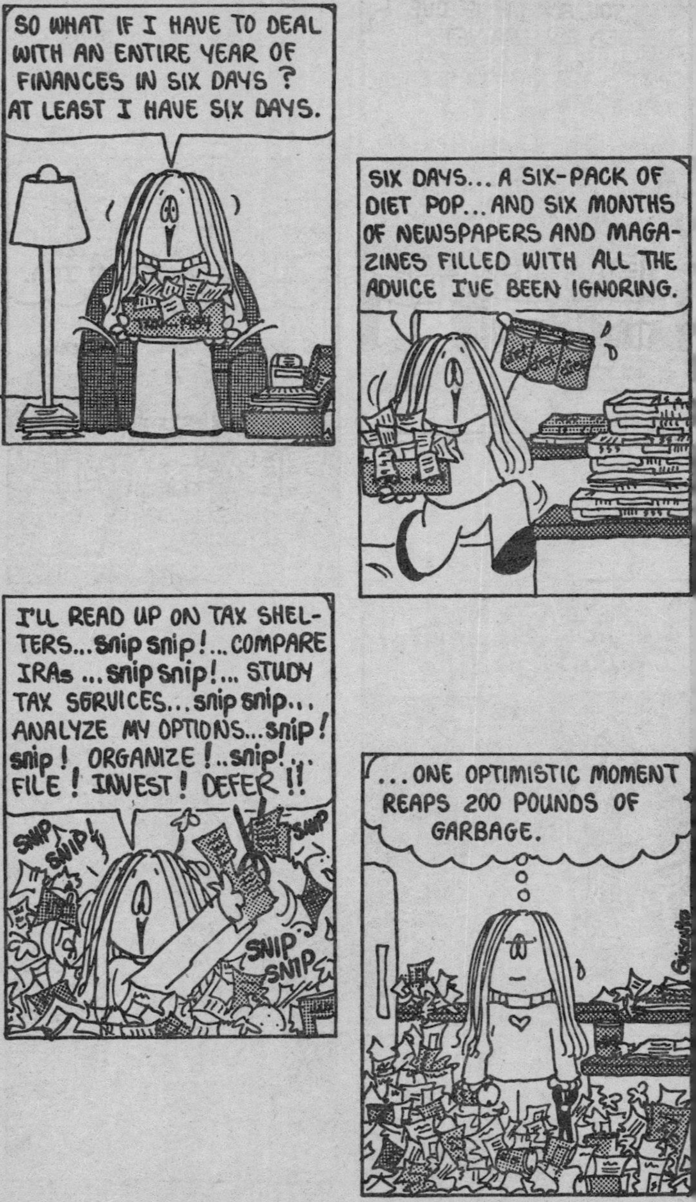
SO WHAT IF I HAVE TO DEAL WITH AN ENTIRE YEAR OF FINANCES IN SIX DAYS? AT LEAST I HAVE SIX DAYS.
SIX DAYS... A SIX-PACK OF DIET POP... AND SIX MONTHS OF NEWSPAPERS AND MAGAZINES FILLED WITH ALL THE ADVICE I'VE BEEN IGNORING.
I'LL READ UP ON TAX SHELTERS...snip snip!... COMPARE IRAs ...snip snip!... STUDY TAX SERVICES...snip snip... ANALYZE MY OPTIONS...snip! snip! ORGANIZE!..snip!... FILE! INVEST! DEFER!!
SNIP
SNIP!
SNIP
SNIP
SNIP
...ONE OPTIMISTIC MOMENT REAPS 200 POUNDS OF GARBAGE.

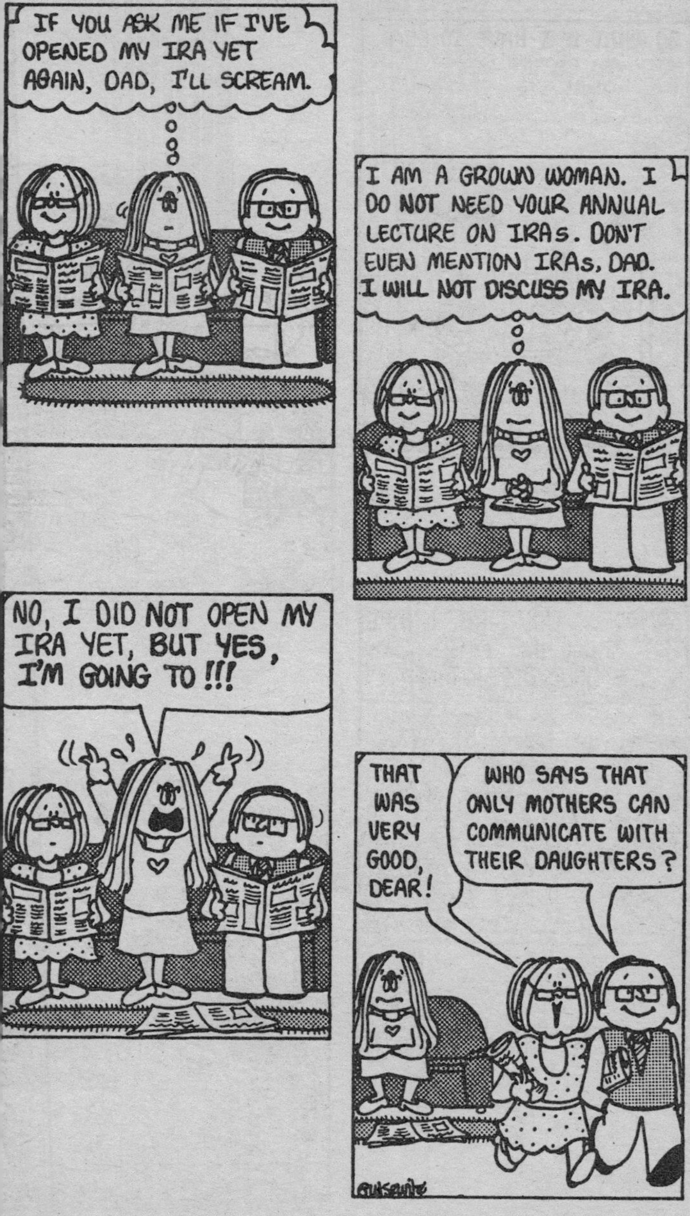
IF YOU ASK ME IF I'VE OPENED MY IRA YET AGAIN, DAD, I'LL SCREAM.
I AM A GROWN WOMAN. I DO NOT NEED YOUR ANNUAL LECTURE ON IRAs. DON'T EVEN MENTION IRAs, DAD. I WILL NOT DISCUSS MY IRA.
NO, I DID NOT OPEN MY IRA YET, BUT YES, I'M GOING TO!!!
THAT WAS VERY GOOD, DEAR!
WHO SAYS THAT ONLY MOTHERS CAN COMMUNICATE WITH THEIR DAUGHTERS?

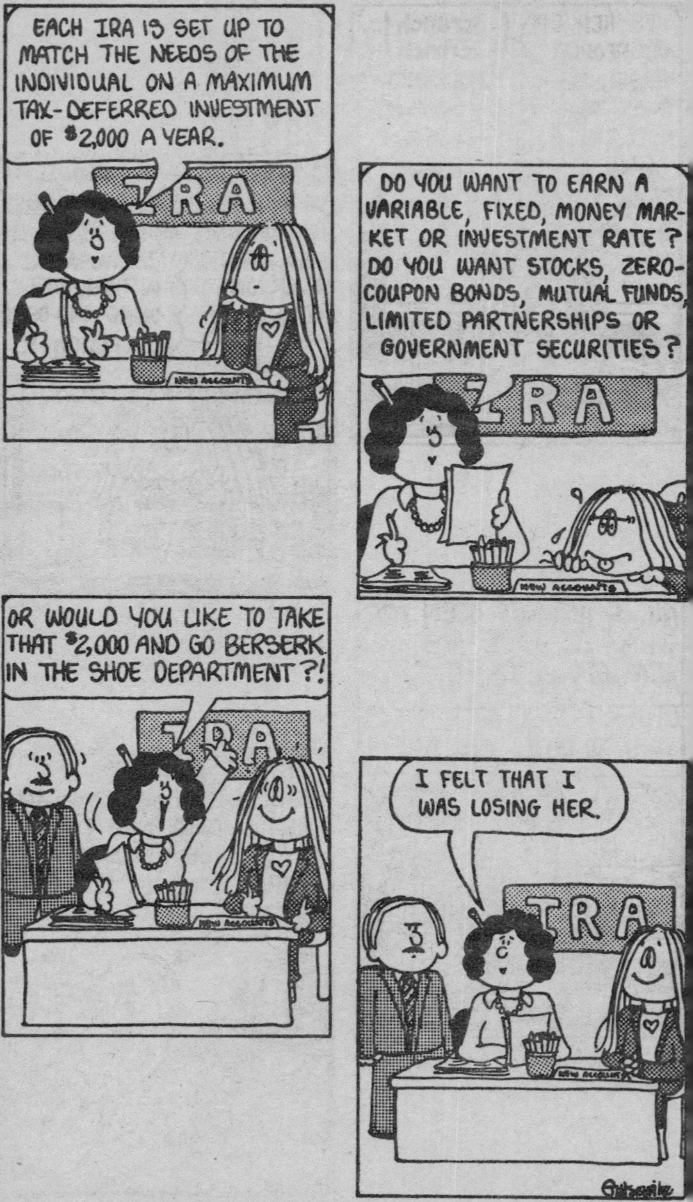
EACH IRA IS SET UP TO MATCH THE NEEDS OF THE INDIVIDUAL ON A MAXIMUM TAX-DEFERRED INVESTMENT OF $2,000 A YEAR.
IRA
DO YOU WANT TO EARN A VARIABLE, FIXED, MONEY MARKET OR INVESTMENT RATE? DO YOU WANT STOCKS, ZERO-COUPON BONDS, MUTUAL FUNDS, LIMITED PARTNERSHIPS OR GOVERNMENT SECURITIES?
IRA
OR WOULD YOU LIKE TO TAKE THAT $2,000 AND GO BERSERK IN THE SHOE DEPARTMENT?!
I FELT THAT I WAS LOSING HER.
IRA
Guisewite

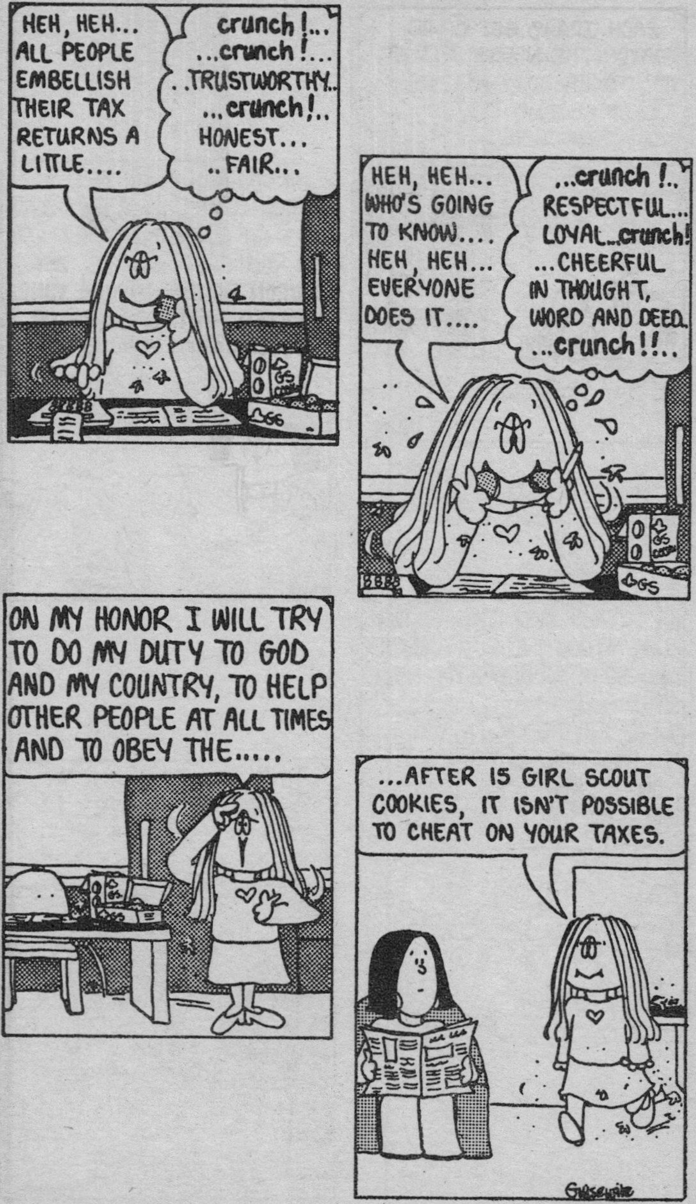
HEH, HEH... ALL PEOPLE EMBELLISH THEIR TAX RETURNS A LITTLE....
crunch!... ...crunch!... ..TRUSTWORTHY.. ...crunch!.. HONEST... ..FAIR...
HEH, HEH... WHO'S GOING TO KNOW.... HEH, HEH... EVERYONE DOES IT....
...crunch!.. RESPECTFUL... LOYAL...crunch! ...CHEERFUL IN THOUGHT, WORD AND DEED. ...crunch!!...
ON MY HONOR I WILL TRY TO DO MY DUTY TO GOD AND MY COUNTRY, TO HELP OTHER PEOPLE AT ALL TIMES AND TO OBEY THE.....
...AFTER 15 GIRL SCOUT COOKIES, IT ISN'T POSSIBLE TO CHEAT ON YOUR TAXES.
Guisewite

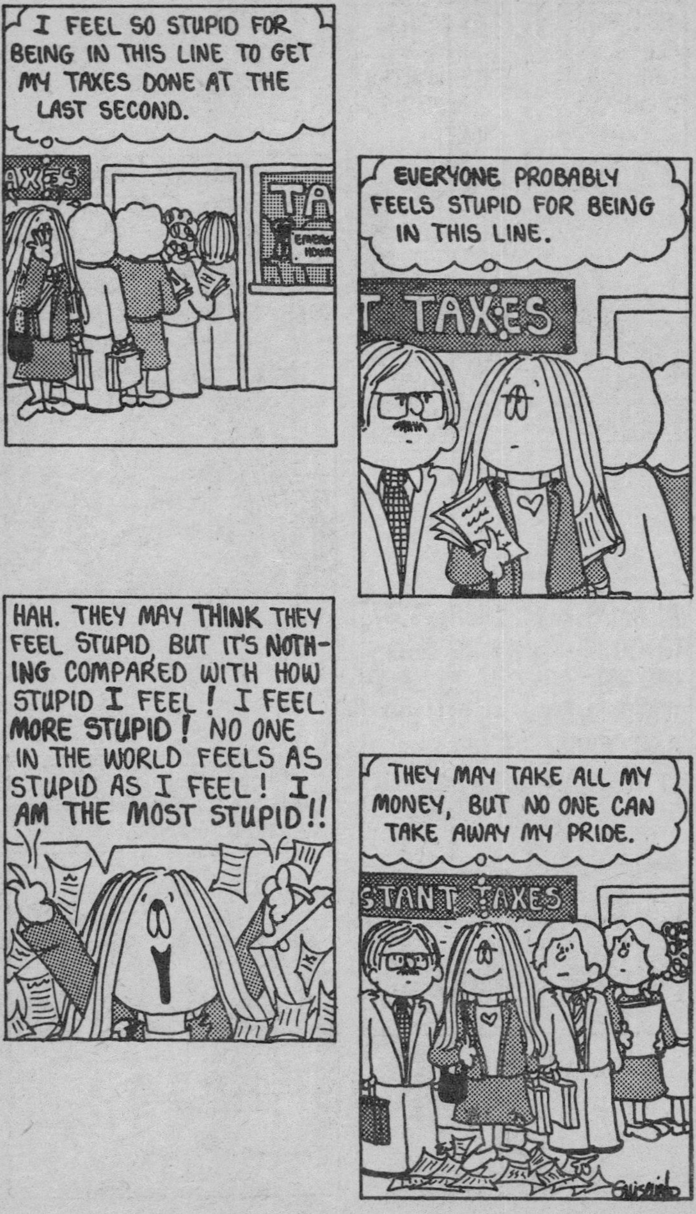
I FEEL SO STUPID FOR BEING IN THIS LINE TO GET MY TAXES DONE AT THE LAST SECOND.
EVERYONE PROBABLY FEELS STUPID FOR BEING IN THIS LINE.
T TAXES
HAH. THEY MAY THINK THEY FEEL STUPID, BUT IT'S NOTHING COMPARED WITH HOW STUPID I FEEL! I FEEL MORE STUPID! NO ONE IN THE WORLD FEELS AS STUPID AS I FEEL! I AM THE MOST STUPID!!
THEY MAY TAKE ALL MY MONEY, BUT NO ONE CAN TAKE AWAY MY PRIDE.
STANT TAXES

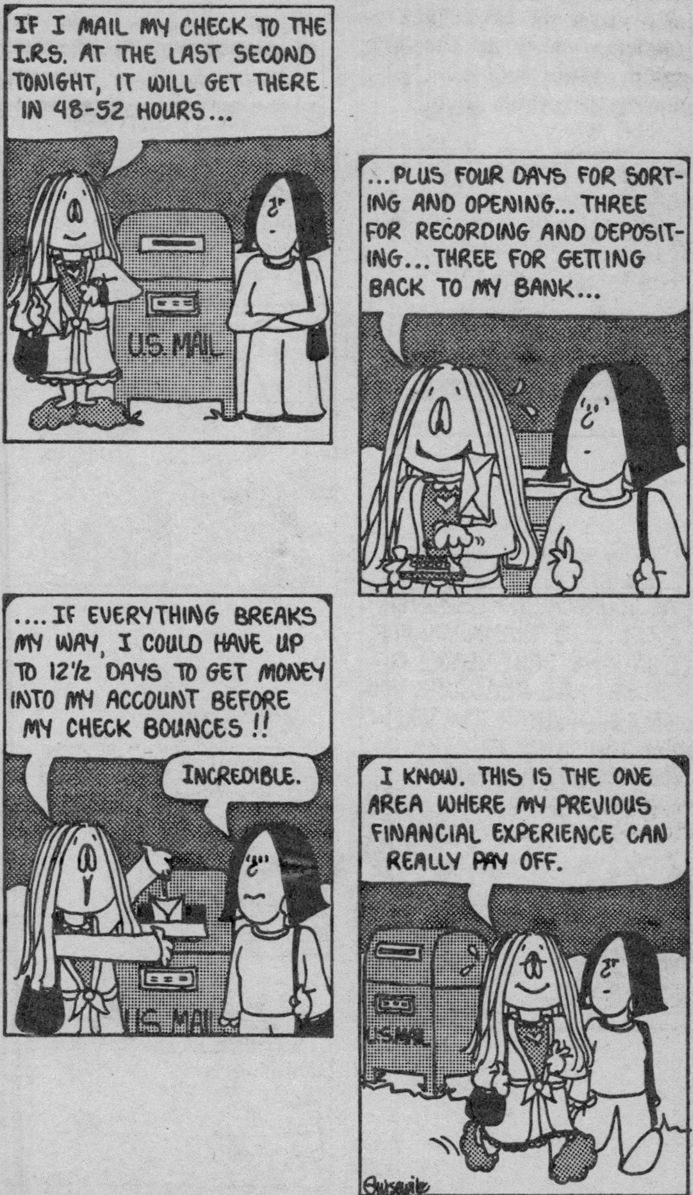
IF I MAIL MY CHECK TO THE I.R.S. AT THE LAST SECOND TONIGHT, IT WILL GET THERE IN 48-52 HOURS...
U.S. MAIL
...PLUS FOUR DAYS FOR SORTING AND OPENING... THREE FOR RECORDING AND DEPOSITING... THREE FOR GETTING BACK TO MY BANK...
....IF EVERYTHING BREAKS MY WAY, I COULD HAVE UP TO 12½ DAYS TO GET MONEY INTO MY ACCOUNT BEFORE MY CHECK BOUNCES !!
INCREDIBLE.
U.S. MAIL
I KNOW. THIS IS THE ONE AREA WHERE MY PREVIOUS FINANCIAL EXPERIENCE CAN REALLY PAY OFF.
U.S. MAIL
Guisewite

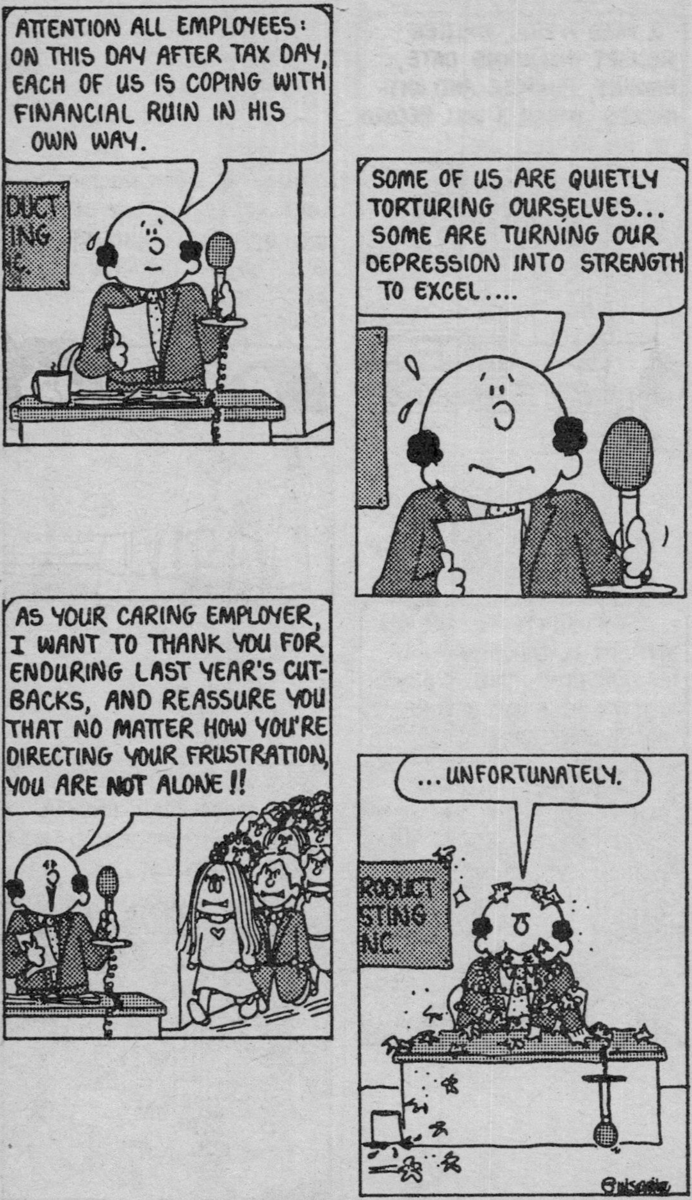
ATTENTION ALL EMPLOYEES: ON THIS DAY AFTER TAX DAY, EACH OF US IS COPING WITH FINANCIAL RUIN IN HIS OWN WAY.
SOME OF US ARE QUIETLY TORTURING OURSELVES... SOME ARE TURNING OUR DEPRESSION INTO STRENGTH TO EXCEL....
AS YOUR CARING EMPLOYER, I WANT TO THANK YOU FOR ENDURING LAST YEAR'S CUT-BACKS, AND REASSURE YOU THAT NO MATTER HOW YOU'RE DIRECTING YOUR FRUSTRATION, YOU ARE NOT ALONE!!
...UNFORTUNATELY.

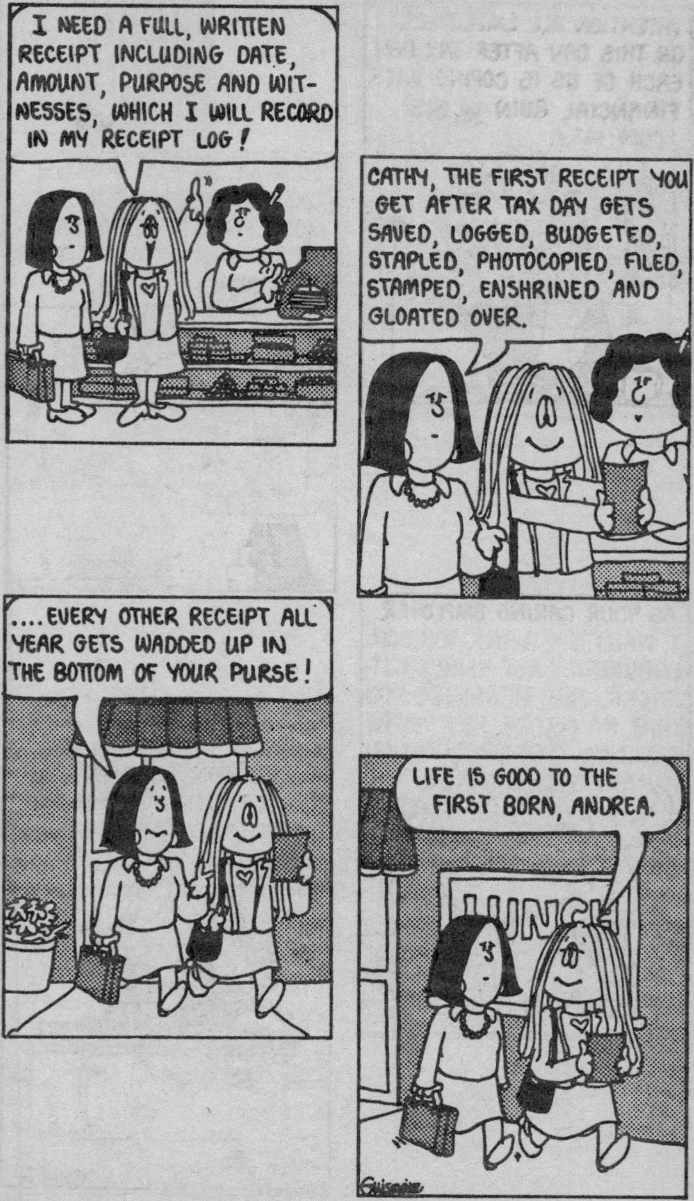
I NEED A FULL, WRITTEN RECEIPT INCLUDING DATE, AMOUNT, PURPOSE AND WITNESSES, WHICH I WILL RECORD IN MY RECEIPT LOG!
CATHY, THE FIRST RECEIPT YOU GET AFTER TAX DAY GETS SAVED, LOGGED, BUDGETED, STAPLED, PHOTOCOPIED, FILED, STAMPED, ENSHRINED AND GLOATED OVER.
....EVERY OTHER RECEIPT ALL YEAR GETS WADDED UP IN THE BOTTOM OF YOUR PURSE!
LIFE IS GOOD TO THE FIRST BORN, ANDREA.
LUNCH
Guisewite

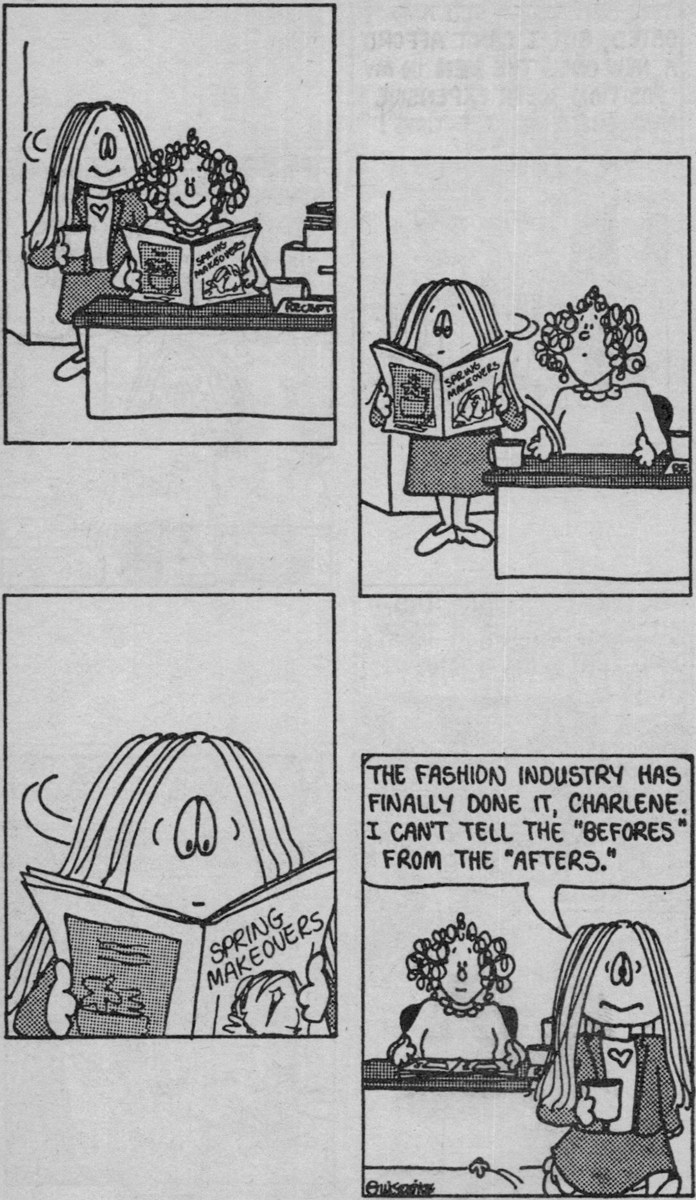
SPRING MAKEOVERS
THE FASHION INDUSTRY HAS FINALLY DONE IT, CHARLENE. I CAN'T TELL THE "BEFORES" FROM THE "AFTERS."

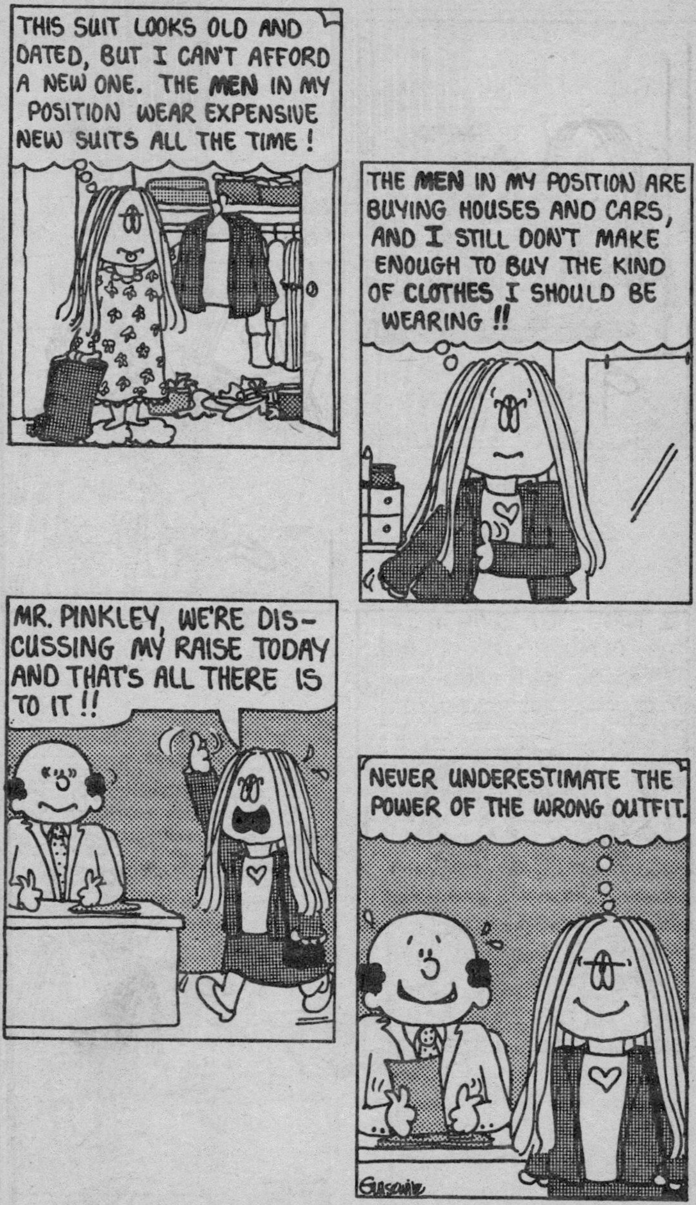
THIS SUIT LOOKS OLD AND DATED, BUT I CAN'T AFFORD A NEW ONE. THE MEN IN MY POSITION WEAR EXPENSIVE NEW SUITS ALL THE TIME!
THE MEN IN MY POSITION ARE BUYING HOUSES AND CARS, AND I STILL DON'T MAKE ENOUGH TO BUY THE KIND OF CLOTHES I SHOULD BE WEARING!!
MR. PINKLEY, WE'RE DISCUSSING MY RAISE TODAY AND THAT'S ALL THERE IS TO IT!!
NEVER UNDERESTIMATE THE POWER OF THE WRONG OUTFIT.
GUISEWITE

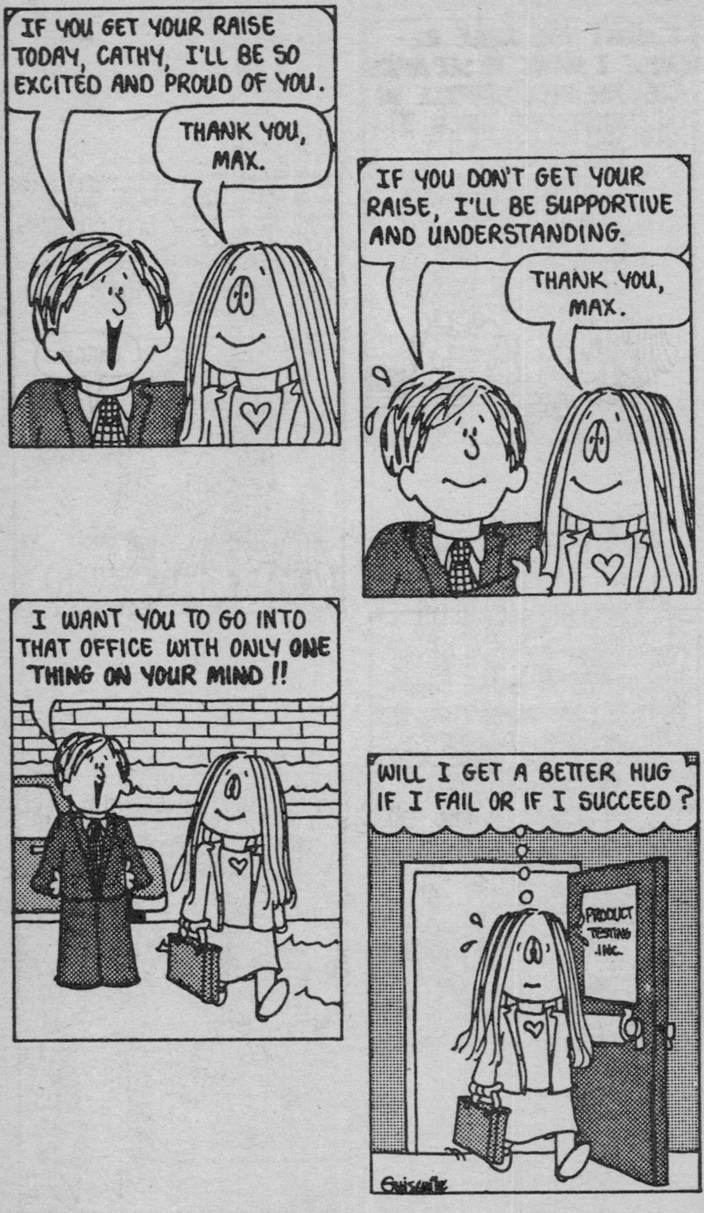
IF YOU GET YOUR RAISE TODAY, CATHY, I'LL BE SO EXCITED AND PROUD OF YOU.
THANK YOU, MAX.
IF YOU DON'T GET YOUR RAISE, I'LL BE SUPPORTIVE AND UNDERSTANDING.
THANK YOU, MAX.
I WANT YOU TO GO INTO THAT OFFICE WITH ONLY ONE THING ON YOUR MIND !!
WILL I GET A BETTER HUG IF I FAIL OR IF I SUCCEED ?
PRODUCT TESTING INC.

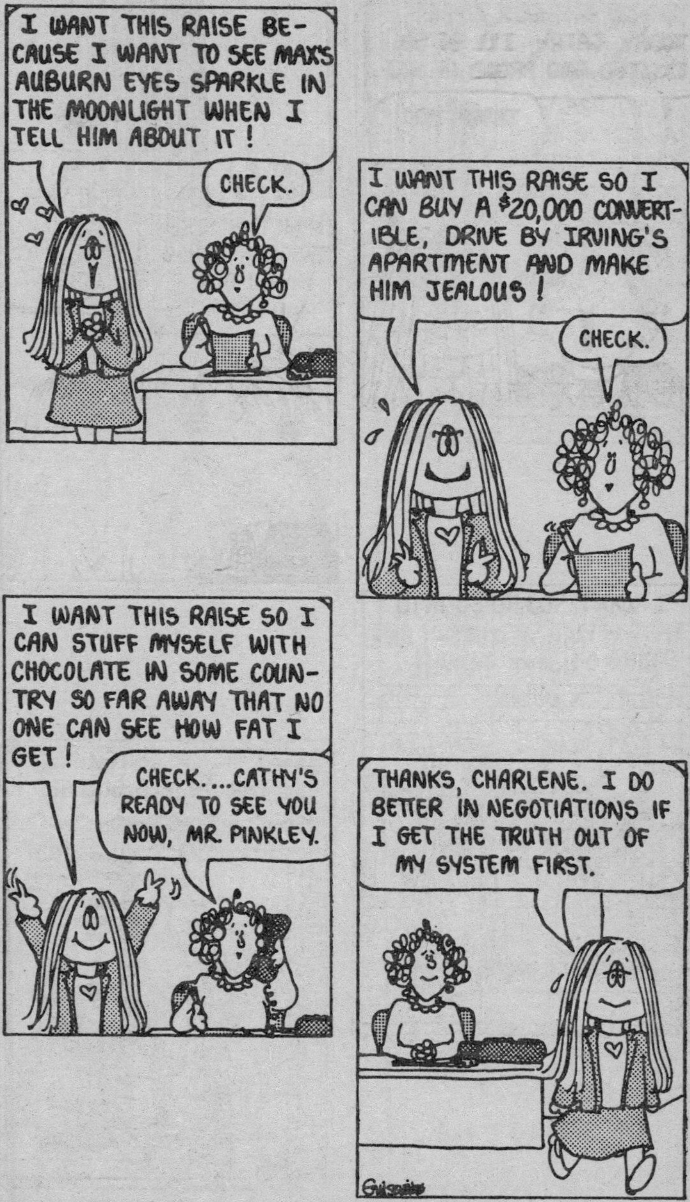
I WANT THIS RAISE BECAUSE I WANT TO SEE MAX'S AUBURN EYES SPARKLE IN THE MOONLIGHT WHEN I TELL HIM ABOUT IT!
CHECK.
I WANT THIS RAISE SO I CAN BUY A $20,000 CONVERTIBLE, DRIVE BY IRVING'S APARTMENT AND MAKE HIM JEALOUS!
CHECK.
I WANT THIS RAISE SO I CAN STUFF MYSELF WITH CHOCOLATE IN SOME COUNTRY SO FAR AWAY THAT NO ONE CAN SEE HOW FAT I GET!
CHECK.....CATHY'S READY TO SEE YOU NOW, MR. PINKLEY.
THANKS, CHARLENE. I DO BETTER IN NEGOTIATIONS IF I GET THE TRUTH OUT OF MY SYSTEM FIRST.
Guisewite

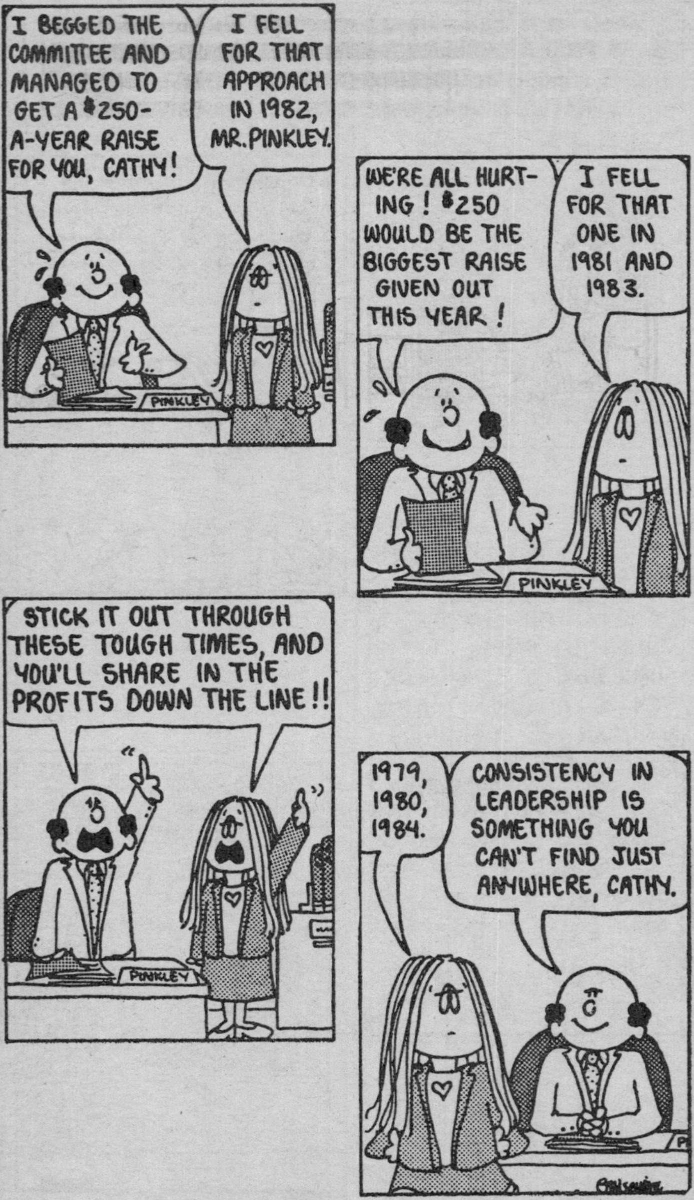
I BEGGED THE COMMITTEE AND MANAGED TO GET A $250-A-YEAR RAISE FOR YOU, CATHY!
I FELL FOR THAT APPROACH IN 1982, MR. PINKLEY.
PINKLEY
WE'RE ALL HURTING! $250 WOULD BE THE BIGGEST RAISE GIVEN OUT THIS YEAR!
I FELL FOR THAT ONE IN 1981 AND 1983.
PINKLEY
STICK IT OUT THROUGH THESE TOUGH TIMES, AND YOU'LL SHARE IN THE PROFITS DOWN THE LINE!!
PINKLEY
1979, 1980, 1984.
CONSISTENCY IN LEADERSHIP IS SOMETHING YOU CAN'T FIND JUST ANYWHERE, CATHY.

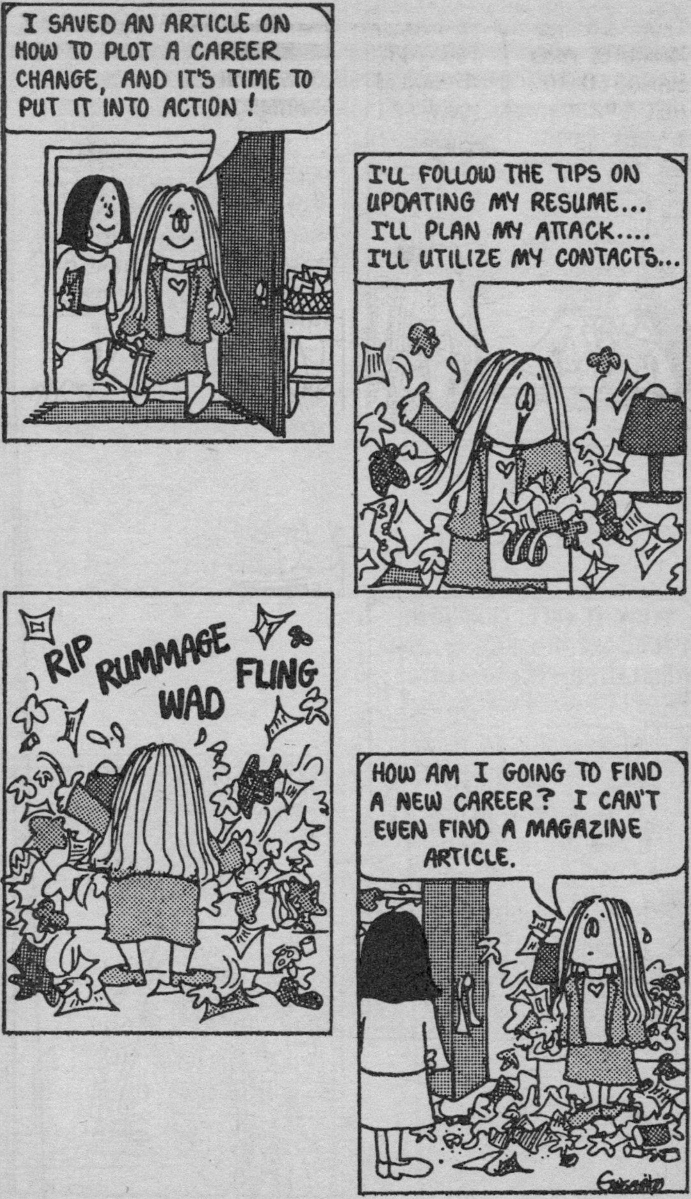
I SAVED AN ARTICLE ON HOW TO PLOT A CAREER CHANGE, AND IT'S TIME TO PUT IT INTO ACTION!
I'LL FOLLOW THE TIPS ON UPDATING MY RESUME... I'LL PLAN MY ATTACK.... I'LL UTILIZE MY CONTACTS...
RIP
RUMMAGE
FLING
WAD
HOW AM I GOING TO FIND A NEW CAREER? I CAN'T EVEN FIND A MAGAZINE ARTICLE.
Guisewite

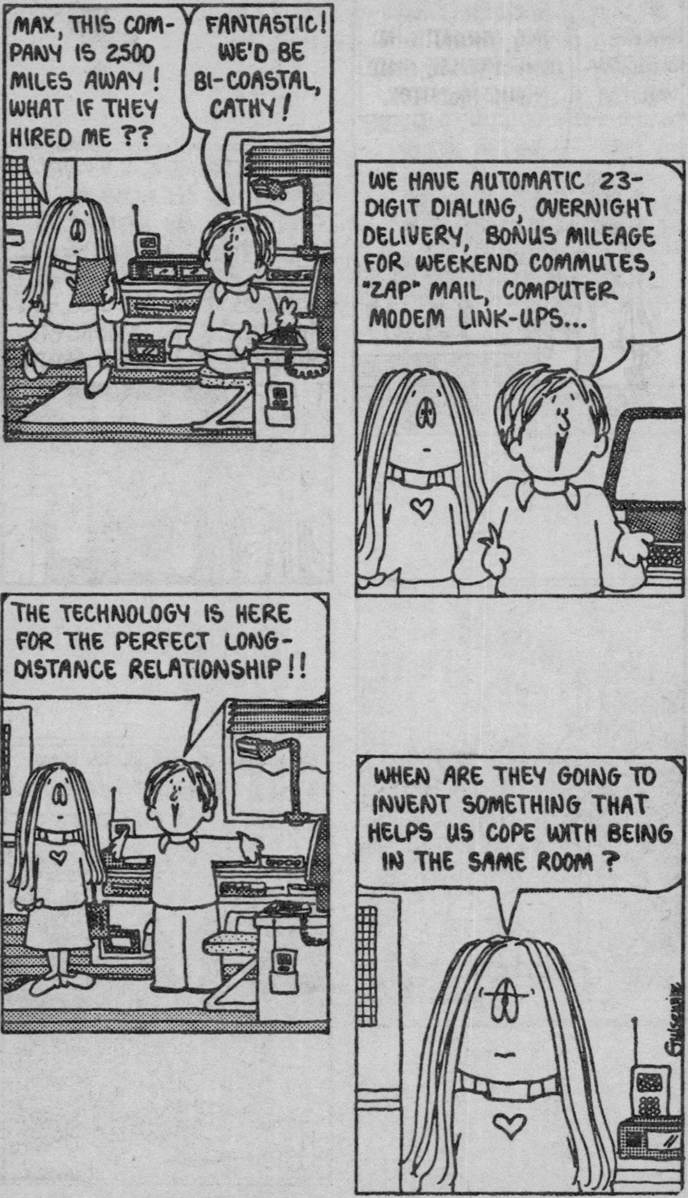
MAX, THIS COMPANY IS 2,500 MILES AWAY! WHAT IF THEY HIRED ME??
FANTASTIC! WE'D BE BI-COASTAL, CATHY!
WE HAVE AUTOMATIC 23-DIGIT DIALING, OVERNIGHT DELIVERY, BONUS MILEAGE FOR WEEKEND COMMUTES, "ZAP" MAIL, COMPUTER MODEM LINK-UPS...
THE TECHNOLOGY IS HERE FOR THE PERFECT LONG-DISTANCE RELATIONSHIP!!
WHEN ARE THEY GOING TO INVENT SOMETHING THAT HELPS US COPE WITH BEING IN THE SAME ROOM?

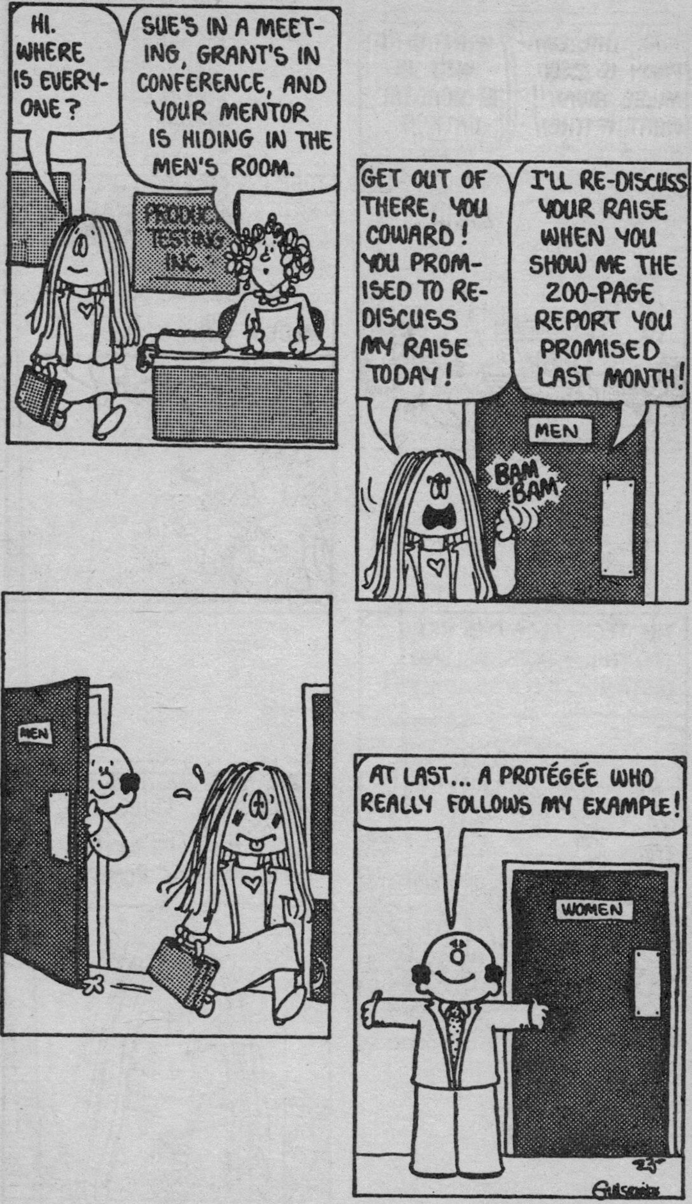
HI. WHERE IS EVERYONE?
SUE'S IN A MEETING, GRANT'S IN CONFERENCE, AND YOUR MENTOR IS HIDING IN THE MEN'S ROOM.
PRODUCT TESTING INC.
GET OUT OF THERE, YOU COWARD! YOU PROMISED TO RE-DISCUSS MY RAISE TODAY!
I'LL RE-DISCUSS YOUR RAISE WHEN YOU SHOW ME THE 200-PAGE REPORT YOU PROMISED LAST MONTH!
MEN
BAM BAM
MEN
AT LAST... A PROTÉGÉE WHO REALLY FOLLOWS MY EXAMPLE!
WOMEN
Guisewite

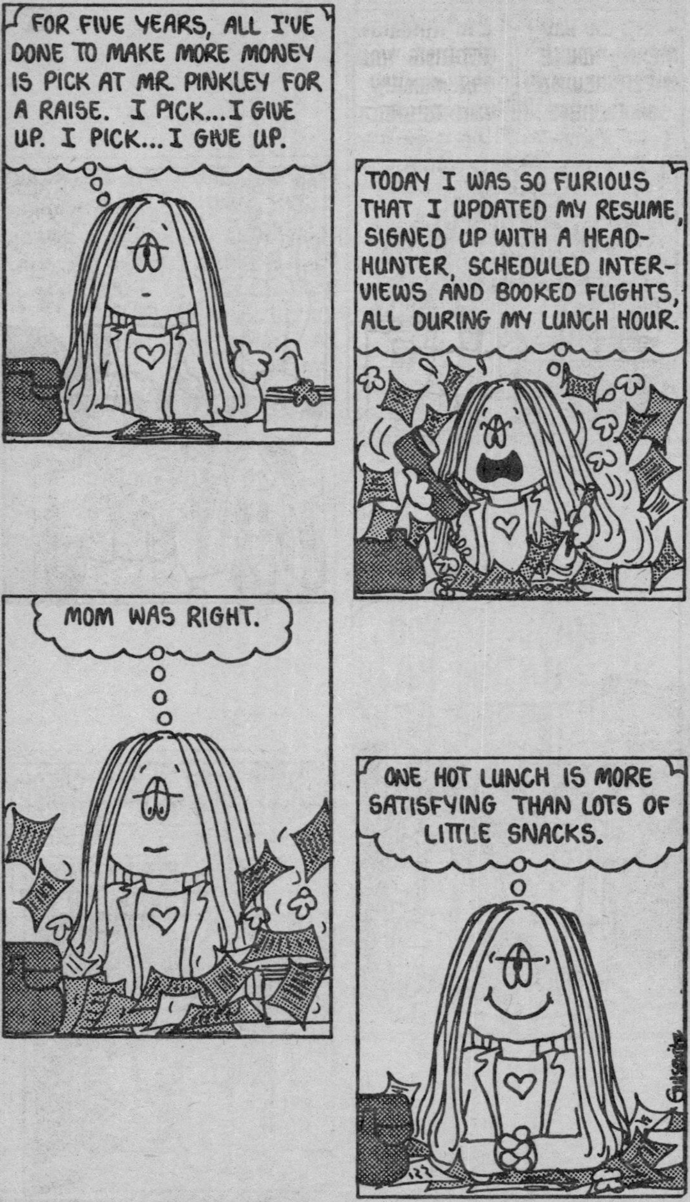
FOR FIVE YEARS, ALL I'VE DONE TO MAKE MORE MONEY IS PICK AT MR. PINKLEY FOR A RAISE. I PICK...I GIVE UP. I PICK...I GIVE UP.
TODAY I WAS SO FURIOUS THAT I UPDATED MY RESUME, SIGNED UP WITH A HEAD-HUNTER, SCHEDULED INTER-VIEWS AND BOOKED FLIGHTS, ALL DURING MY LUNCH HOUR.
MOM WAS RIGHT.
ONE HOT LUNCH IS MORE SATISFYING THAN LOTS OF LITTLE SNACKS.
Guisewite

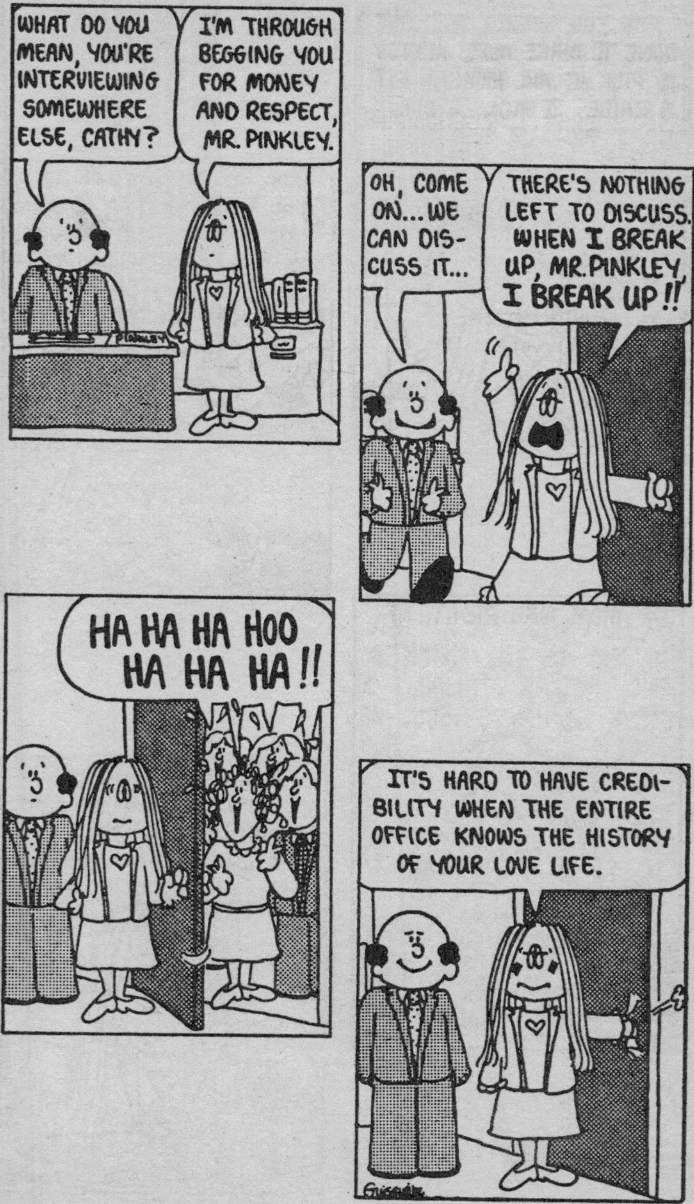
WHAT DO YOU MEAN, YOU'RE INTERVIEWING SOMEWHERE ELSE, CATHY?
I'M THROUGH BEGGING YOU FOR MONEY AND RESPECT, MR. PINKLEY.
PINKLEY
OH, COME ON... WE CAN DISCUSS IT...
THERE'S NOTHING LEFT TO DISCUSS. WHEN I BREAK UP, MR. PINKLEY, I BREAK UP!!
HA HA HA HOO HA HA HA!!
IT'S HARD TO HAVE CREDIBILITY WHEN THE ENTIRE OFFICE KNOWS THE HISTORY OF YOUR LOVE LIFE.
Guisewite

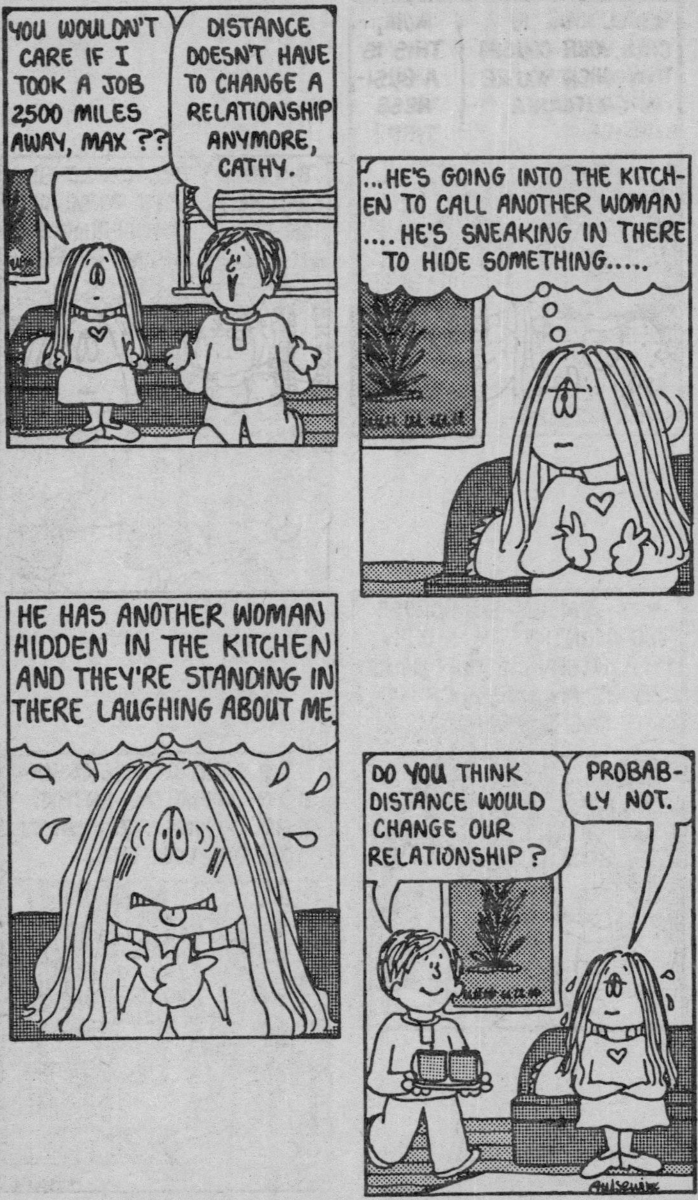
YOU WOULDN'T CARE IF I TOOK A JOB 2500 MILES AWAY, MAX ??
DISTANCE DOESN'T HAVE TO CHANGE A RELATIONSHIP ANYMORE, CATHY.
...HE'S GOING INTO THE KITCHEN TO CALL ANOTHER WOMAN .... HE'S SNEAKING IN THERE TO HIDE SOMETHING.....
HE HAS ANOTHER WOMAN HIDDEN IN THE KITCHEN AND THEY'RE STANDING IN THERE LAUGHING ABOUT ME.
DO YOU THINK DISTANCE WOULD CHANGE OUR RELATIONSHIP ?
PROBABLY NOT.

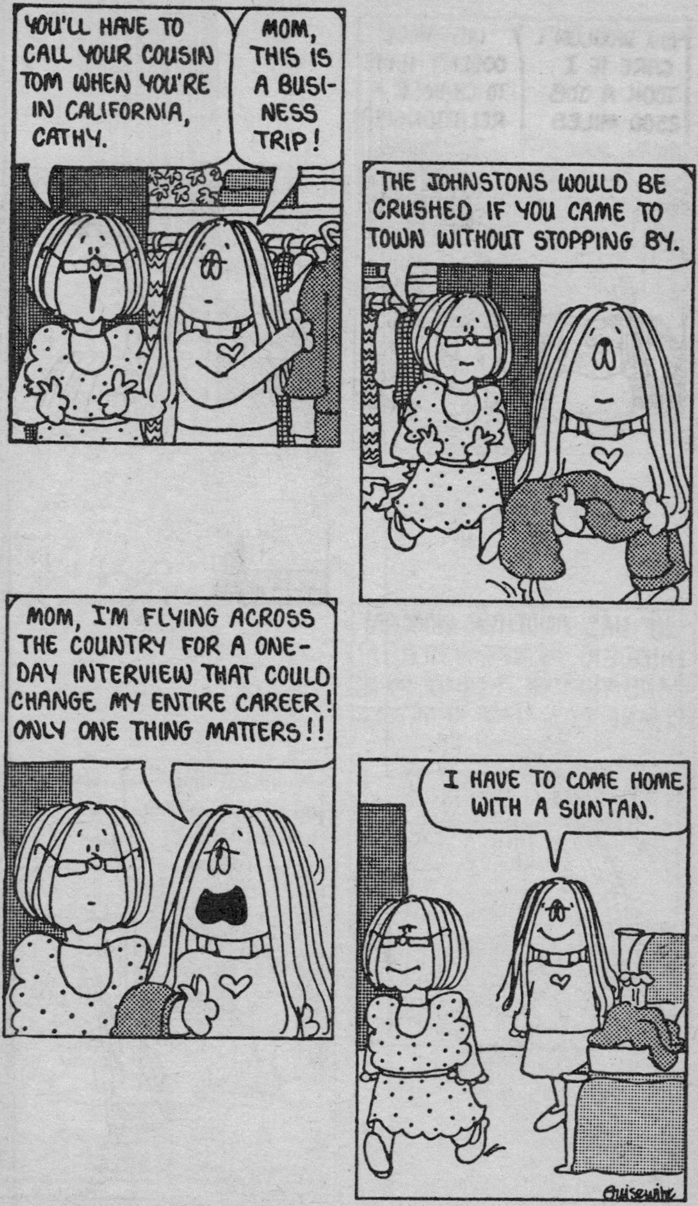
YOU'LL HAVE TO CALL YOUR COUSIN TOM WHEN YOU'RE IN CALIFORNIA, CATHY.
MOM, THIS IS A BUSINESS TRIP!
THE JOHNSTONS WOULD BE CRUSHED IF YOU CAME TO TOWN WITHOUT STOPPING BY.
MOM, I'M FLYING ACROSS THE COUNTRY FOR A ONE-DAY INTERVIEW THAT COULD CHANGE MY ENTIRE CAREER! ONLY ONE THING MATTERS!!
I HAVE TO COME HOME WITH A SUNTAN.
Guisewite

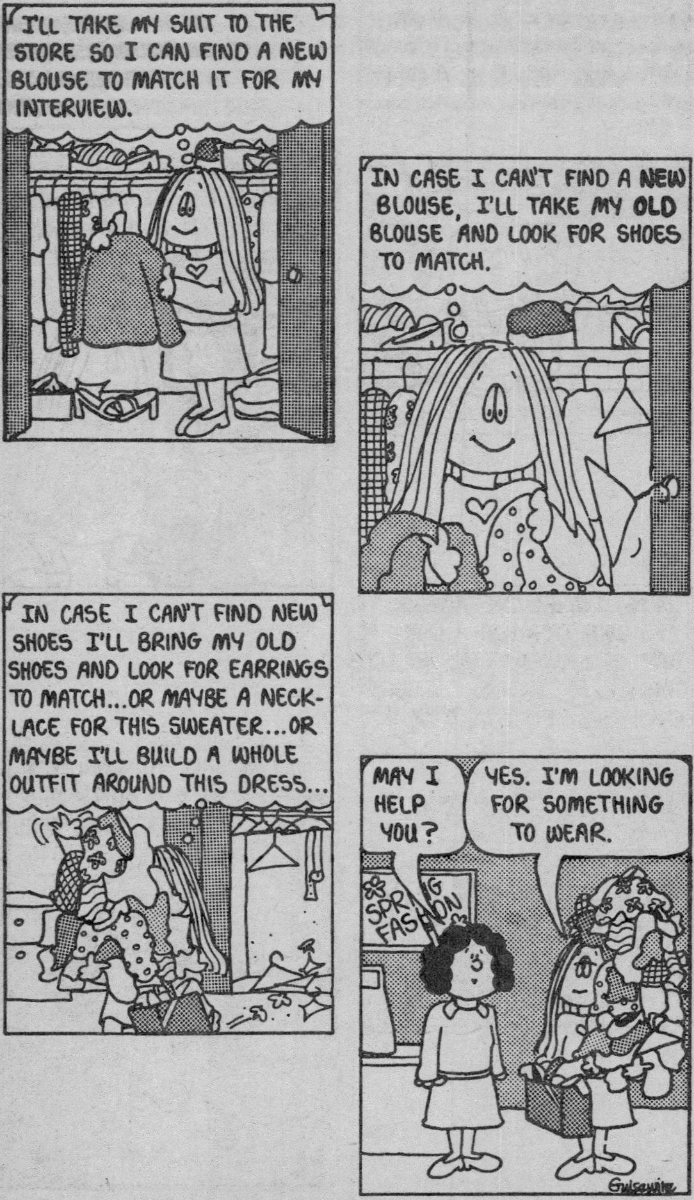
I'LL TAKE MY SUIT TO THE STORE SO I CAN FIND A NEW BLOUSE TO MATCH IT FOR MY INTERVIEW.
IN CASE I CAN'T FIND A NEW BLOUSE, I'LL TAKE MY OLD BLOUSE AND LOOK FOR SHOES TO MATCH.
IN CASE I CAN'T FIND NEW SHOES I'LL BRING MY OLD SHOES AND LOOK FOR EARRINGS TO MATCH...OR MAYBE A NECKLACE FOR THIS SWEATER...OR MAYBE I'LL BUILD A WHOLE OUTFIT AROUND THIS DRESS...
MAY I HELP YOU?
YES. I'M LOOKING FOR SOMETHING TO WEAR.

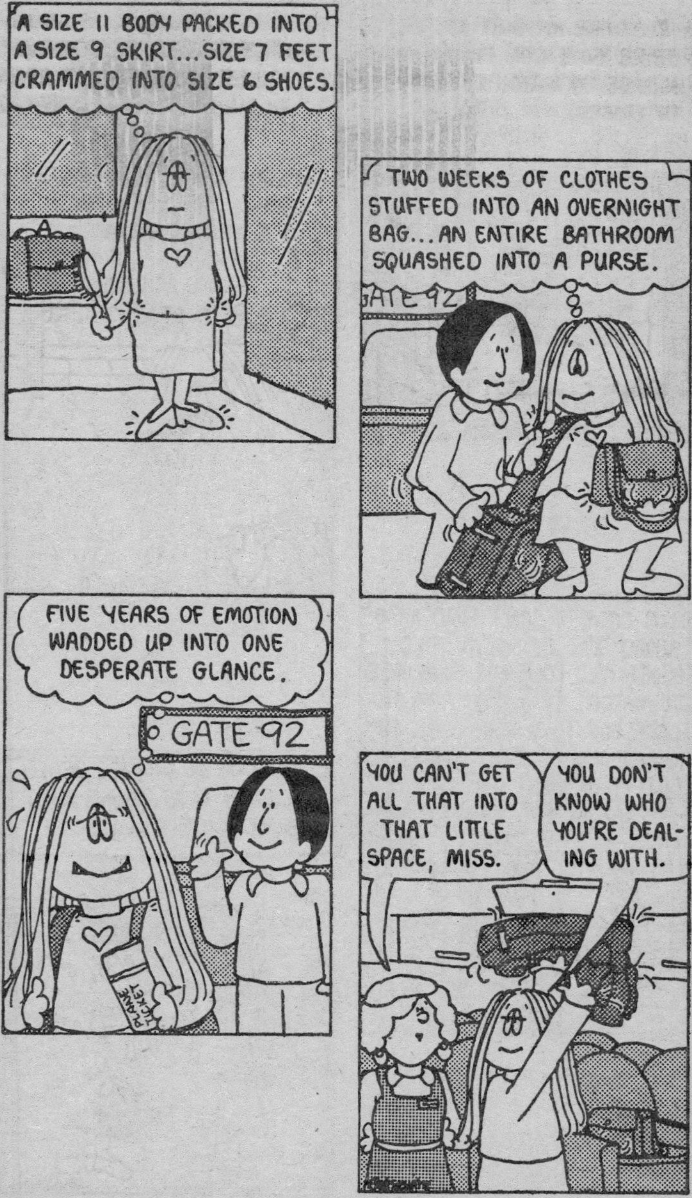
A SIZE 11 BODY PACKED INTO A SIZE 9 SKIRT... SIZE 7 FEET CRAMMED INTO SIZE 6 SHOES.
TWO WEEKS OF CLOTHES STUFFED INTO AN OVERNIGHT BAG... AN ENTIRE BATHROOM SQUASHED INTO A PURSE.
GATE 92
FIVE YEARS OF EMOTION WADDED UP INTO ONE DESPERATE GLANCE.
GATE 92
PLANE TICKET
YOU CAN'T GET ALL THAT INTO THAT LITTLE SPACE, MISS.
YOU DON'T KNOW WHO YOU'RE DEALING WITH.

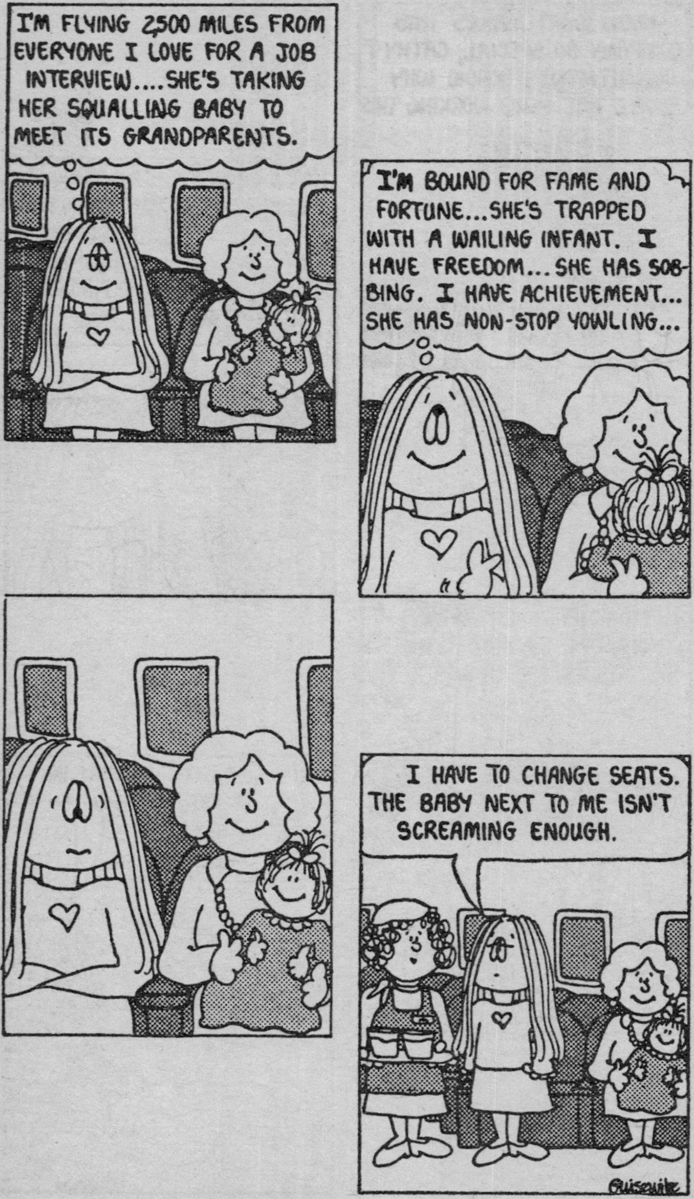
I'M FLYING 2,500 MILES FROM EVERYONE I LOVE FOR A JOB INTERVIEW.....SHE'S TAKING HER SQUALLING BABY TO MEET ITS GRANDPARENTS.
I'M BOUND FOR FAME AND FORTUNE...SHE'S TRAPPED WITH A WAILING INFANT. I HAVE FREEDOM...SHE HAS SOBBING. I HAVE ACHIEVEMENT...SHE HAS NON-STOP YOWLING...
I HAVE TO CHANGE SEATS. THE BABY NEXT TO ME ISN'T SCREAMING ENOUGH.
Guisewite

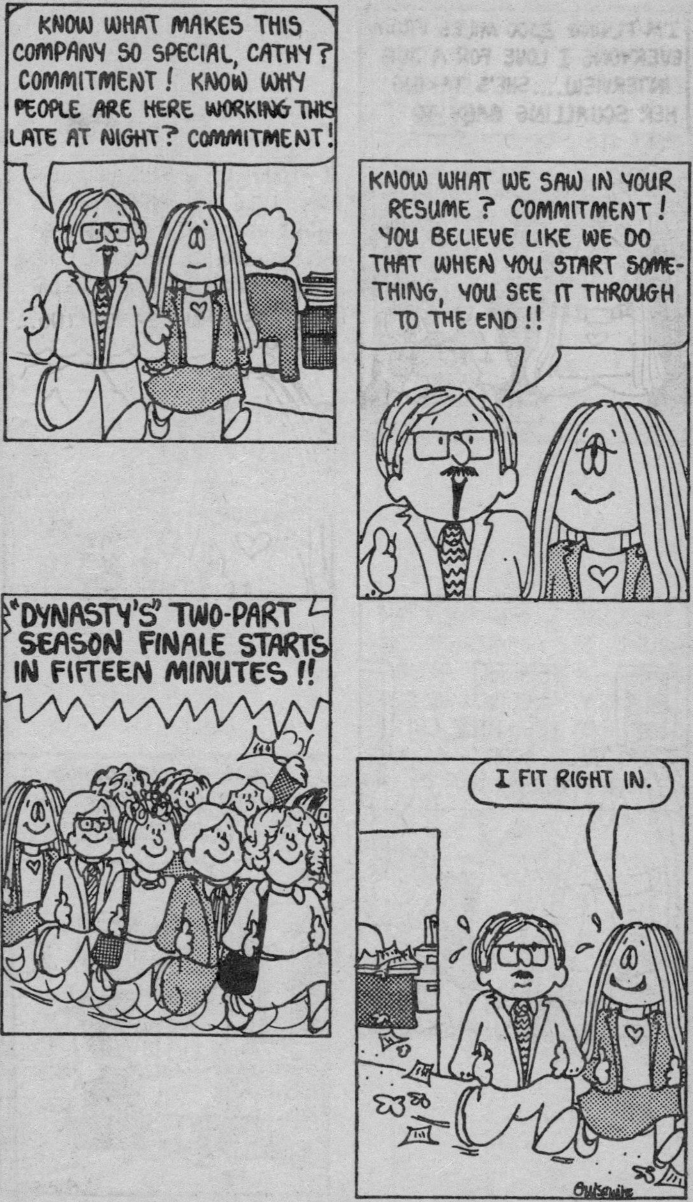
KNOW WHAT MAKES THIS COMPANY SO SPECIAL, CATHY? COMMITMENT! KNOW WHY PEOPLE ARE HERE WORKING THIS LATE AT NIGHT? COMMITMENT!
KNOW WHAT WE SAW IN YOUR RESUME? COMMITMENT! YOU BELIEVE LIKE WE DO THAT WHEN YOU START SOMETHING, YOU SEE IT THROUGH TO THE END!!
"DYNASTY'S" TWO-PART SEASON FINALE STARTS IN FIFTEEN MINUTES!!
I FIT RIGHT IN.

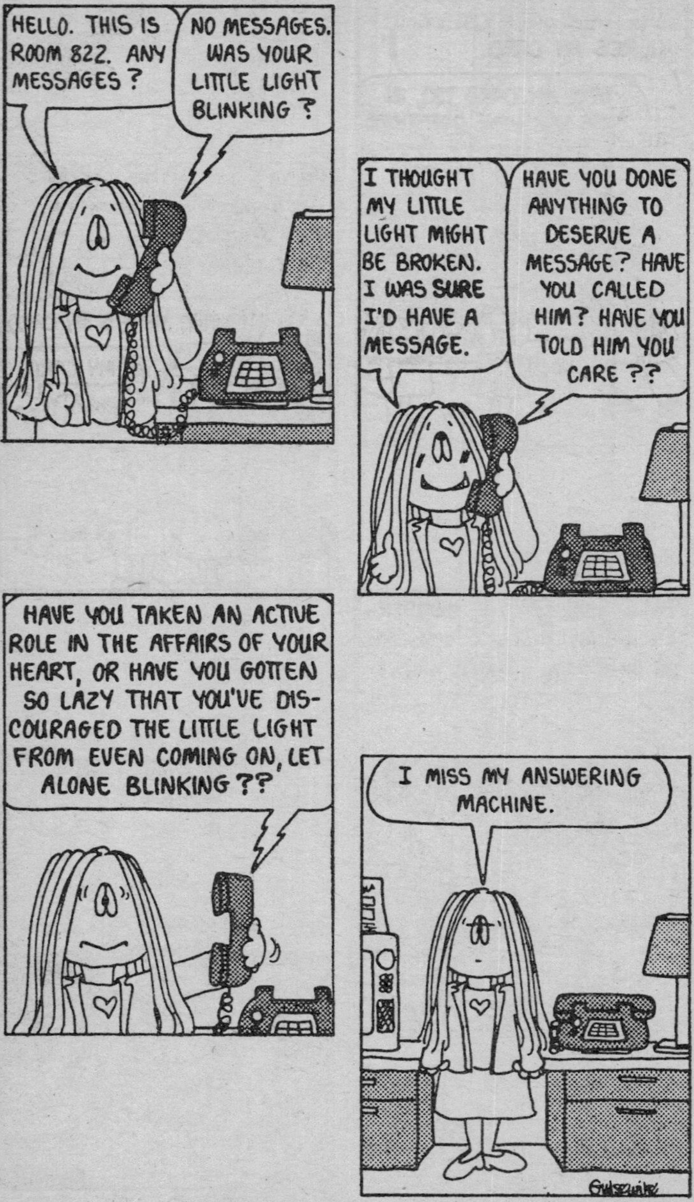

HELLO. THIS IS ROOM 822. ANY MESSAGES?
NO MESSAGES. WAS YOUR LITTLE LIGHT BLINKING?
I THOUGHT MY LITTLE LIGHT MIGHT BE BROKEN. I WAS SURE I'D HAVE A MESSAGE.
HAVE YOU DONE ANYTHING TO DESERVE A MESSAGE? HAVE YOU CALLED HIM? HAVE YOU TOLD HIM YOU CARE??
HAVE YOU TAKEN AN ACTIVE ROLE IN THE AFFAIRS OF YOUR HEART, OR HAVE YOU GOTTEN SO LAZY THAT YOU'VE DISCOURAGED THE LITTLE LIGHT FROM EVEN COMING ON, LET ALONE BLINKING??
I MISS MY ANSWERING MACHINE.
GUISEWITE

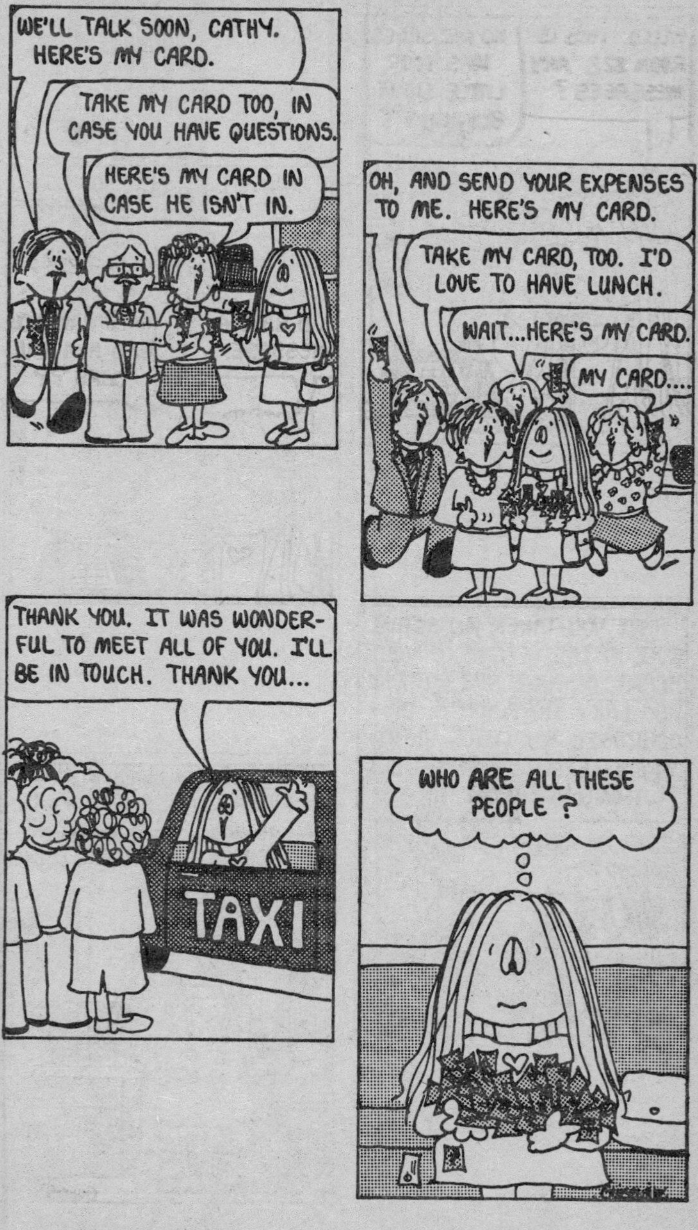
WE'LL TALK SOON, CATHY. HERE'S MY CARD.
TAKE MY CARD TOO, IN CASE YOU HAVE QUESTIONS.
HERE'S MY CARD IN CASE HE ISN'T IN.
OH, AND SEND YOUR EXPENSES TO ME. HERE'S MY CARD.
TAKE MY CARD, TOO. I'D LOVE TO HAVE LUNCH.
WAIT...HERE'S MY CARD.
MY CARD....
THANK YOU. IT WAS WONDER-FUL TO MEET ALL OF YOU. I'LL BE IN TOUCH. THANK YOU...
TAXI
WHO ARE ALL THESE PEOPLE ?

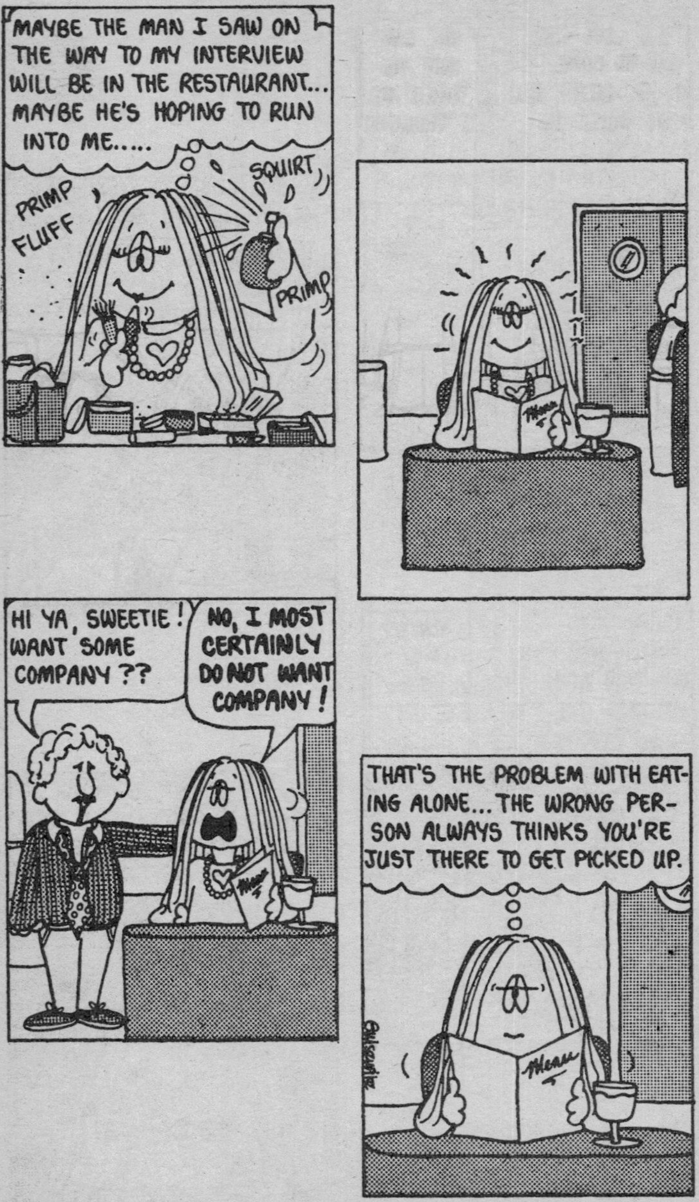
MAYBE THE MAN I SAW ON THE WAY TO MY INTERVIEW WILL BE IN THE RESTAURANT... MAYBE HE'S HOPING TO RUN INTO ME.....
PRIMP
FLUFF
SQUIRT
PRIMP
HI YA, SWEETIE! WANT SOME COMPANY??
NO, I MOST CERTAINLY DO NOT WANT COMPANY!
THAT'S THE PROBLEM WITH EATING ALONE... THE WRONG PERSON ALWAYS THINKS YOU'RE JUST THERE TO GET PICKED UP.

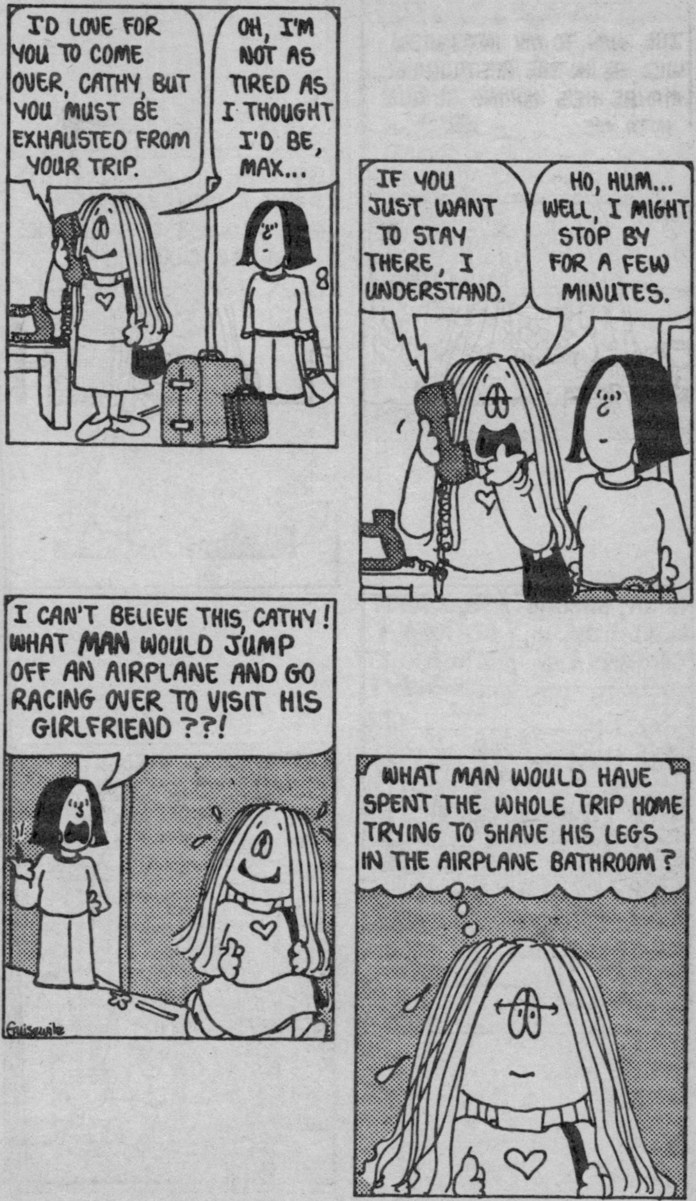
I'D LOVE FOR YOU TO COME OVER, CATHY, BUT YOU MUST BE EXHAUSTED FROM YOUR TRIP.
OH, I'M NOT AS TIRED AS I THOUGHT I'D BE, MAX...
IF YOU JUST WANT TO STAY THERE, I UNDERSTAND.
HO, HUM... WELL, I MIGHT STOP BY FOR A FEW MINUTES.
I CAN'T BELIEVE THIS, CATHY! WHAT MAN WOULD JUMP OFF AN AIRPLANE AND GO RACING OVER TO VISIT HIS GIRLFRIEND ??!
Guisewite
WHAT MAN WOULD HAVE SPENT THE WHOLE TRIP HOME TRYING TO SHAVE HIS LEGS IN THE AIRPLANE BATHROOM?

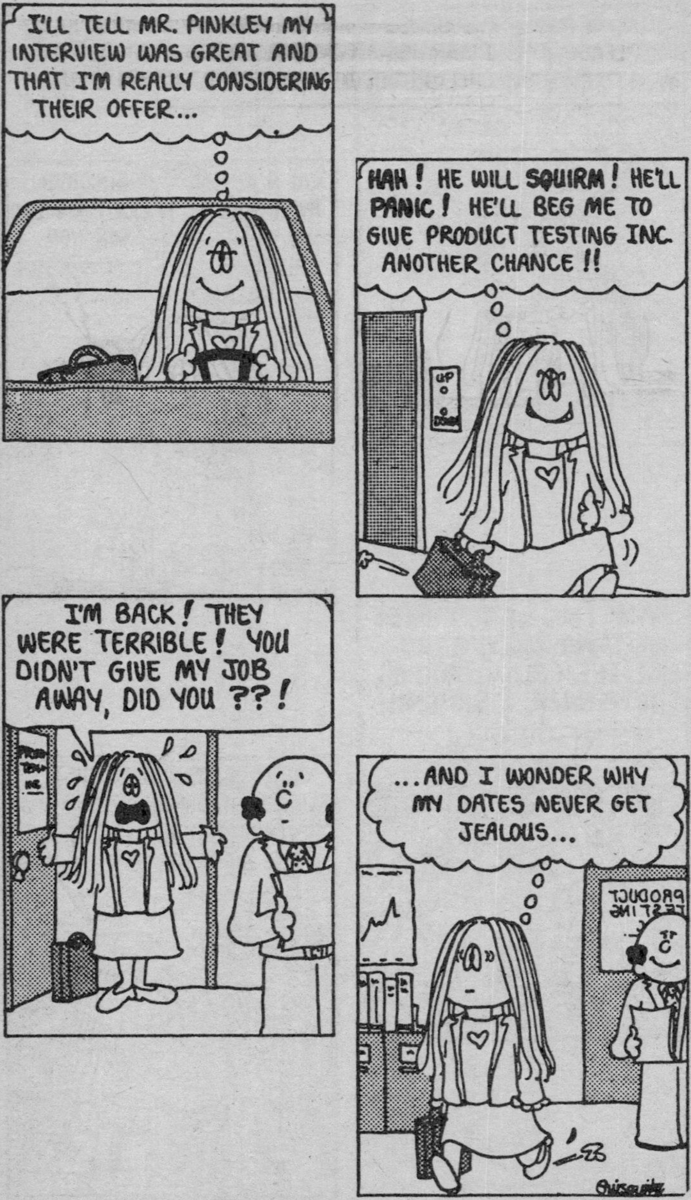
I'LL TELL MR. PINKLEY MY INTERVIEW WAS GREAT AND THAT I'M REALLY CONSIDERING THEIR OFFER...
HAH! HE WILL SQUIRM! HE'LL PANIC! HE'LL BEG ME TO GIVE PRODUCT TESTING INC. ANOTHER CHANCE!!
UP
I'M BACK! THEY WERE TERRIBLE! YOU DIDN'T GIVE MY JOB AWAY, DID YOU??!
...AND I WONDER WHY MY DATES NEVER GET JEALOUS...
Guisewite

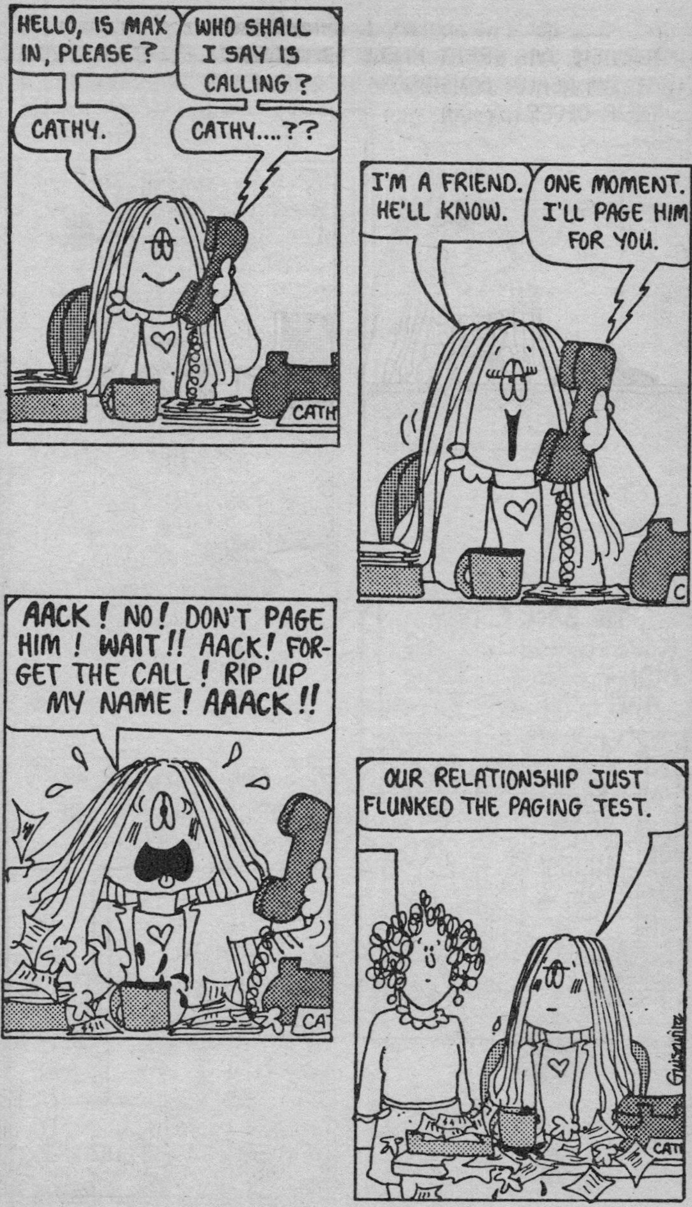
HELLO, IS MAX IN, PLEASE?
WHO SHALL I SAY IS CALLING?
CATHY.
CATHY....??
I'M A FRIEND. HE'LL KNOW.
ONE MOMENT. I'LL PAGE HIM FOR YOU.
AACK! NO! DON'T PAGE HIM! WAIT!! AACK! FORGET THE CALL! RIP UP MY NAME! AAACK!!
OUR RELATIONSHIP JUST FLUNKED THE PAGING TEST.
Guisewite

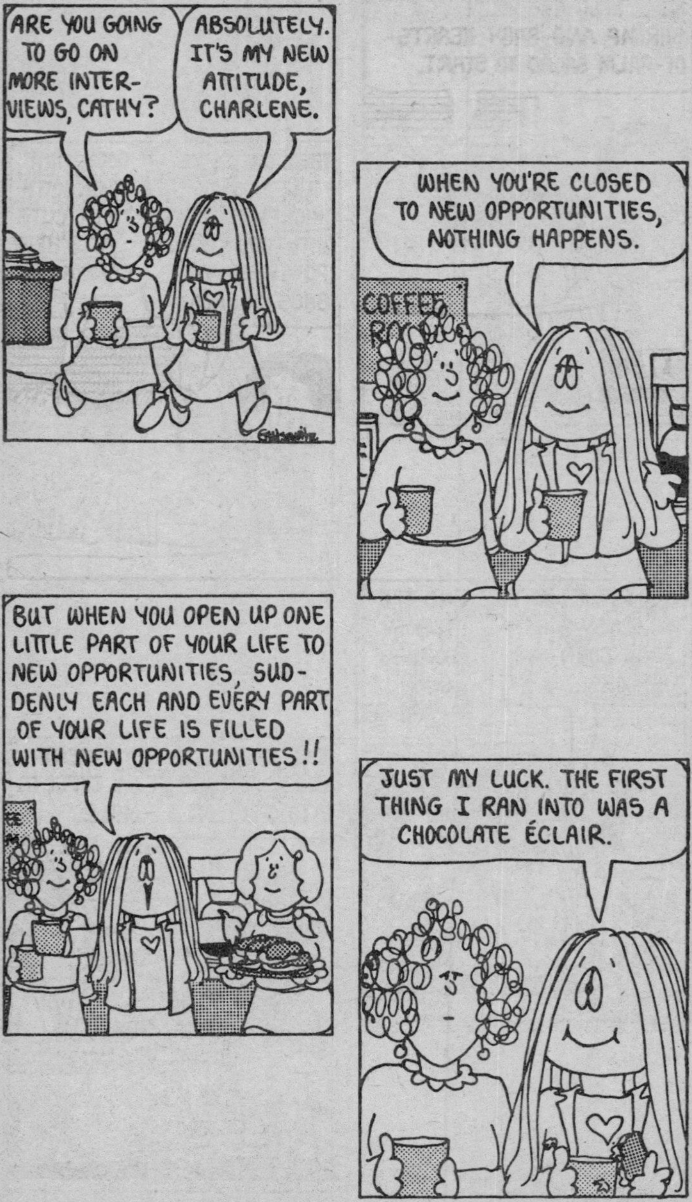
ARE YOU GOING TO GO ON MORE INTER-VIEWS, CATHY?
ABSOLUTELY. IT'S MY NEW ATTITUDE, CHARLENE.
WHEN YOU'RE CLOSED TO NEW OPPORTUNITIES, NOTHING HAPPENS.
COFFEE RO
BUT WHEN YOU OPEN UP ONE LITTLE PART OF YOUR LIFE TO NEW OPPORTUNITIES, SUD-DENLY EACH AND EVERY PART OF YOUR LIFE IS FILLED WITH NEW OPPORTUNITIES!!
JUST MY LUCK. THE FIRST THING I RAN INTO WAS A CHOCOLATE ÉCLAIR.

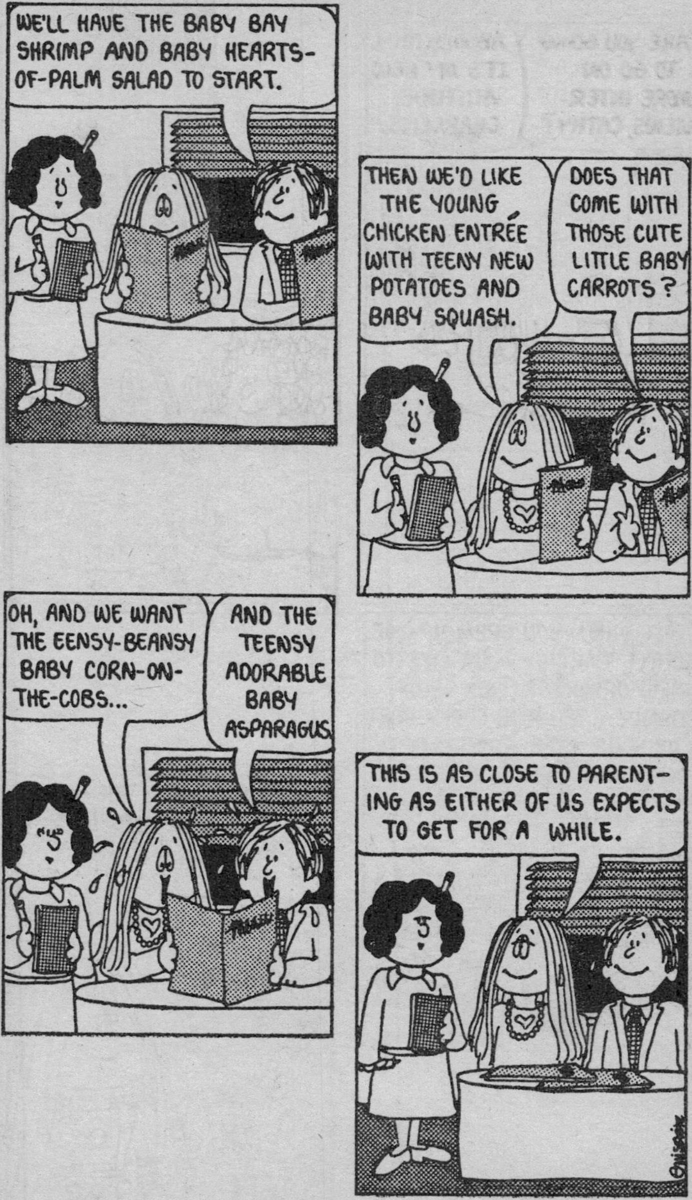
WE'LL HAVE THE BABY BAY SHRIMP AND BABY HEARTS-OF-PALM SALAD TO START.
THEN WE'D LIKE THE YOUNG CHICKEN ENTRÉE WITH TEENY NEW POTATOES AND BABY SQUASH.
DOES THAT COME WITH THOSE CUTE LITTLE BABY CARROTS?
OH, AND WE WANT THE EENSY-BEANSY BABY CORN-ON-THE-COBS...
AND THE TEENSY ADORABLE BABY ASPARAGUS
THIS IS AS CLOSE TO PARENTING AS EITHER OF US EXPECTS TO GET FOR A WHILE.

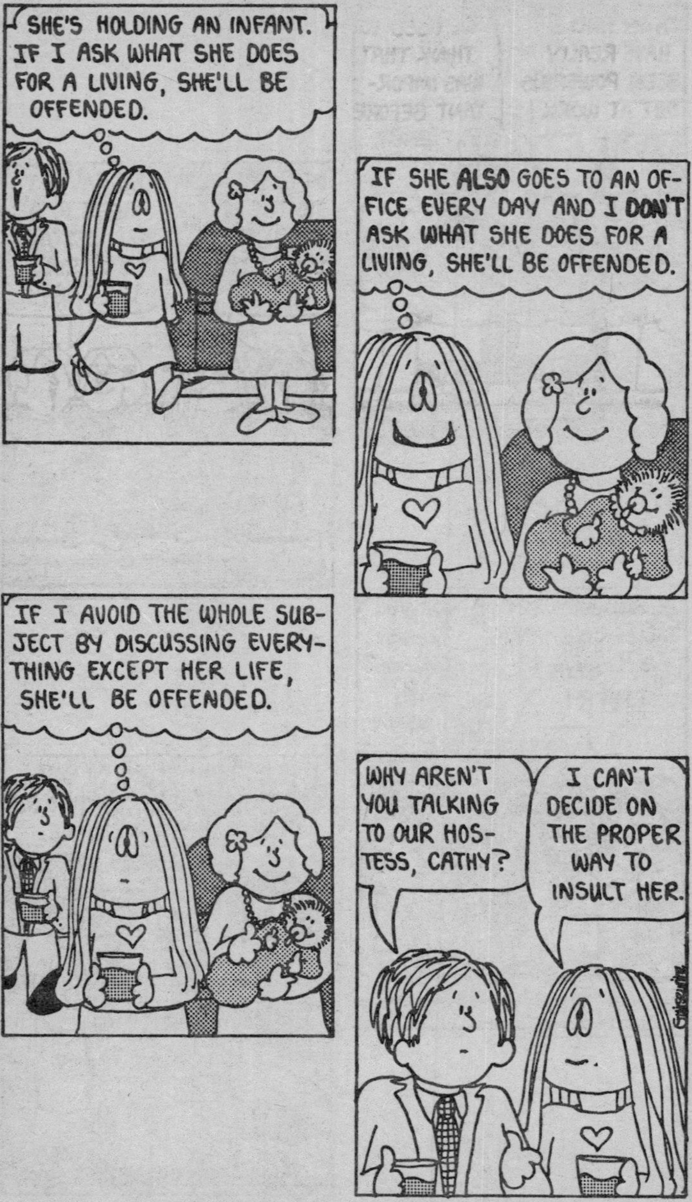
SHE'S HOLDING AN INFANT. IF I ASK WHAT SHE DOES FOR A LIVING, SHE'LL BE OFFENDED.
IF SHE **ALSO** GOES TO AN OFFICE EVERY DAY AND I **DON'T** ASK WHAT SHE DOES FOR A LIVING, SHE'LL BE OFFENDED.
IF I AVOID THE WHOLE SUBJECT BY DISCUSSING EVERYTHING EXCEPT HER LIFE, SHE'LL BE OFFENDED.
WHY AREN'T YOU TALKING TO OUR HOSTESS, CATHY?
I CAN'T DECIDE ON THE PROPER WAY TO INSULT HER.

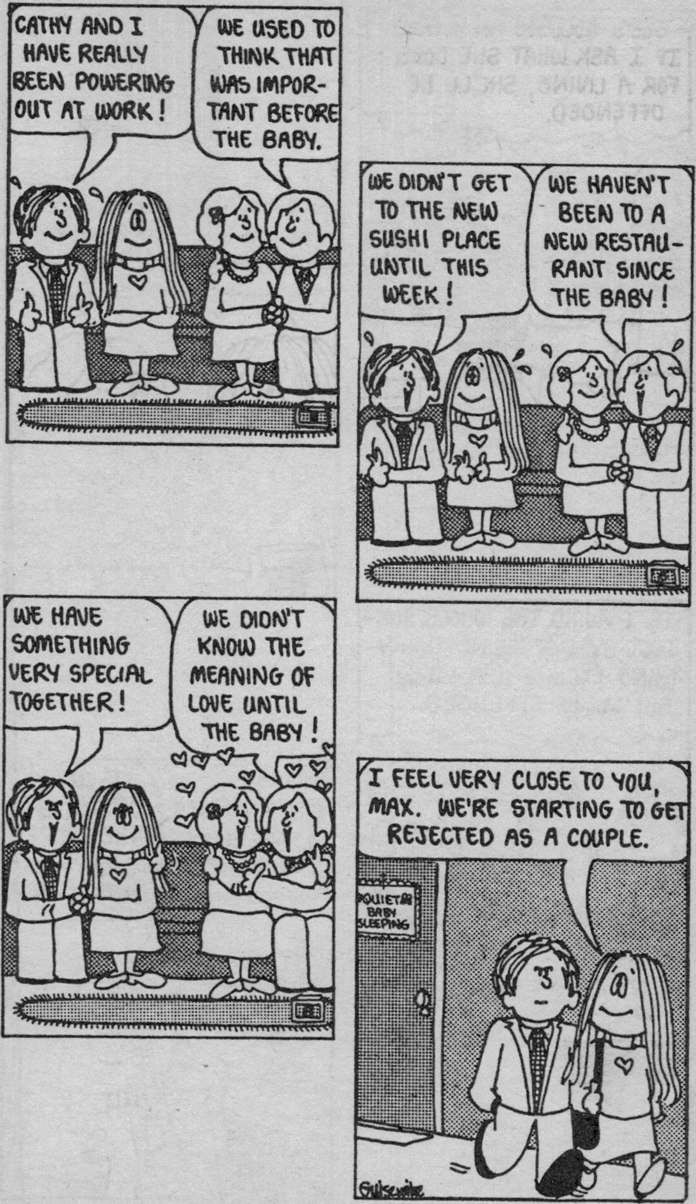
CATHY AND I HAVE REALLY BEEN POWERING OUT AT WORK!
WE USED TO THINK THAT WAS IMPORTANT BEFORE THE BABY.
WE DIDN'T GET TO THE NEW SUSHI PLACE UNTIL THIS WEEK!
WE HAVEN'T BEEN TO A NEW RESTAURANT SINCE THE BABY!
WE HAVE SOMETHING VERY SPECIAL TOGETHER!
WE DIDN'T KNOW THE MEANING OF LOVE UNTIL THE BABY!
I FEEL VERY CLOSE TO YOU, MAX. WE'RE STARTING TO GET REJECTED AS A COUPLE.
QUIET BABY SLEEPING
Guisewite

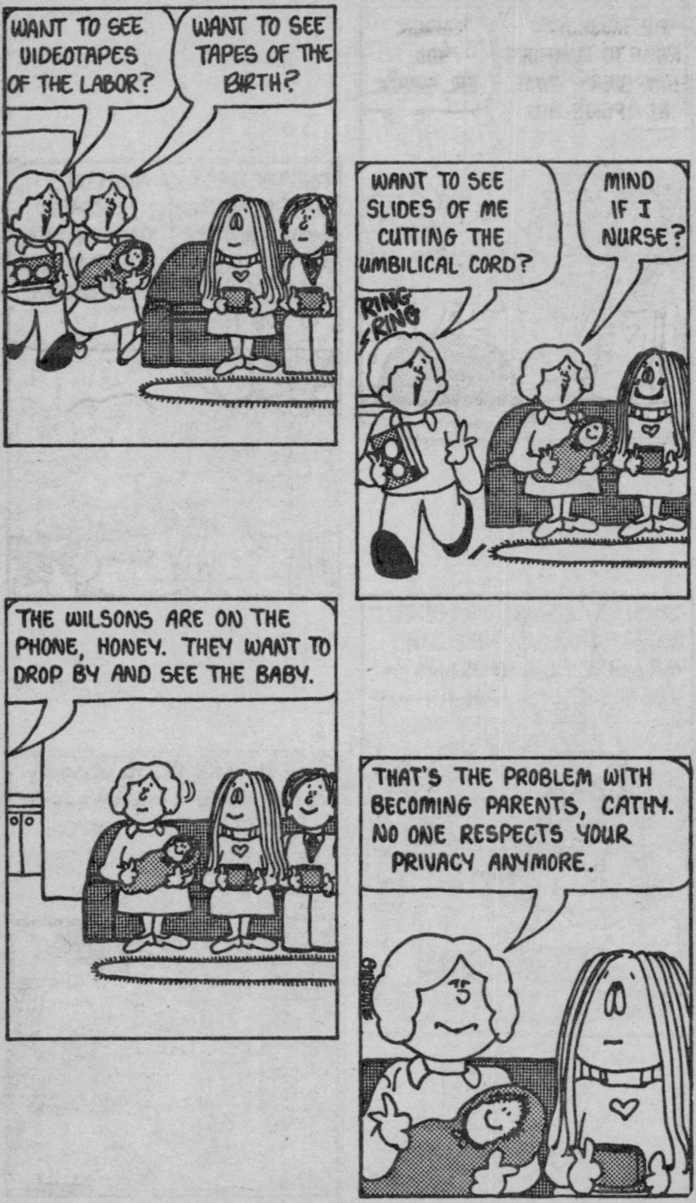
WANT TO SEE VIDEOTAPES OF THE LABOR?
WANT TO SEE TAPES OF THE BIRTH?
WANT TO SEE SLIDES OF ME CUTTING THE UMBILICAL CORD?
MIND IF I NURSE?
RING RING
THE WILSONS ARE ON THE PHONE, HONEY. THEY WANT TO DROP BY AND SEE THE BABY.
THAT'S THE PROBLEM WITH BECOMING PARENTS, CATHY. NO ONE RESPECTS YOUR PRIVACY ANYMORE.

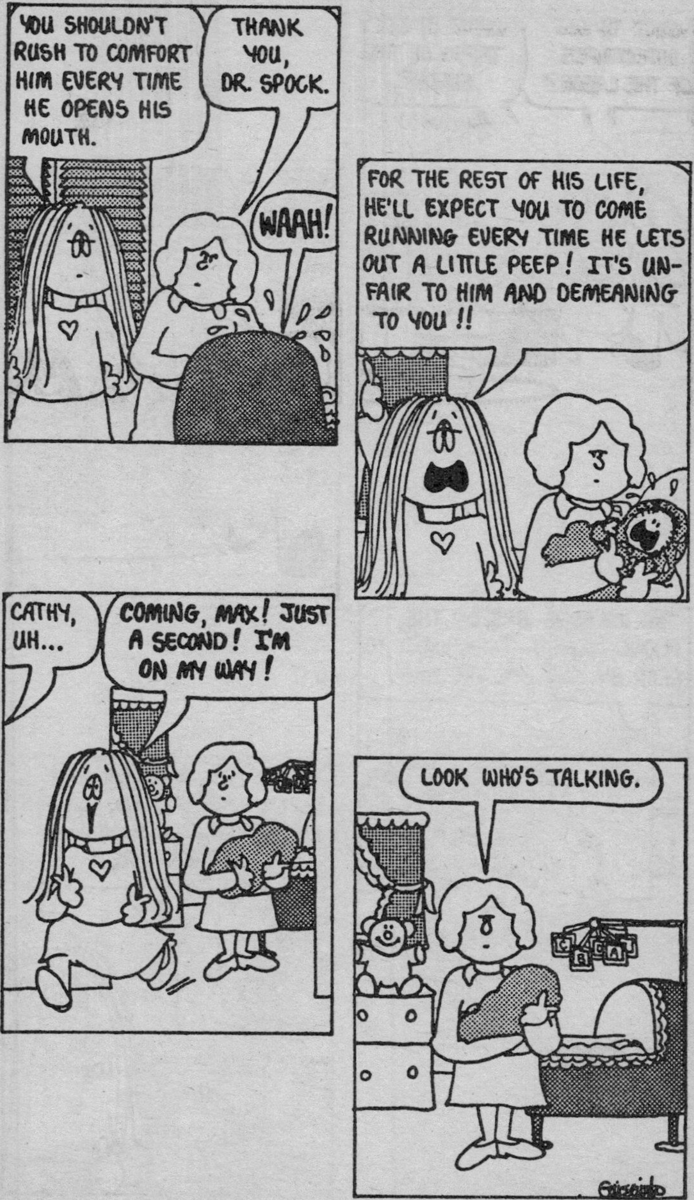
YOU SHOULDN'T RUSH TO COMFORT HIM EVERY TIME HE OPENS HIS MOUTH.
THANK YOU, DR. SPOCK.
WAAH!
FOR THE REST OF HIS LIFE, HE'LL EXPECT YOU TO COME RUNNING EVERY TIME HE LETS OUT A LITTLE PEEP! IT'S UN-FAIR TO HIM AND DEMEANING TO YOU!!
CATHY, UH...
COMING, MAX! JUST A SECOND! I'M ON MY WAY!
LOOK WHO'S TALKING.

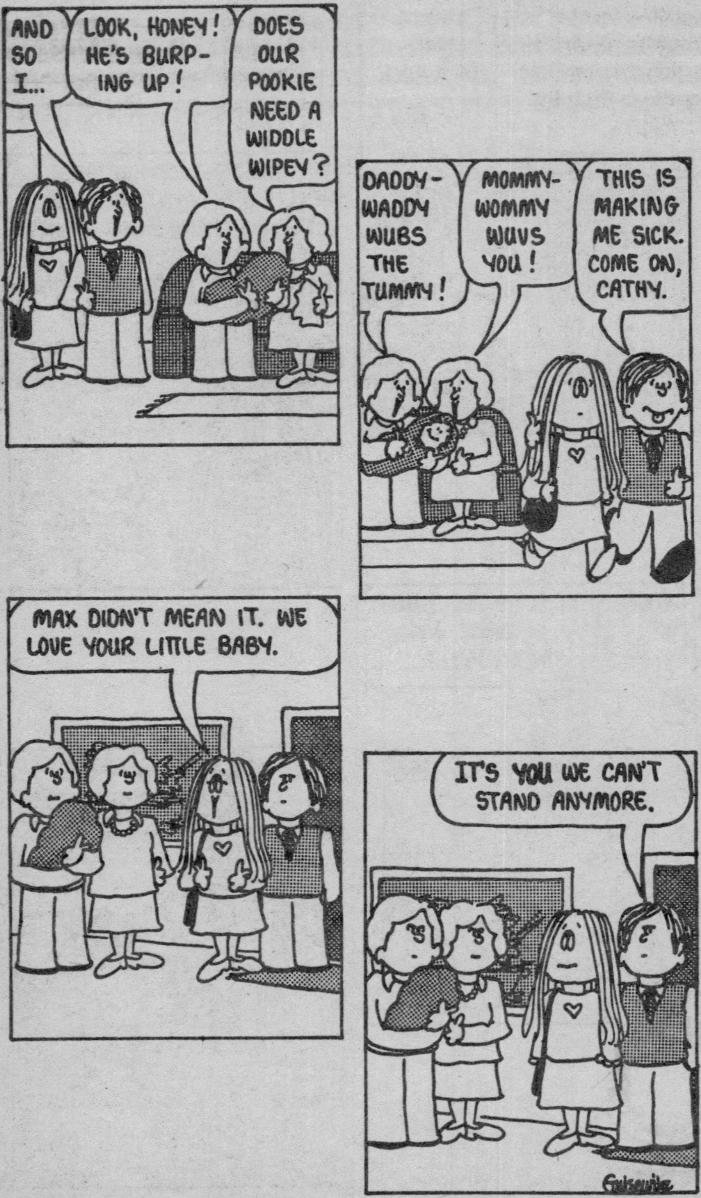
AND SO I...
LOOK, HONEY! HE'S BURP-ING UP!
DOES OUR POOKIE NEED A WIDDLE WIPEY?
DADDY-WADDY WUBS THE TUMMY!
MOMMY-WOMMY WUVS YOU!
THIS IS MAKING ME SICK. COME ON, CATHY.
MAX DIDN'T MEAN IT. WE LOVE YOUR LITTLE BABY.
IT'S YOU WE CAN'T STAND ANYMORE.
Guisewite

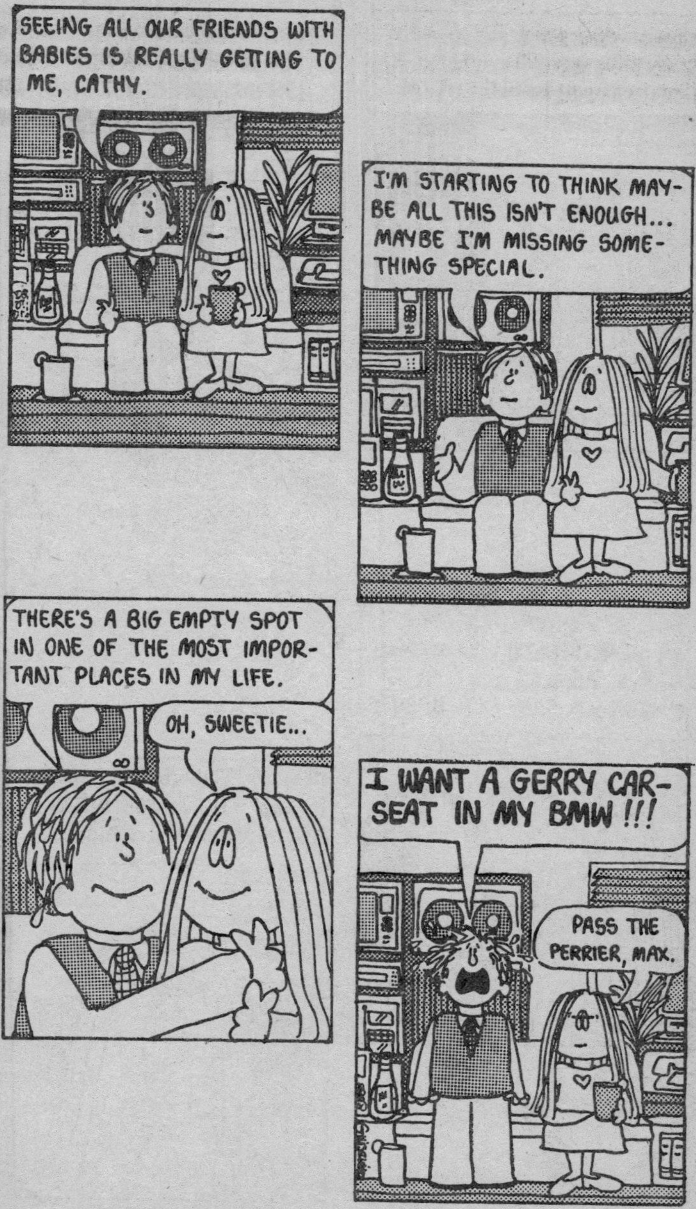
SEEING ALL OUR FRIENDS WITH BABIES IS REALLY GETTING TO ME, CATHY.
I'M STARTING TO THINK MAYBE ALL THIS ISN'T ENOUGH... MAYBE I'M MISSING SOMETHING SPECIAL.
THERE'S A BIG EMPTY SPOT IN ONE OF THE MOST IMPORTANT PLACES IN MY LIFE.
OH, SWEETIE...
I WANT A GERRY CAR-SEAT IN MY BMW !!!
PASS THE PERRIER, MAX.

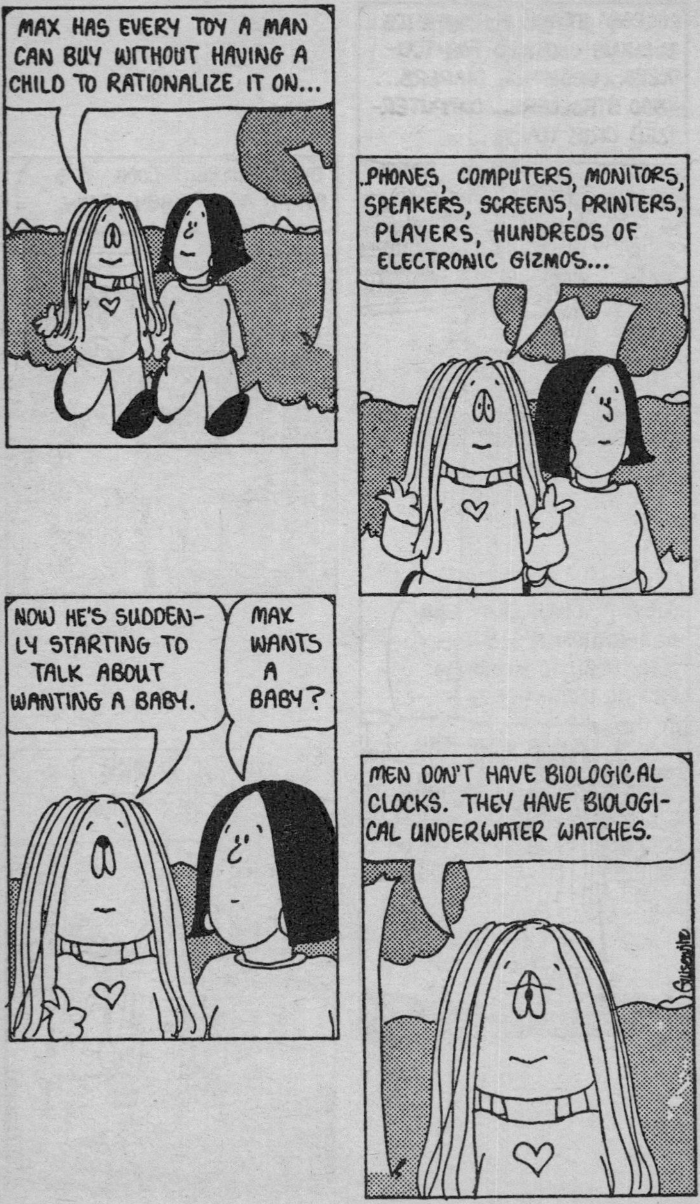

MAX HAS EVERY TOY A MAN CAN BUY WITHOUT HAVING A CHILD TO RATIONALIZE IT ON...
...PHONES, COMPUTERS, MONITORS, SPEAKERS, SCREENS, PRINTERS, PLAYERS, HUNDREDS OF ELECTRONIC GIZMOS...
NOW HE'S SUDDEN-LY STARTING TO TALK ABOUT WANTING A BABY.
MAX WANTS A BABY?
MEN DON'T HAVE BIOLOGICAL CLOCKS. THEY HAVE BIOLOGI-CAL UNDERWATER WATCHES.

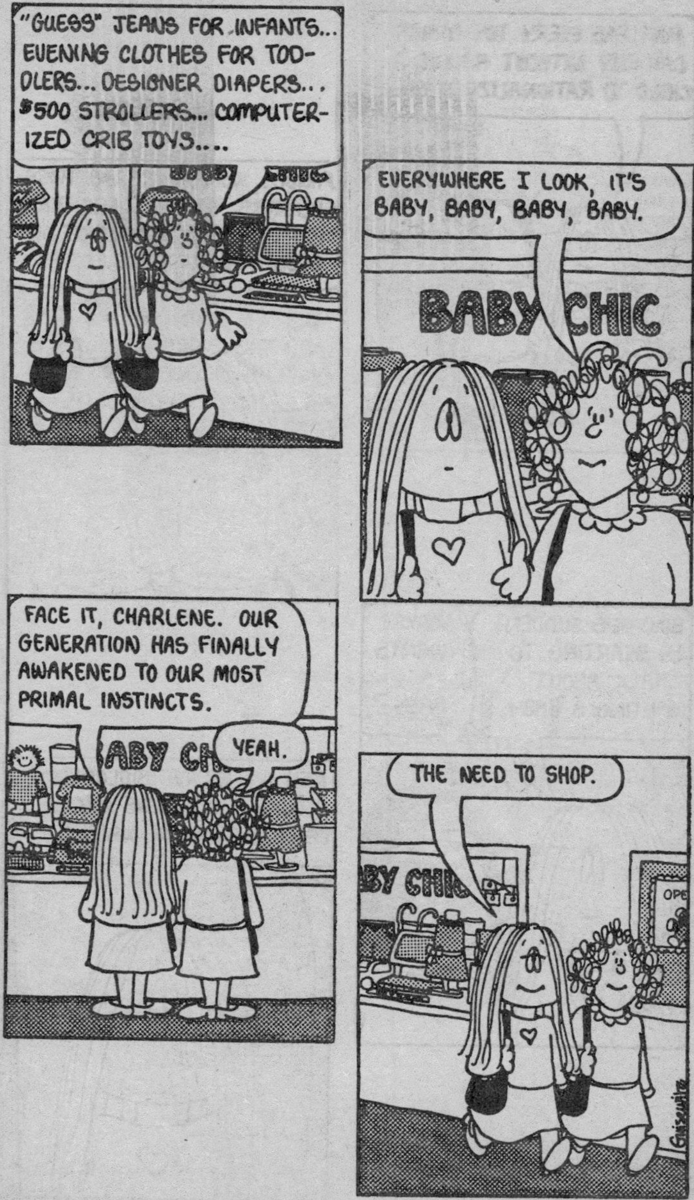
"GUESS" JEANS FOR INFANTS... EVENING CLOTHES FOR TODDLERS... DESIGNER DIAPERS... $500 STROLLERS... COMPUTERIZED CRIB TOYS....
EVERYWHERE I LOOK, IT'S BABY, BABY, BABY, BABY.
BABY CHIC
FACE IT, CHARLENE. OUR GENERATION HAS FINALLY AWAKENED TO OUR MOST PRIMAL INSTINCTS.
YEAH.
THE NEED TO SHOP.
Guisewite

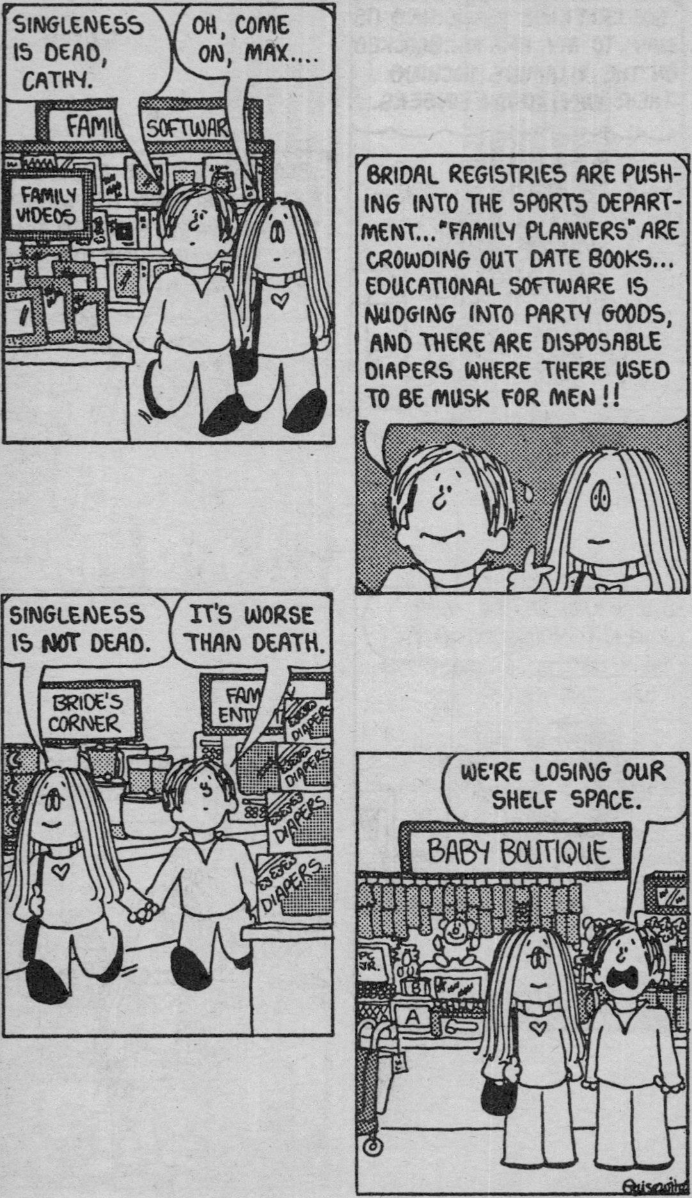
SINGLENESS IS DEAD, CATHY.
OH, COME ON, MAX....
FAMIL
SOFTWAR
FAMILY VIDEOS
BRIDAL REGISTRIES ARE PUSHING INTO THE SPORTS DEPARTMENT..."FAMILY PLANNERS" ARE CROWDING OUT DATE BOOKS... EDUCATIONAL SOFTWARE IS NUDGING INTO PARTY GOODS, AND THERE ARE DISPOSABLE DIAPERS WHERE THERE USED TO BE MUSK FOR MEN!!
SINGLENESS IS NOT DEAD.
IT'S WORSE THAN DEATH.
BRIDE'S CORNER
DIAPERS
DIAPERS
DIAPERS
DIAPERS
WE'RE LOSING OUR SHELF SPACE.
BABY BOUTIQUE
PC JR.
A

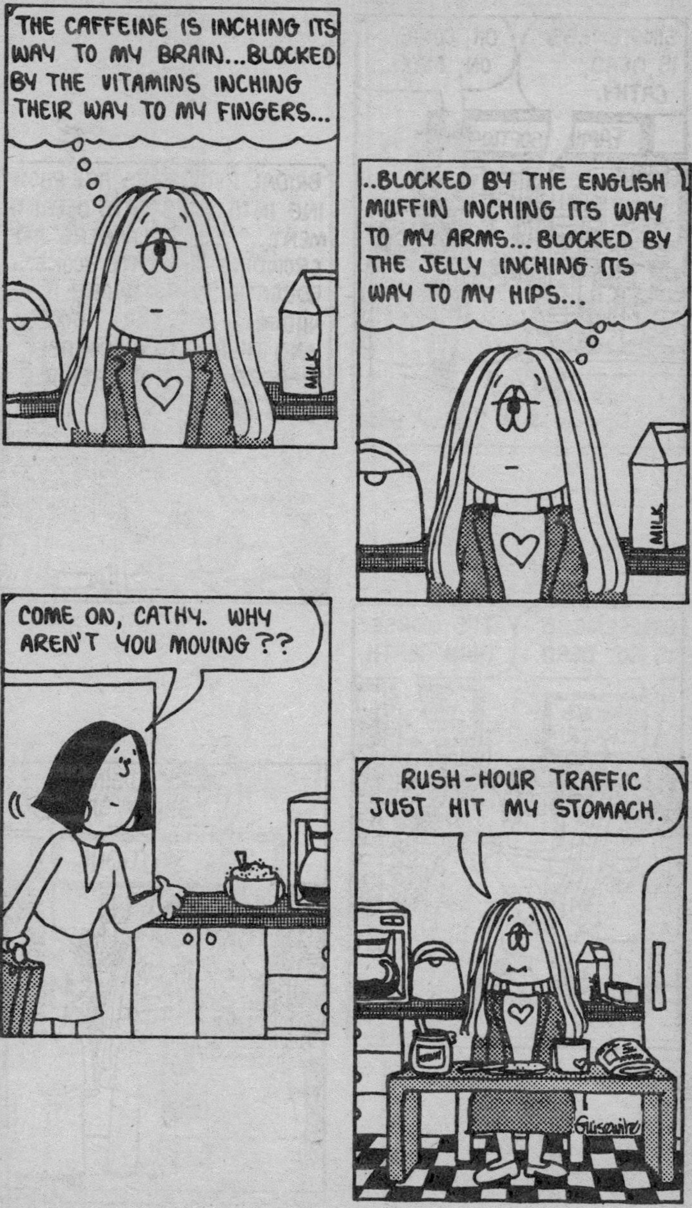
THE CAFFEINE IS INCHING ITS WAY TO MY BRAIN...BLOCKED BY THE VITAMINS INCHING THEIR WAY TO MY FINGERS...
MILK
..BLOCKED BY THE ENGLISH MUFFIN INCHING ITS WAY TO MY ARMS... BLOCKED BY THE JELLY INCHING ITS WAY TO MY HIPS...
MILK
COME ON, CATHY. WHY AREN'T YOU MOVING??
RUSH-HOUR TRAFFIC JUST HIT MY STOMACH.
Guisewite

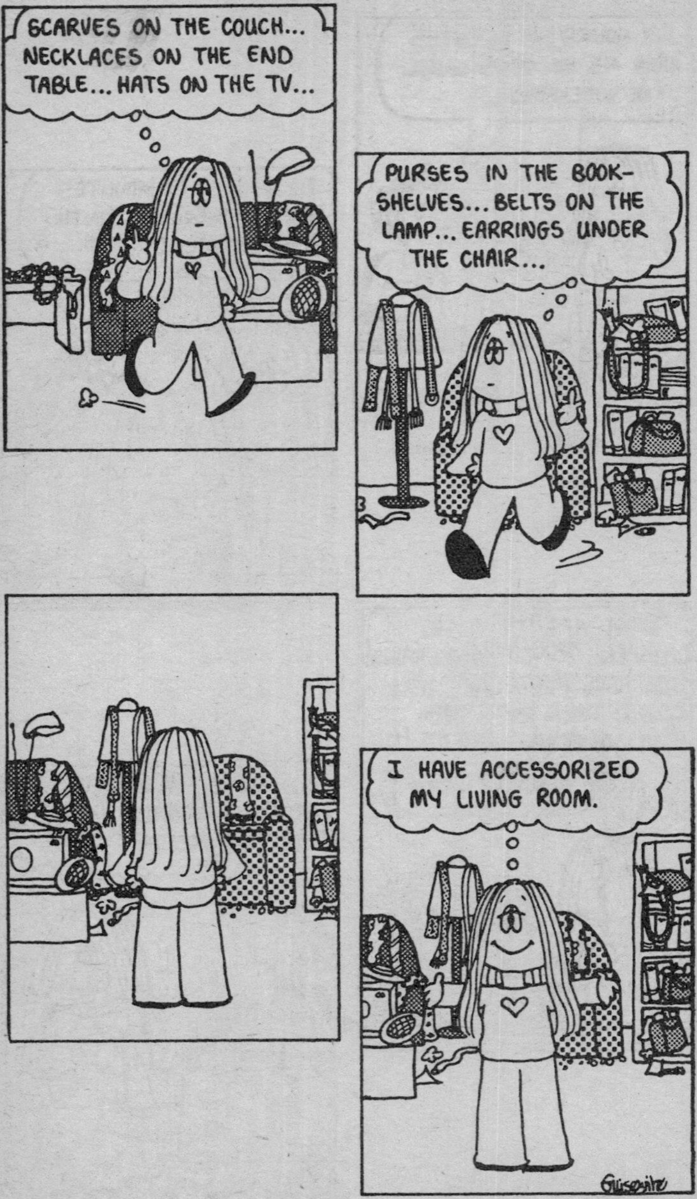
SCARVES ON THE COUCH... NECKLACES ON THE END TABLE... HATS ON THE TV...
PURSES IN THE BOOK-SHELVES... BELTS ON THE LAMP... EARRINGS UNDER THE CHAIR...
I HAVE ACCESSORIZED MY LIVING ROOM.

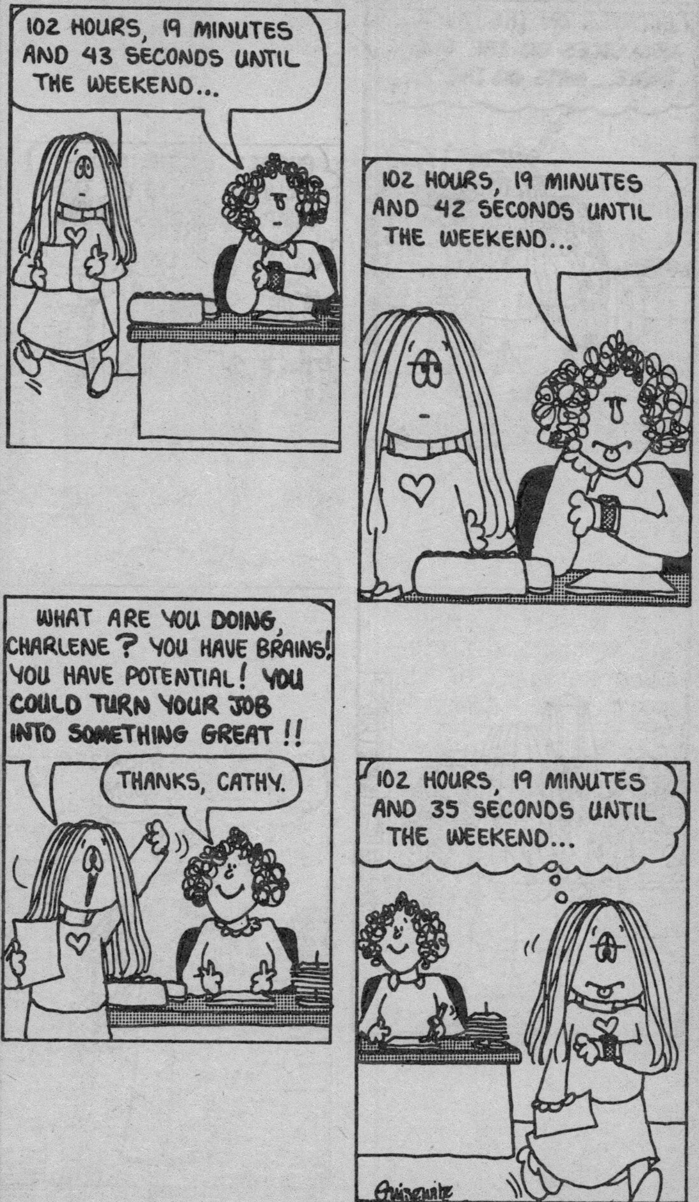
102 HOURS, 19 MINUTES AND 43 SECONDS UNTIL THE WEEKEND...
102 HOURS, 19 MINUTES AND 42 SECONDS UNTIL THE WEEKEND...
WHAT ARE YOU DOING, CHARLENE? YOU HAVE BRAINS! YOU HAVE POTENTIAL! YOU COULD TURN YOUR JOB INTO SOMETHING GREAT!!
THANKS, CATHY.
102 HOURS, 19 MINUTES AND 35 SECONDS UNTIL THE WEEKEND...

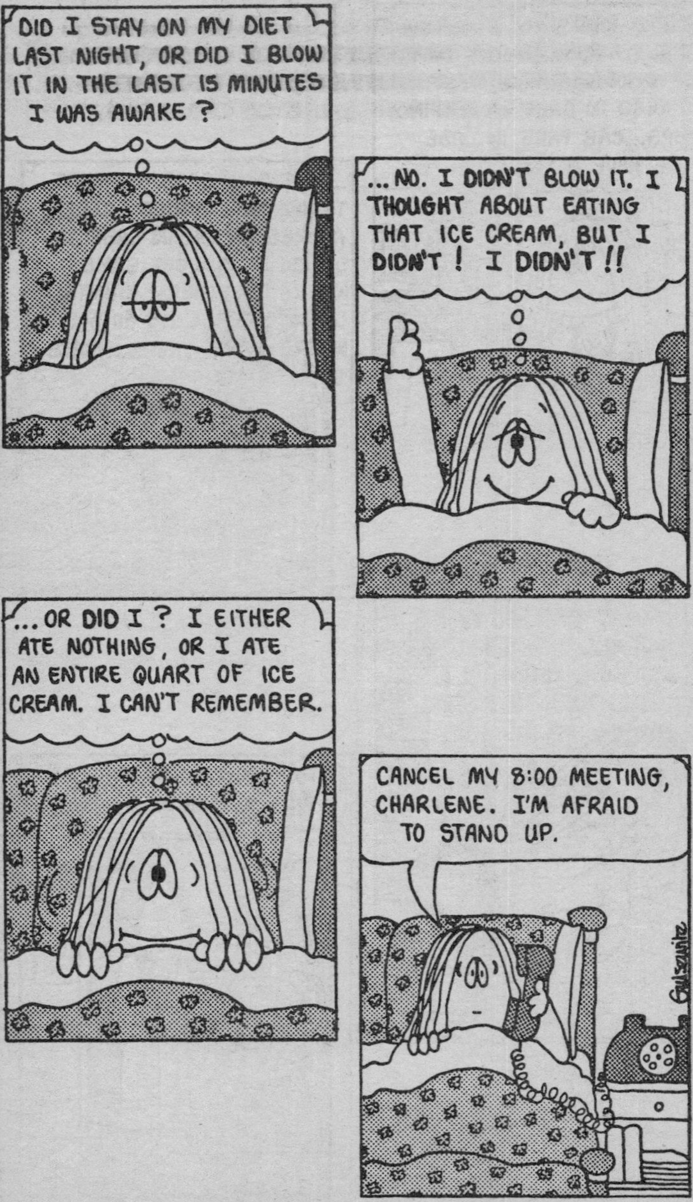
DID I STAY ON MY DIET LAST NIGHT, OR DID I BLOW IT IN THE LAST 15 MINUTES I WAS AWAKE?
...NO. I DIDN'T BLOW IT. I THOUGHT ABOUT EATING THAT ICE CREAM, BUT I DIDN'T! I DIDN'T!!
...OR DID I? I EITHER ATE NOTHING, OR I ATE AN ENTIRE QUART OF ICE CREAM. I CAN'T REMEMBER.
CANCEL MY 8:00 MEETING, CHARLENE. I'M AFRAID TO STAND UP.
Guisewite

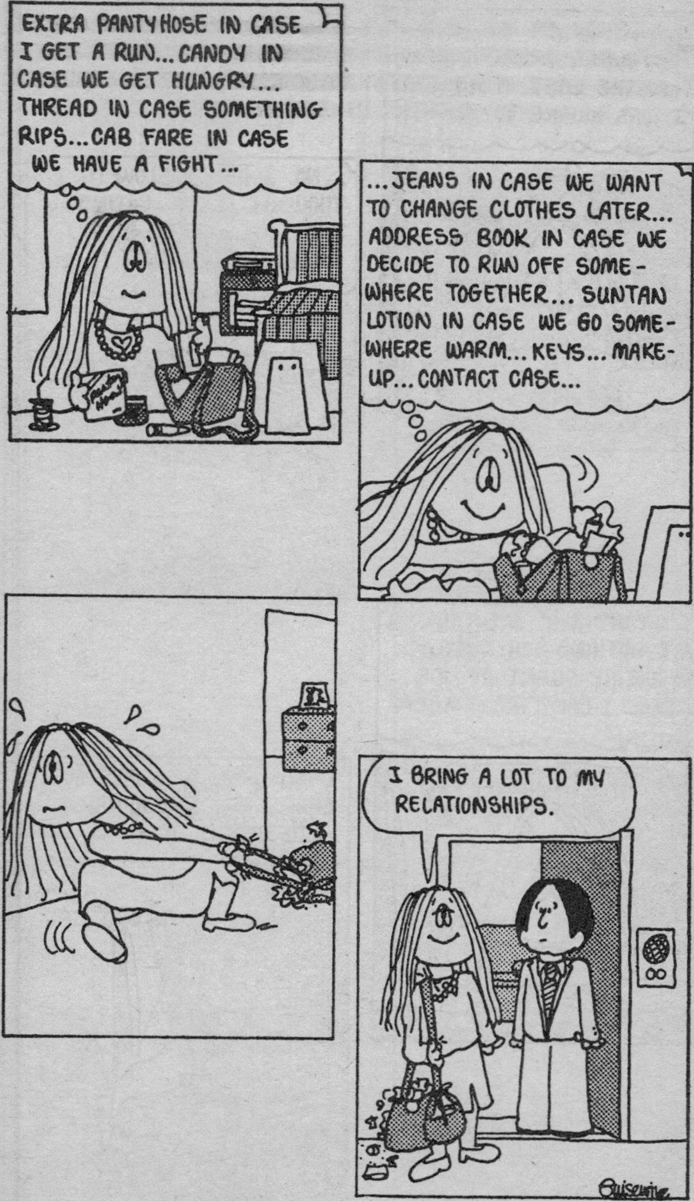
EXTRA PANTYHOSE IN CASE I GET A RUN... CANDY IN CASE WE GET HUNGRY... THREAD IN CASE SOMETHING RIPS... CAB FARE IN CASE WE HAVE A FIGHT...
...JEANS IN CASE WE WANT TO CHANGE CLOTHES LATER... ADDRESS BOOK IN CASE WE DECIDE TO RUN OFF SOMEWHERE TOGETHER... SUNTAN LOTION IN CASE WE GO SOMEWHERE WARM... KEYS... MAKE-UP... CONTACT CASE...
I BRING A LOT TO MY RELATIONSHIPS.
Guisewite

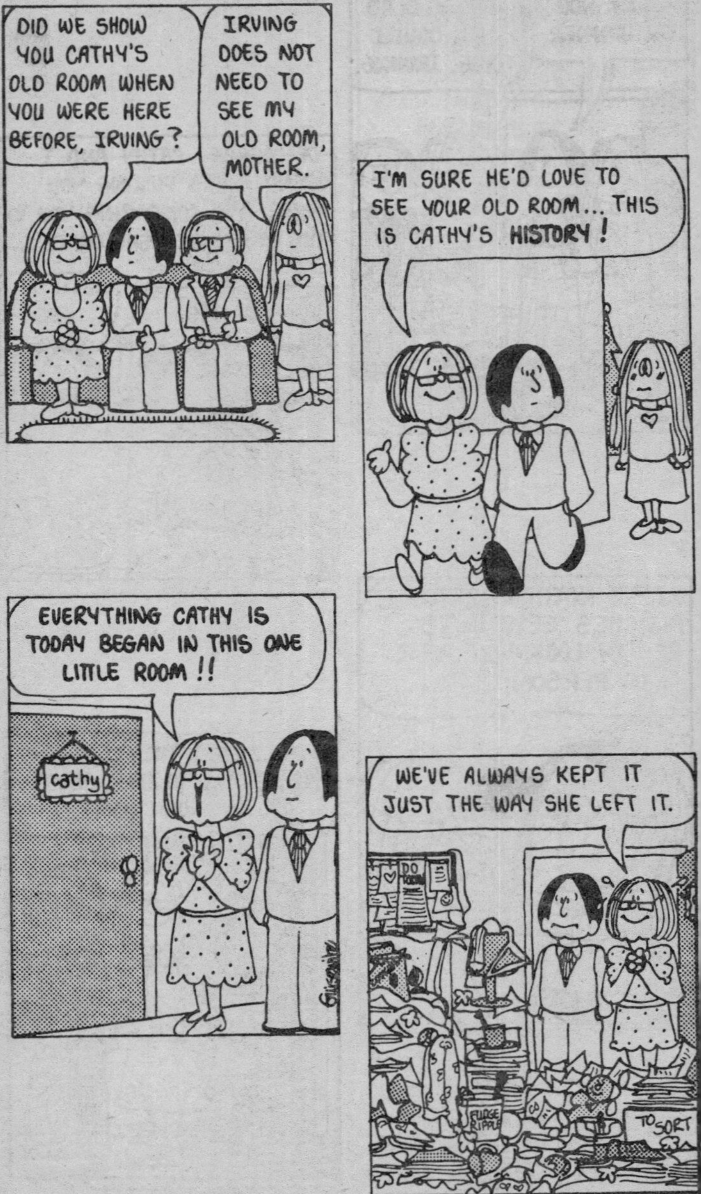
DID WE SHOW YOU CATHY'S OLD ROOM WHEN YOU WERE HERE BEFORE, IRVING?
IRVING DOES NOT NEED TO SEE MY OLD ROOM, MOTHER.
I'M SURE HE'D LOVE TO SEE YOUR OLD ROOM... THIS IS CATHY'S HISTORY!
EVERYTHING CATHY IS TODAY BEGAN IN THIS ONE LITTLE ROOM!!
cathy
WE'VE ALWAYS KEPT IT JUST THE WAY SHE LEFT IT.
FUDGE RIPPLE
TO SORT

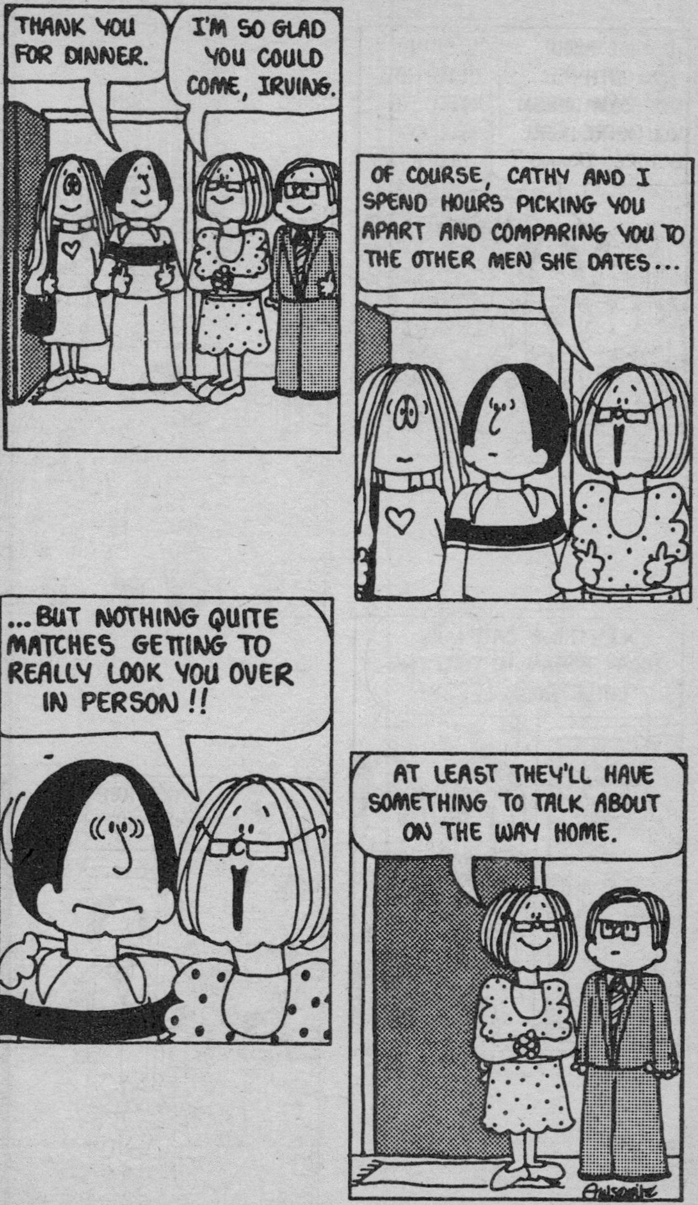
THANK YOU FOR DINNER.
I'M SO GLAD YOU COULD COME, IRVING.
OF COURSE, CATHY AND I SPEND HOURS PICKING YOU APART AND COMPARING YOU TO THE OTHER MEN SHE DATES...
...BUT NOTHING QUITE MATCHES GETTING TO REALLY LOOK YOU OVER IN PERSON!!
AT LEAST THEY'LL HAVE SOMETHING TO TALK ABOUT ON THE WAY HOME.

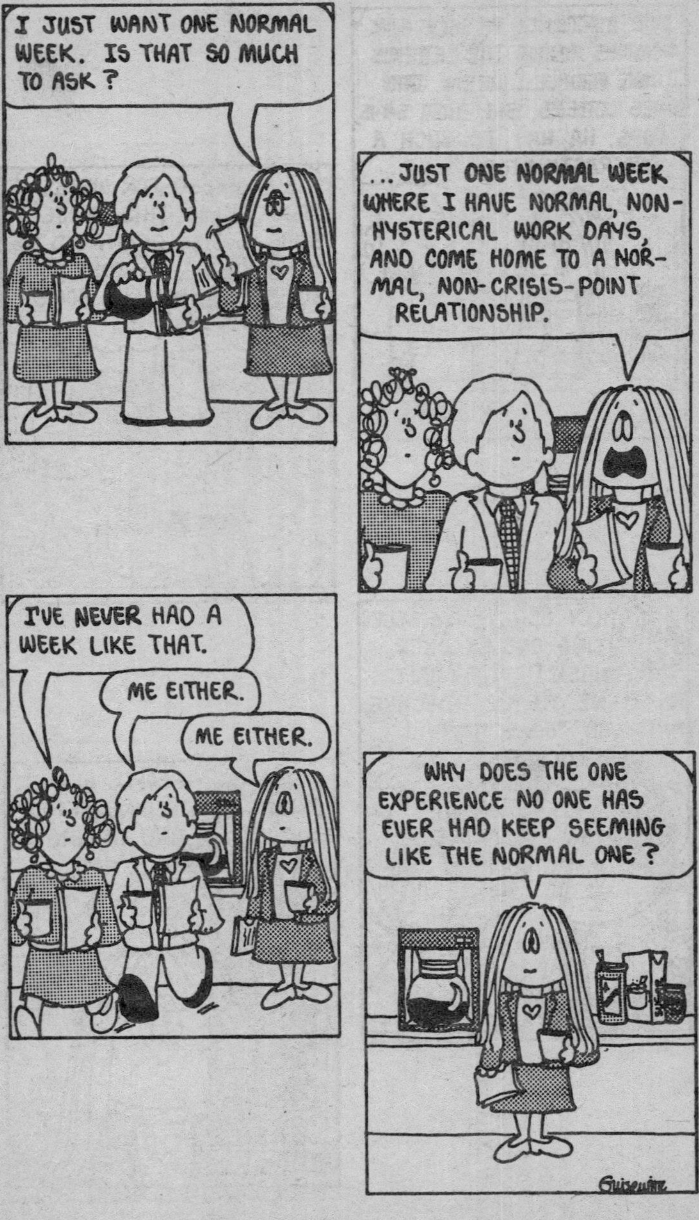
I JUST WANT ONE NORMAL WEEK. IS THAT SO MUCH TO ASK?
...JUST ONE NORMAL WEEK WHERE I HAVE NORMAL, NON-HYSTERICAL WORK DAYS, AND COME HOME TO A NORMAL, NON-CRISIS-POINT RELATIONSHIP.
I'VE NEVER HAD A WEEK LIKE THAT.
ME EITHER.
ME EITHER.
WHY DOES THE ONE EXPERIENCE NO ONE HAS EVER HAD KEEP SEEMING LIKE THE NORMAL ONE?
Guisewite

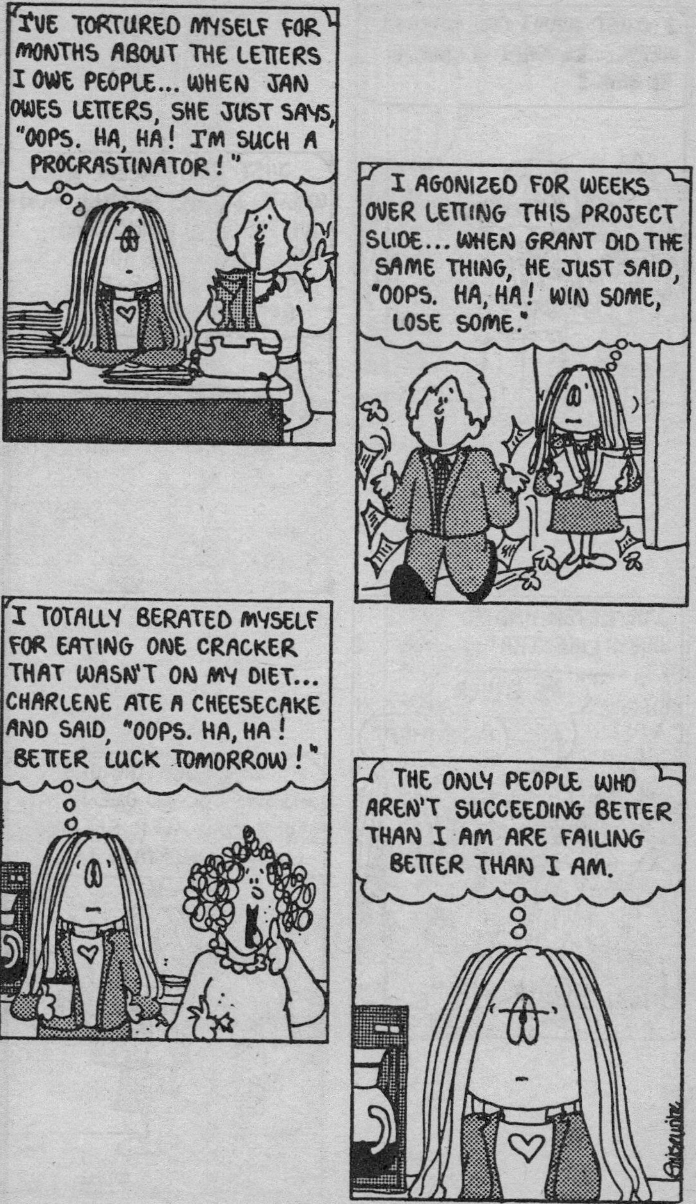
I'VE TORTURED MYSELF FOR MONTHS ABOUT THE LETTERS I OWE PEOPLE... WHEN JAN OWES LETTERS, SHE JUST SAYS, "OOPS. HA, HA! I'M SUCH A PROCRASTINATOR!"
I AGONIZED FOR WEEKS OVER LETTING THIS PROJECT SLIDE... WHEN GRANT DID THE SAME THING, HE JUST SAID, "OOPS. HA, HA! WIN SOME, LOSE SOME."
I TOTALLY BERATED MYSELF FOR EATING ONE CRACKER THAT WASN'T ON MY DIET... CHARLENE ATE A CHEESECAKE AND SAID, "OOPS. HA, HA! BETTER LUCK TOMORROW!"
THE ONLY PEOPLE WHO AREN'T SUCCEEDING BETTER THAN I AM ARE FAILING BETTER THAN I AM.

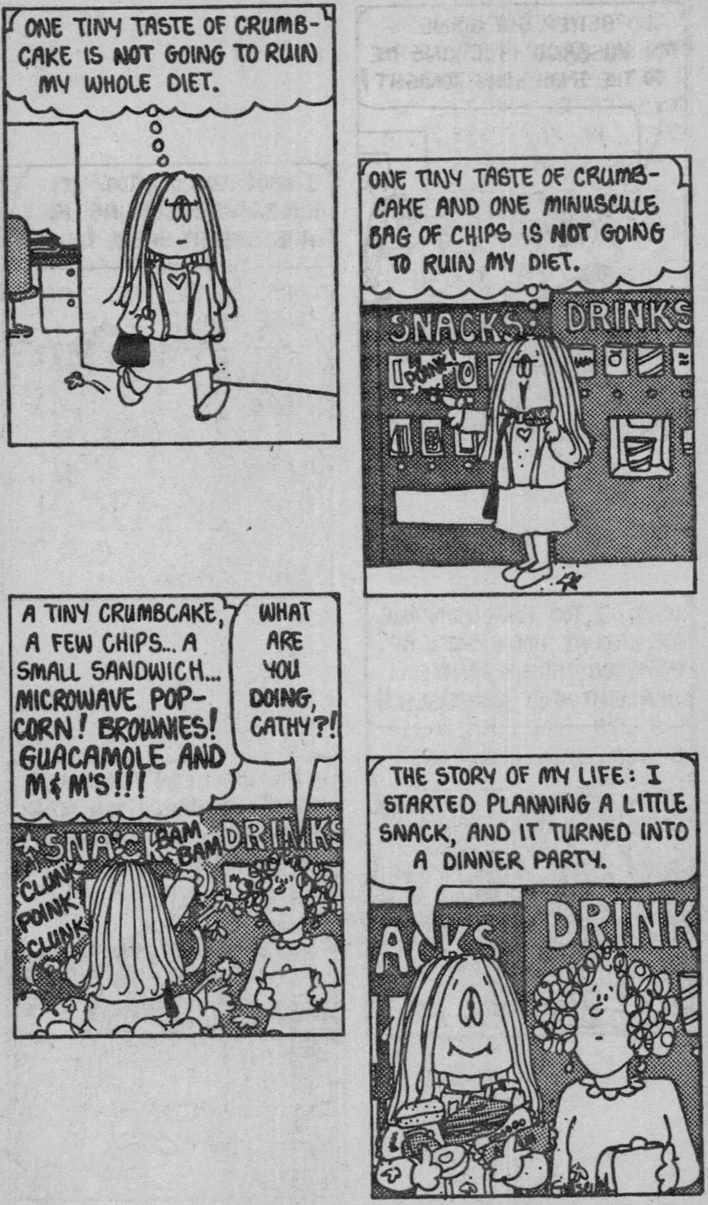
ONE TINY TASTE OF CRUMB-CAKE IS NOT GOING TO RUIN MY WHOLE DIET.
ONE TINY TASTE OF CRUMB-CAKE AND ONE MINUSCULE BAG OF CHIPS IS NOT GOING TO RUIN MY DIET.
SNACKS
DRINKS
POINK!
A TINY CRUMBCAKE, A FEW CHIPS... A SMALL SANDWICH... MICROWAVE POP-CORN! BROWNIES! GUACAMOLE AND M&M'S!!!
WHAT ARE YOU DOING, CATHY?!
SNACKS
DRINKS
BAM BAM
CLUNK POINK CLUNK
THE STORY OF MY LIFE: I STARTED PLANNING A LITTLE SNACK, AND IT TURNED INTO A DINNER PARTY.
ACKS
DRINK

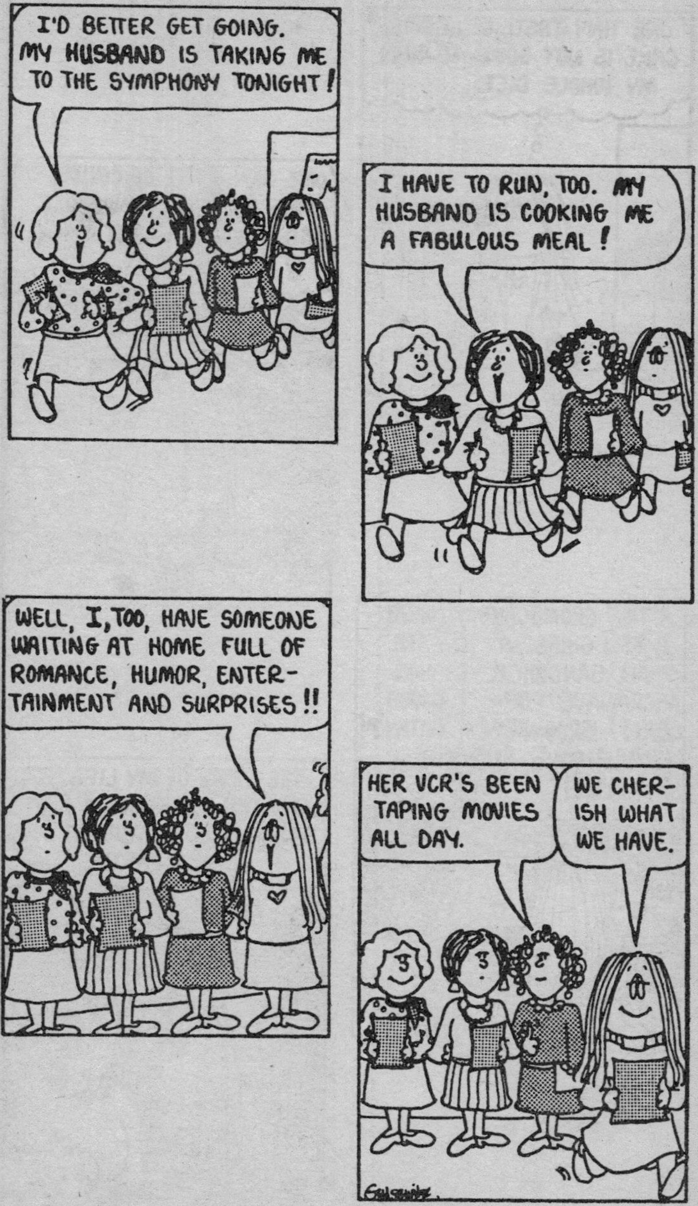
I'D BETTER GET GOING. MY HUSBAND IS TAKING ME TO THE SYMPHONY TONIGHT!
I HAVE TO RUN, TOO. MY HUSBAND IS COOKING ME A FABULOUS MEAL!
WELL, I, TOO, HAVE SOMEONE WAITING AT HOME FULL OF ROMANCE, HUMOR, ENTERTAINMENT AND SURPRISES!!
HER VCR'S BEEN TAPING MOVIES ALL DAY.
WE CHERISH WHAT WE HAVE.

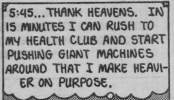

5:45... THANK HEAVENS. IN 15 MINUTES I CAN RUSH TO MY HEALTH CLUB AND START PUSHING GIANT MACHINES AROUND THAT I MAKE HEAVIER ON PURPOSE.

IF I HURRY I CAN EVEN SPEND 30 MINUTES TORTURING MY MUSCLES IN A SWEATY ROOM WHILE SOMEONE SCREAMS AT ME OVER PUNK ROCK LOVE SONGS.

EVERY YEAR THIS DESK MAKES SOMETHING WORSE SEEM LIKE FUN.

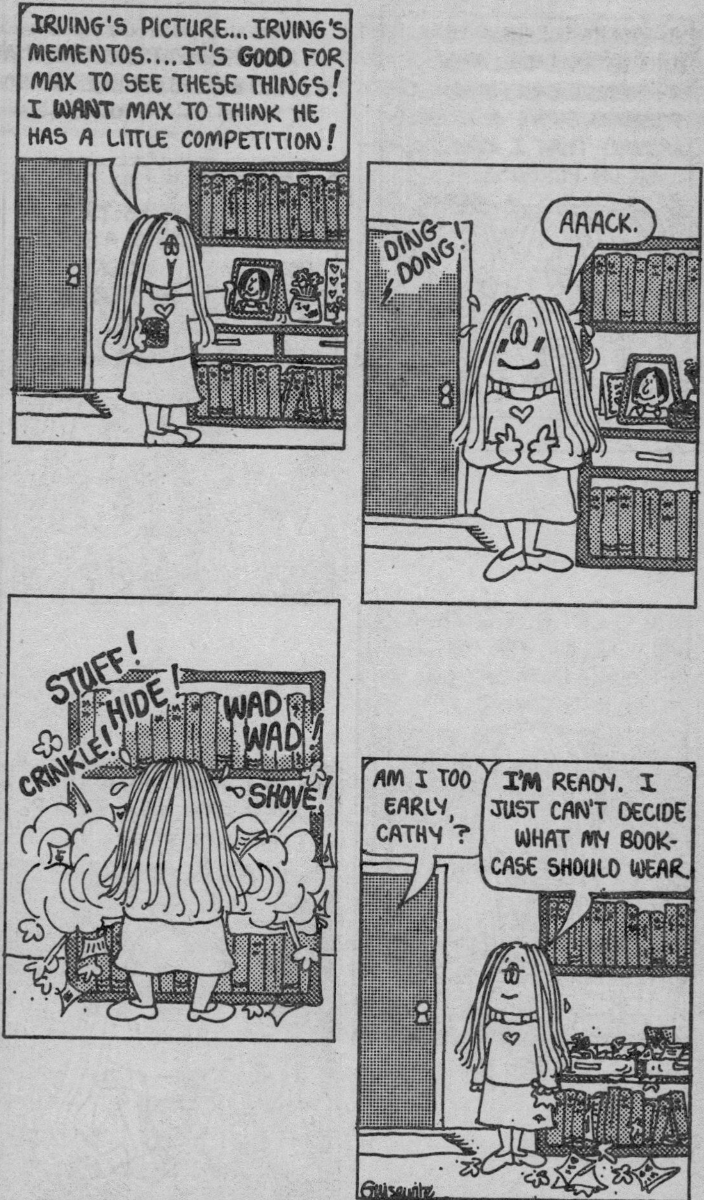
IRVING'S PICTURE... IRVING'S MEMENTOS.... IT'S GOOD FOR MAX TO SEE THESE THINGS! I WANT MAX TO THINK HE HAS A LITTLE COMPETITION!
DING DONG!
AAACK.
STUFF!
HIDE!
WAD WAD!
CRINKLE!
SHOVE!
AM I TOO EARLY, CATHY?
I'M READY. I JUST CAN'T DECIDE WHAT MY BOOK-CASE SHOULD WEAR.
Guisewite

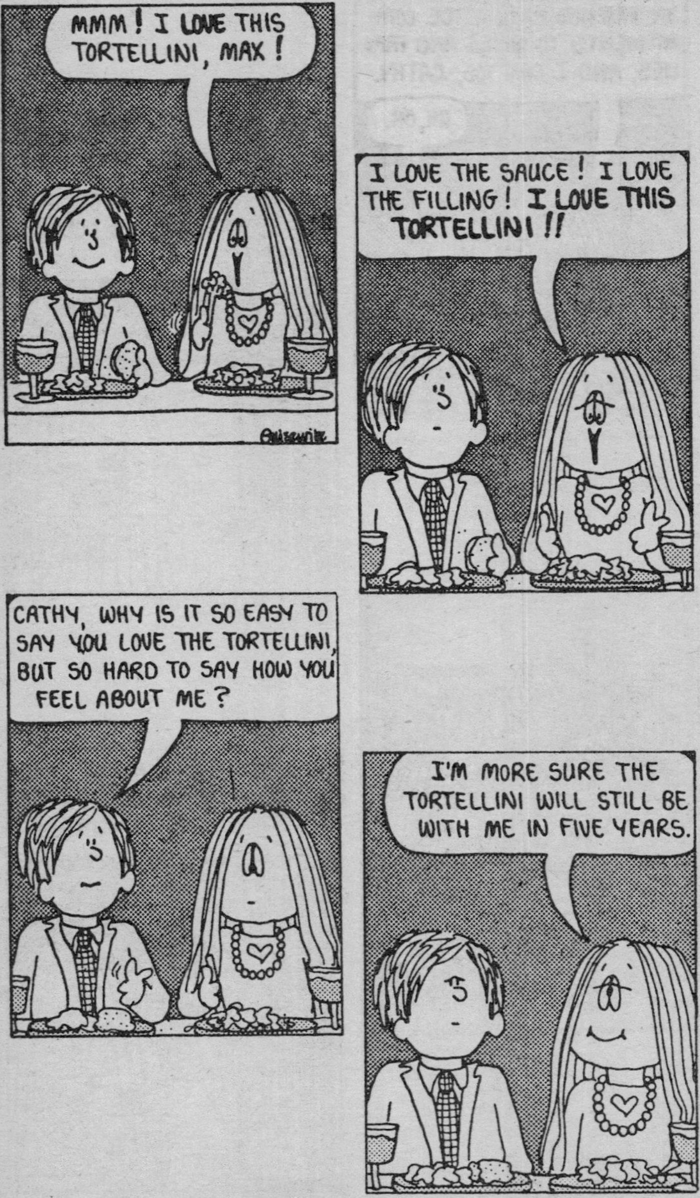
MMM! I LOVE THIS TORTELLINI, MAX!
I LOVE THE SAUCE! I LOVE THE FILLING! I LOVE THIS TORTELLINI!!
CATHY, WHY IS IT SO EASY TO SAY YOU LOVE THE TORTELLINI, BUT SO HARD TO SAY HOW YOU FEEL ABOUT ME?
I'M MORE SURE THE TORTELLINI WILL STILL BE WITH ME IN FIVE YEARS.

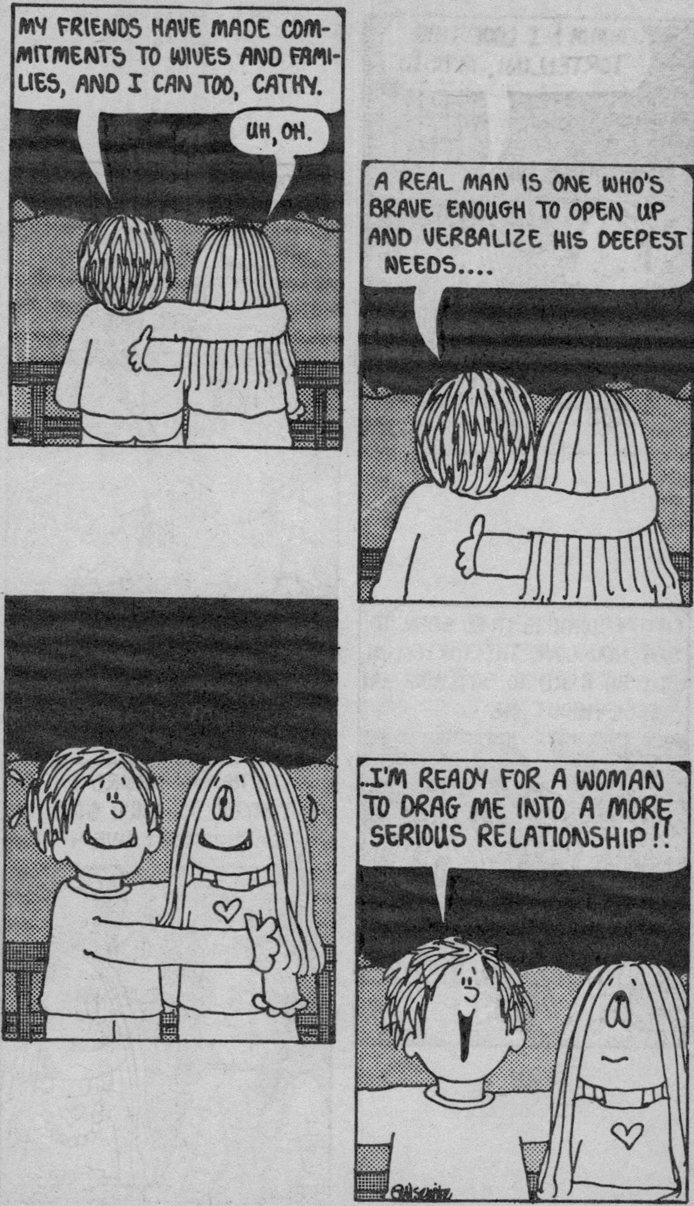
MY FRIENDS HAVE MADE COMMITMENTS TO WIVES AND FAMILIES, AND I CAN TOO, CATHY.
UH, OH.
A REAL MAN IS ONE WHO'S BRAVE ENOUGH TO OPEN UP AND VERBALIZE HIS DEEPEST NEEDS....
..I'M READY FOR A WOMAN TO DRAG ME INTO A MORE SERIOUS RELATIONSHIP!!

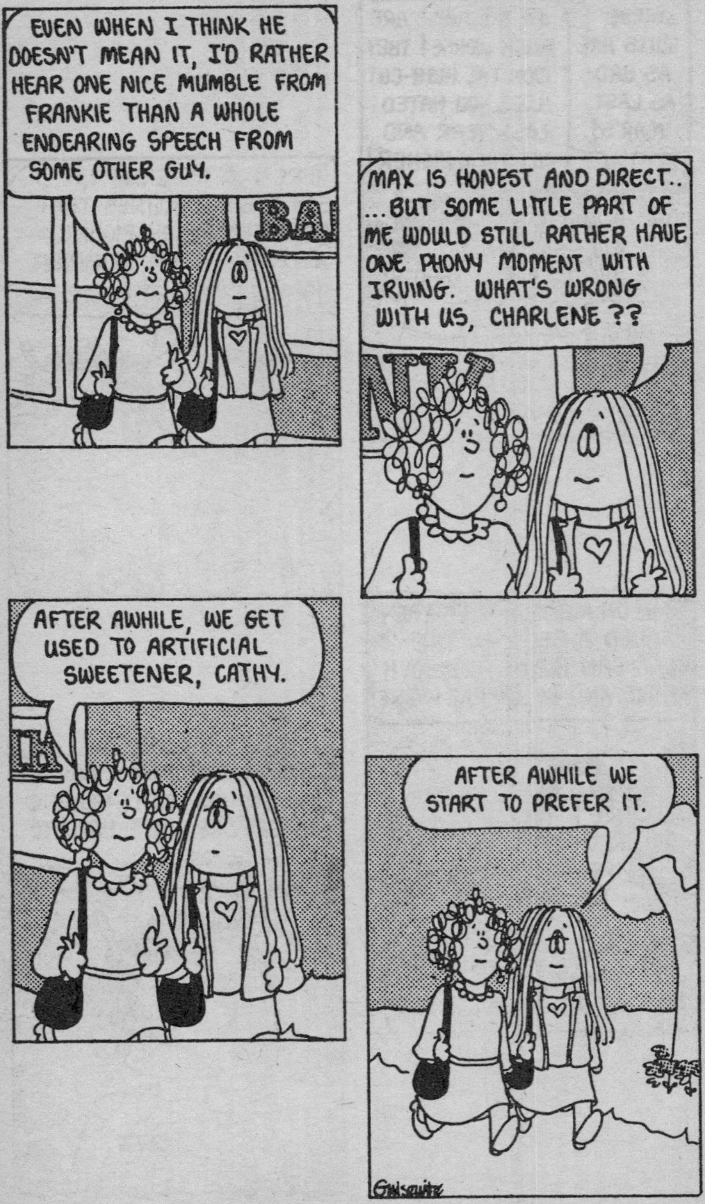
EVEN WHEN I THINK HE DOESN'T MEAN IT, I'D RATHER HEAR ONE NICE MUMBLE FROM FRANKIE THAN A WHOLE ENDEARING SPEECH FROM SOME OTHER GUY.
MAX IS HONEST AND DIRECT.. ...BUT SOME LITTLE PART OF ME WOULD STILL RATHER HAVE ONE PHONY MOMENT WITH IRVING. WHAT'S WRONG WITH US, CHARLENE??
AFTER AWHILE, WE GET USED TO ARTIFICIAL SWEETENER, CATHY.
AFTER AWHILE WE START TO PREFER IT.

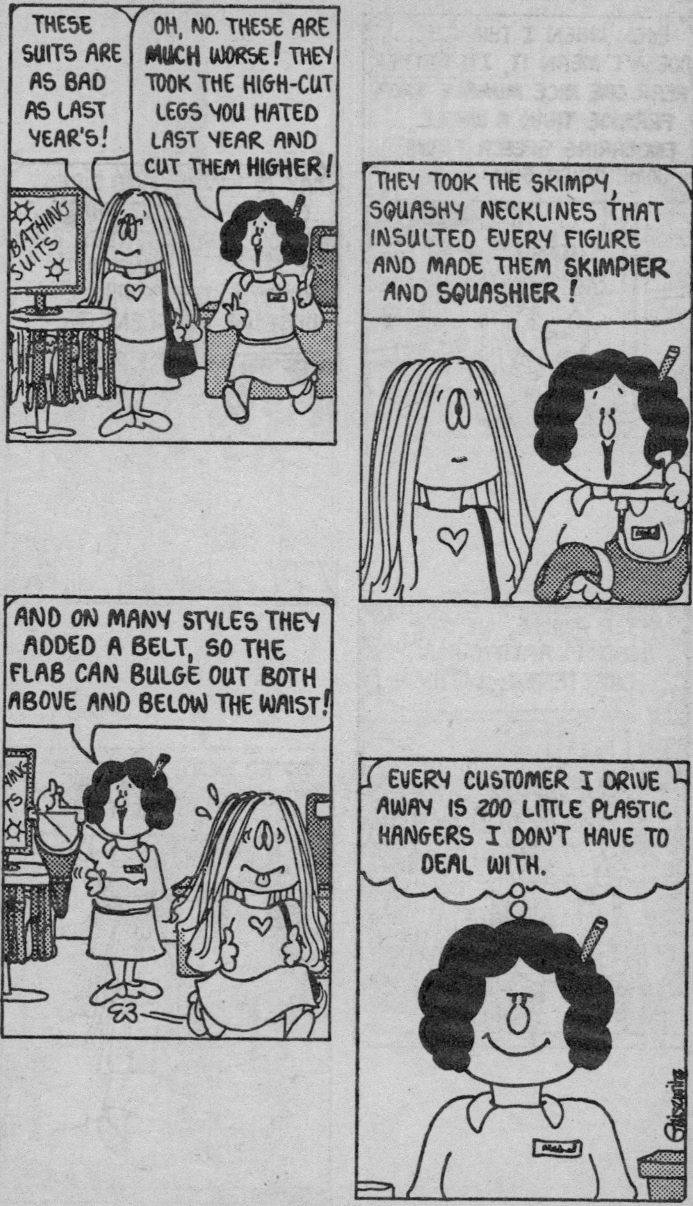
THESE SUITS ARE AS BAD AS LAST YEAR'S!
OH, NO. THESE ARE MUCH WORSE! THEY TOOK THE HIGH-CUT LEGS YOU HATED LAST YEAR AND CUT THEM HIGHER!
BATHING SUITS
THEY TOOK THE SKIMPY, SQUASHY NECKLINES THAT INSULTED EVERY FIGURE AND MADE THEM SKIMPIER AND SQUASHIER!
AND ON MANY STYLES THEY ADDED A BELT, SO THE FLAB CAN BULGE OUT BOTH ABOVE AND BELOW THE WAIST!
EVERY CUSTOMER I DRIVE AWAY IS 200 LITTLE PLASTIC HANGERS I DON'T HAVE TO DEAL WITH.

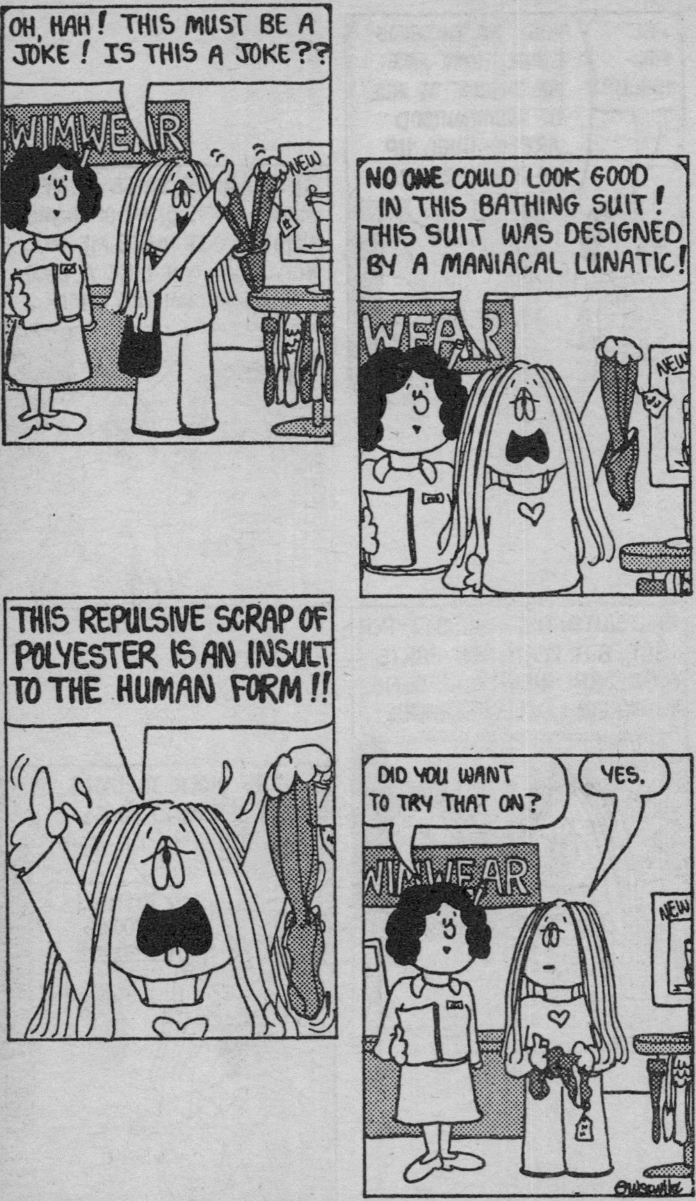
OH, HAH! THIS MUST BE A JOKE! IS THIS A JOKE??
NEW
NO ONE COULD LOOK GOOD IN THIS BATHING SUIT! THIS SUIT WAS DESIGNED BY A MANIACAL LUNATIC!
NEW
THIS REPULSIVE SCRAP OF POLYESTER IS AN INSULT TO THE HUMAN FORM!!
DID YOU WANT TO TRY THAT ON?
YES.
NEW

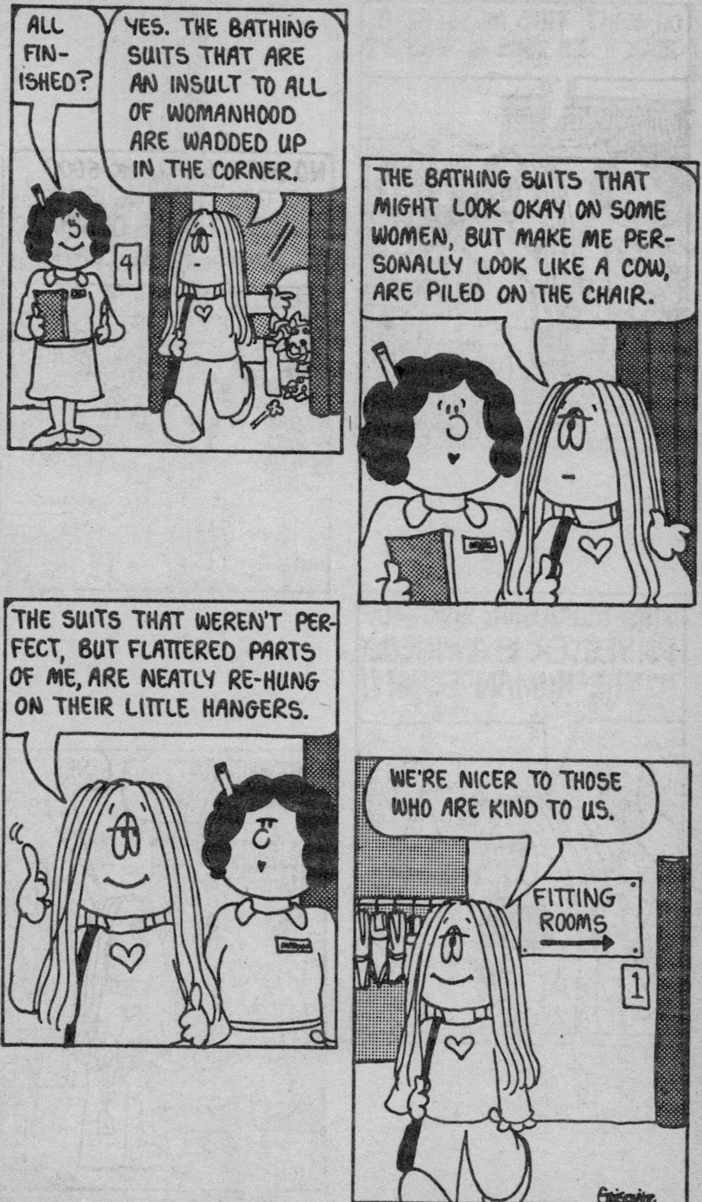
ALL FIN-ISHED?
YES. THE BATHING SUITS THAT ARE AN INSULT TO ALL OF WOMANHOOD ARE WADDED UP IN THE CORNER.
4
THE BATHING SUITS THAT MIGHT LOOK OKAY ON SOME WOMEN, BUT MAKE ME PER-SONALLY LOOK LIKE A COW, ARE PILED ON THE CHAIR.
THE SUITS THAT WEREN'T PER-FECT, BUT FLATTERED PARTS OF ME, ARE NEATLY RE-HUNG ON THEIR LITTLE HANGERS.
WE'RE NICER TO THOSE WHO ARE KIND TO US.
FITTING ROOMS
1

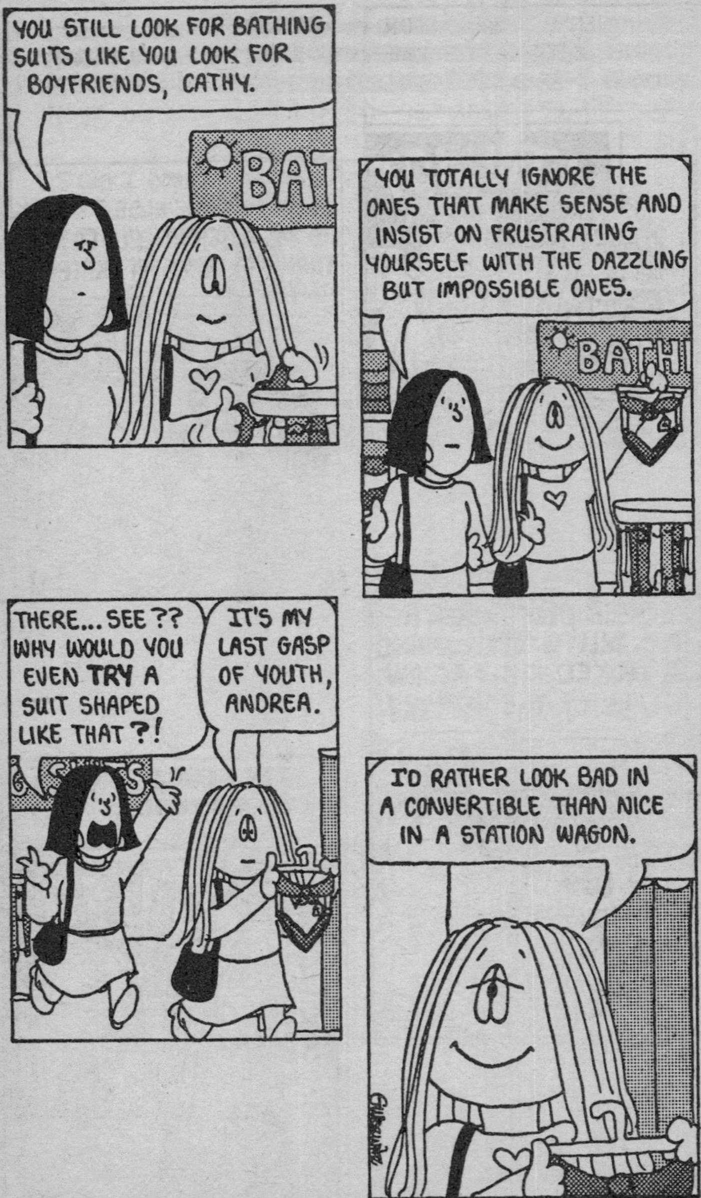
YOU STILL LOOK FOR BATHING SUITS LIKE YOU LOOK FOR BOYFRIENDS, CATHY.
BAT
YOU TOTALLY IGNORE THE ONES THAT MAKE SENSE AND INSIST ON FRUSTRATING YOURSELF WITH THE DAZZLING BUT IMPOSSIBLE ONES.
BATHI
THERE... SEE?? WHY WOULD YOU EVEN TRY A SUIT SHAPED LIKE THAT?!
IT'S MY LAST GASP OF YOUTH, ANDREA.
I'D RATHER LOOK BAD IN A CONVERTIBLE THAN NICE IN A STATION WAGON.
GUISEWITE

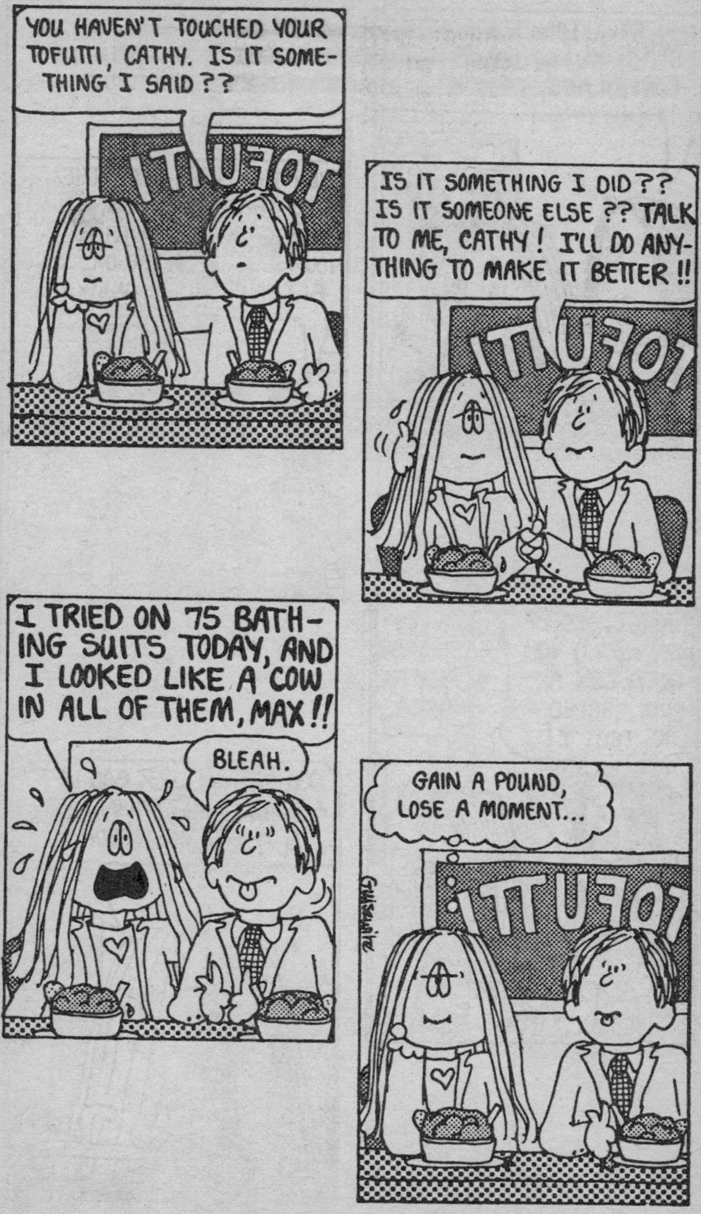
YOU HAVEN'T TOUCHED YOUR TOFUTTI, CATHY. IS IT SOMETHING I SAID??
IS IT SOMETHING I DID?? IS IT SOMEONE ELSE?? TALK TO ME, CATHY! I'LL DO ANYTHING TO MAKE IT BETTER!!
I TRIED ON 75 BATHING SUITS TODAY, AND I LOOKED LIKE A COW IN ALL OF THEM, MAX!!
BLEAH.
GUISEWITE
GAIN A POUND, LOSE A MOMENT...

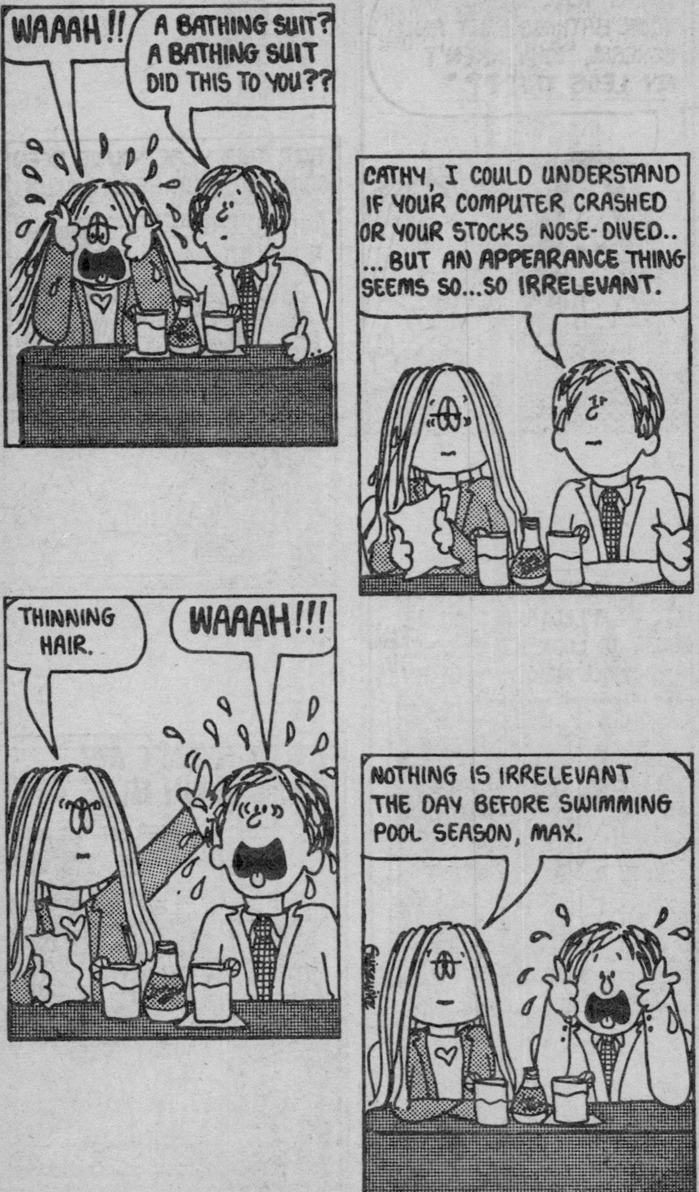
WAAAH!!
A BATHING SUIT? A BATHING SUIT DID THIS TO YOU??
CATHY, I COULD UNDERSTAND IF YOUR COMPUTER CRASHED OR YOUR STOCKS NOSE-DIVED.. ... BUT AN APPEARANCE THING SEEMS SO... SO IRRELEVANT.
THINNING HAIR.
WAAAH!!!
NOTHING IS IRRELEVANT THE DAY BEFORE SWIMMING POOL SEASON, MAX.

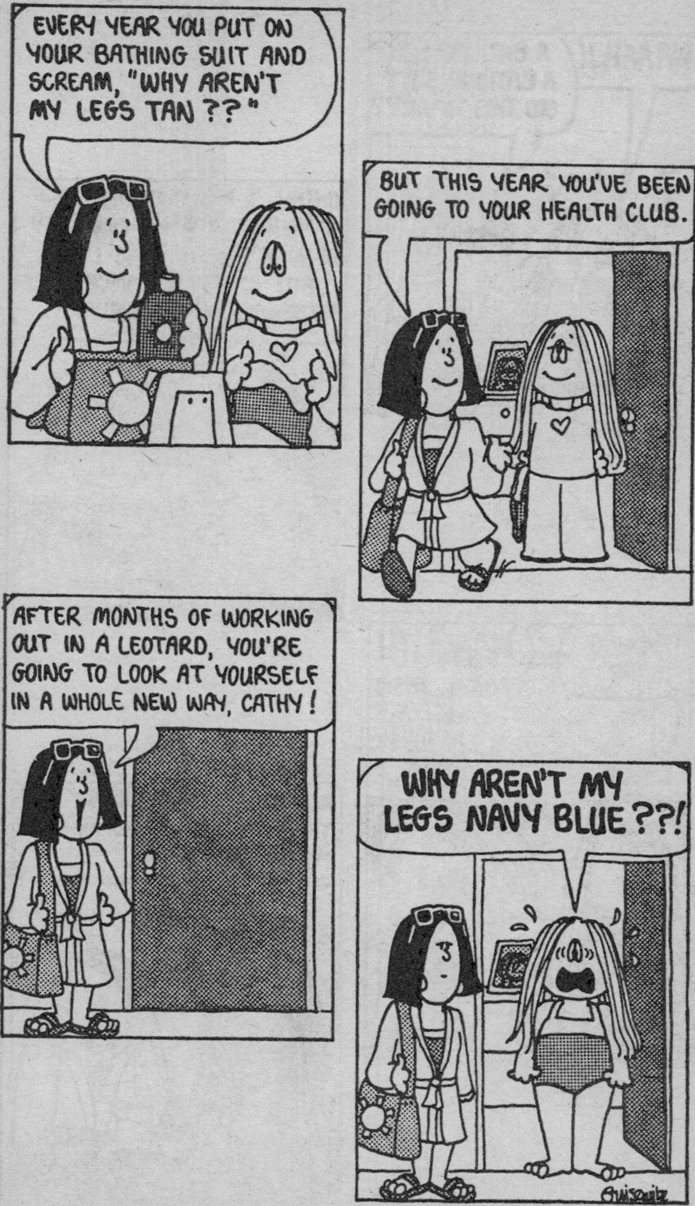
EVERY YEAR YOU PUT ON YOUR BATHING SUIT AND SCREAM, "WHY AREN'T MY LEGS TAN ??"
BUT THIS YEAR YOU'VE BEEN GOING TO YOUR HEALTH CLUB.
AFTER MONTHS OF WORKING OUT IN A LEOTARD, YOU'RE GOING TO LOOK AT YOURSELF IN A WHOLE NEW WAY, CATHY!
WHY AREN'T MY LEGS NAVY BLUE ??!
Guisewite

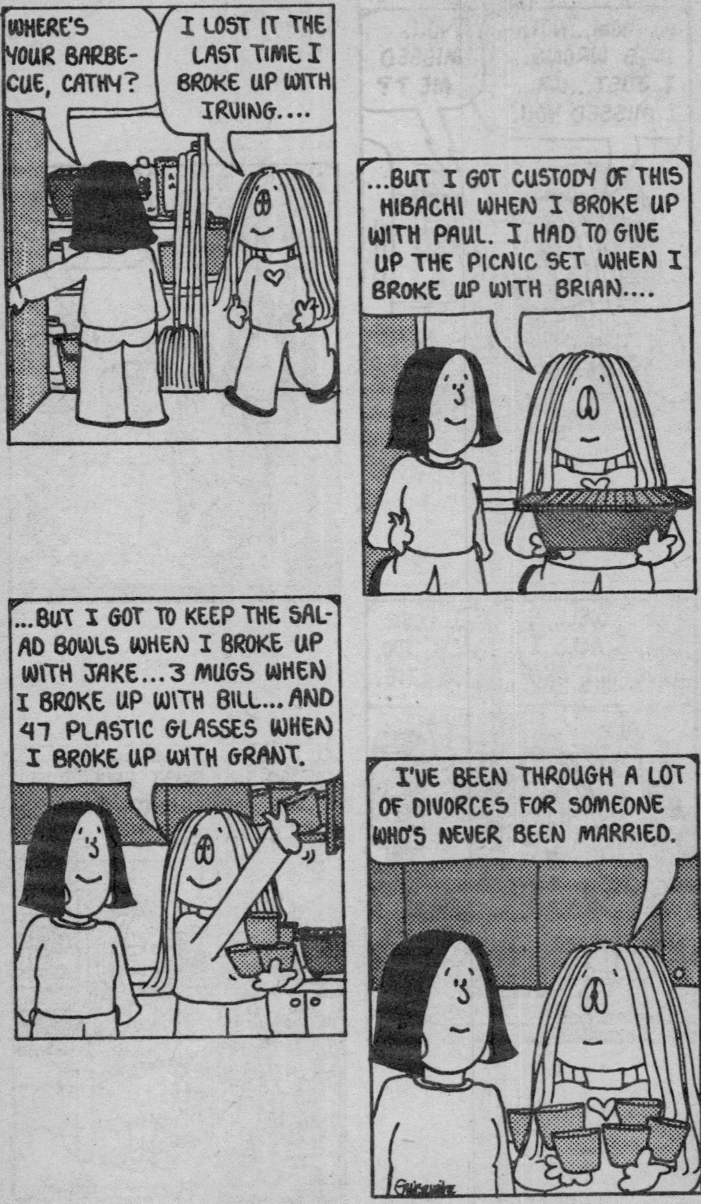
WHERE'S YOUR BARBECUE, CATHY?
I LOST IT THE LAST TIME I BROKE UP WITH IRVING....
...BUT I GOT CUSTODY OF THIS HIBACHI WHEN I BROKE UP WITH PAUL. I HAD TO GIVE UP THE PICNIC SET WHEN I BROKE UP WITH BRIAN....
...BUT I GOT TO KEEP THE SALAD BOWLS WHEN I BROKE UP WITH JAKE...3 MUGS WHEN I BROKE UP WITH BILL...AND 47 PLASTIC GLASSES WHEN I BROKE UP WITH GRANT.
I'VE BEEN THROUGH A LOT OF DIVORCES FOR SOMEONE WHO'S NEVER BEEN MARRIED.
Guisewite

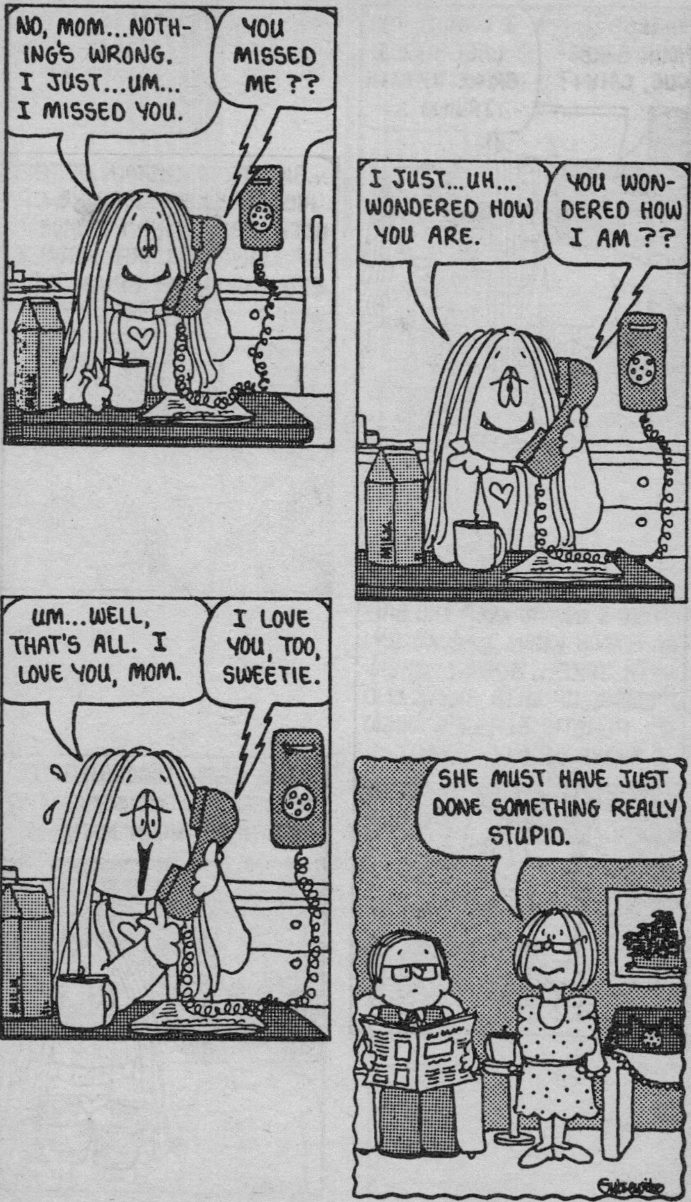
NO, MOM...NOTHING'S WRONG. I JUST...UM... I MISSED YOU.
YOU MISSED ME ??
I JUST...UH... WONDERED HOW YOU ARE.
YOU WONDERED HOW I AM ??
UM...WELL, THAT'S ALL. I LOVE YOU, MOM.
I LOVE YOU, TOO, SWEETIE.
SHE MUST HAVE JUST DONE SOMETHING REALLY STUPID.

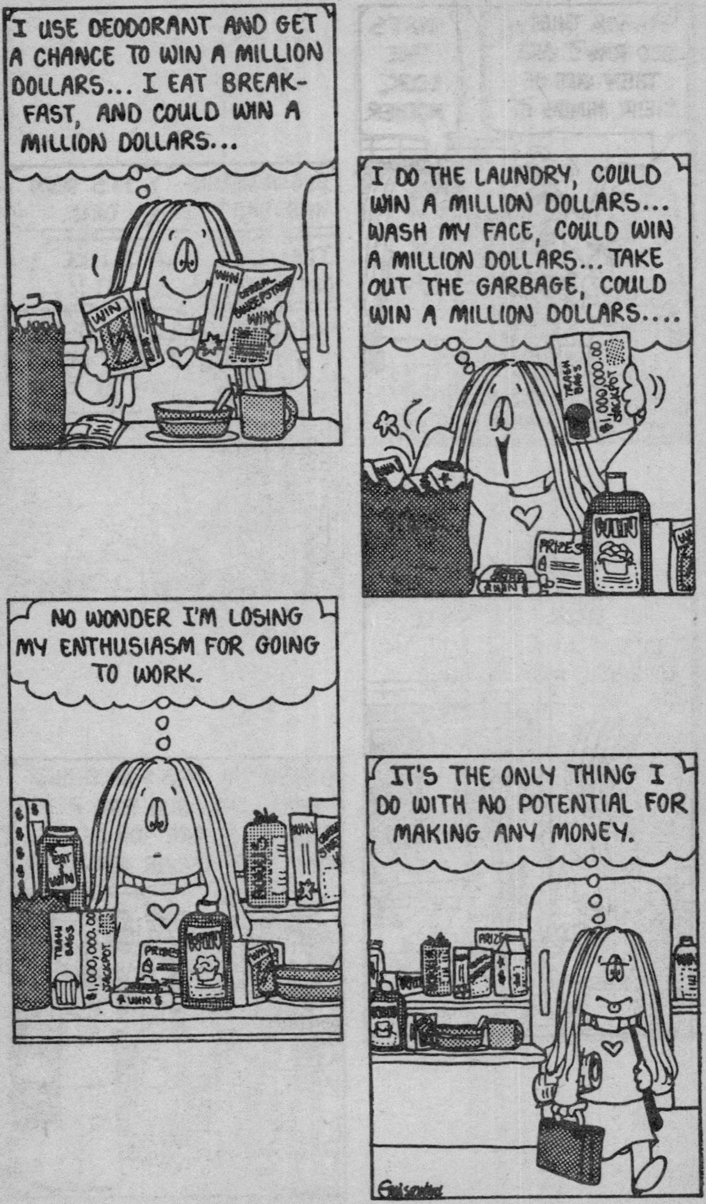
I USE DEODORANT AND GET A CHANCE TO WIN A MILLION DOLLARS... I EAT BREAK-FAST, AND COULD WIN A MILLION DOLLARS...
I DO THE LAUNDRY, COULD WIN A MILLION DOLLARS... WASH MY FACE, COULD WIN A MILLION DOLLARS... TAKE OUT THE GARBAGE, COULD WIN A MILLION DOLLARS....
NO WONDER I'M LOSING MY ENTHUSIASM FOR GOING TO WORK.
IT'S THE ONLY THING I DO WITH NO POTENTIAL FOR MAKING ANY MONEY.
Guisewite

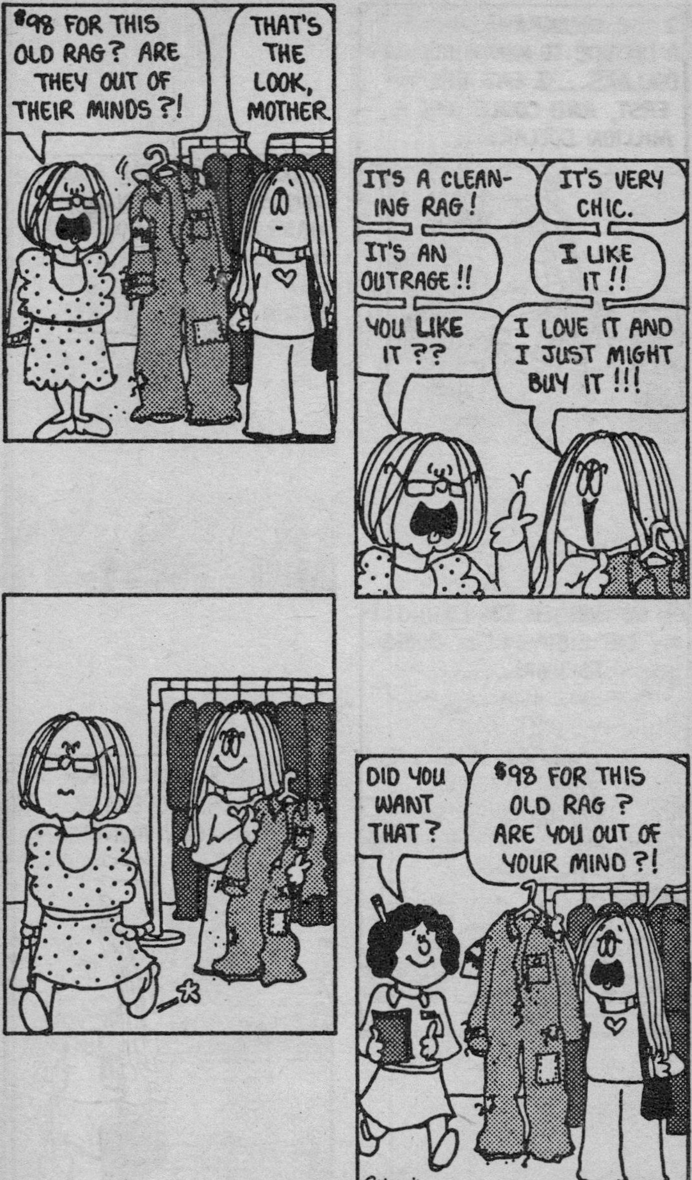
$98 FOR THIS OLD RAG? ARE THEY OUT OF THEIR MINDS?!
THAT'S THE LOOK, MOTHER.
IT'S A CLEANING RAG!
IT'S VERY CHIC.
IT'S AN OUTRAGE!!
I LIKE IT!!
YOU LIKE IT??
I LOVE IT AND I JUST MIGHT BUY IT!!!
DID YOU WANT THAT?
$98 FOR THIS OLD RAG? ARE YOU OUT OF YOUR MIND?!

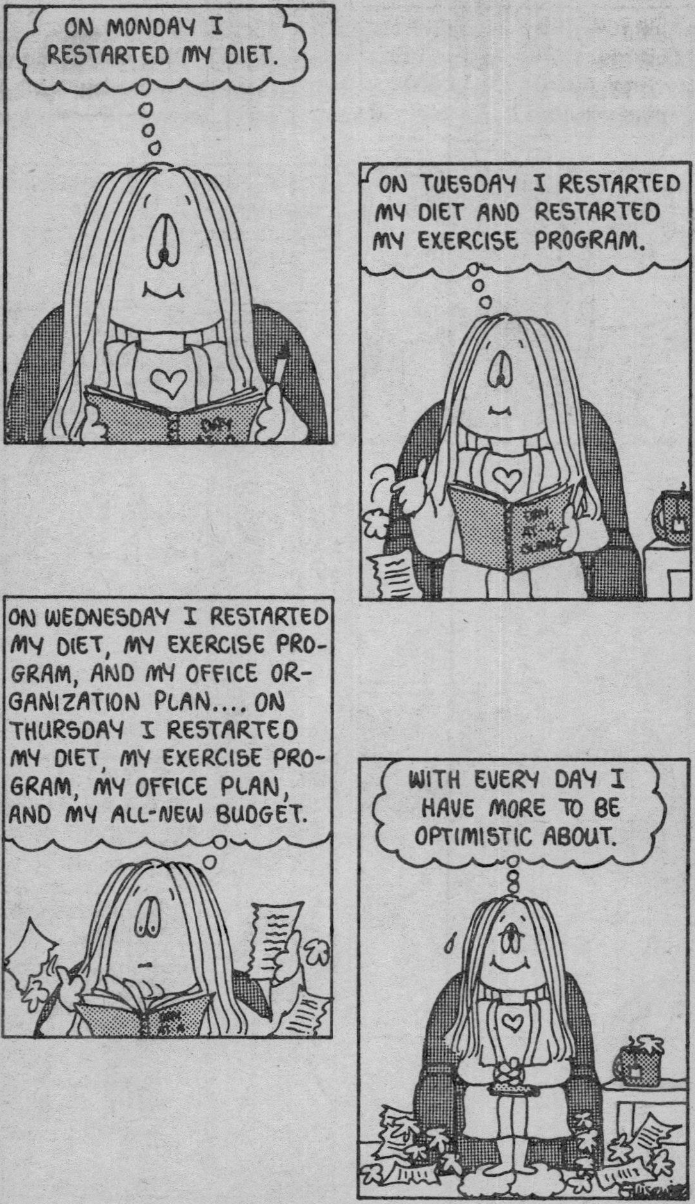
ON MONDAY I RESTARTED MY DIET.
ON TUESDAY I RESTARTED MY DIET AND RESTARTED MY EXERCISE PROGRAM.
ON WEDNESDAY I RESTARTED MY DIET, MY EXERCISE PROGRAM, AND MY OFFICE ORGANIZATION PLAN.... ON THURSDAY I RESTARTED MY DIET, MY EXERCISE PROGRAM, MY OFFICE PLAN, AND MY ALL-NEW BUDGET.
WITH EVERY DAY I HAVE MORE TO BE OPTIMISTIC ABOUT.